For Eema

CONTENTS

PREFACE

The licence plate says "Friendly." It should also say "Undervisited," "Underappreciated," and "Undiscovered," even by most of the people who live within its borders.

Manitoba, in the minds of most Canadians, is a land of endless grain fields populated by parka-wearing bumpkins with a fondness for snowmobiles and ice fishing. Or at least that's what Canadians would think if they stopped to consider Manitoba for a nanosecond.

Locked away in a mid-continental netherworld between Nunavut and North Dakota is a province that defies simple categorization. Manitoba is neither Eastern nor Western, refusing to identify with either urbane Ontario or antagonistic Alberta and – wrongly, perhaps – turning up its nose at simple Saskatchewan. It's also neither urban nor rural, as its 1.3 million souls are divided between quirky, metropolitan Winnipeg and the rest of this farflung land of 650,000 square kilometres. And it's not even a real Prairie province, as fertile farmland only covers a southwestern triangle hemmed in by boreal forests, some of the largest lakes in the nation, and the rugged Canadian Shield.

Manitoba is a place few travellers really know, whether they live in Winnipeg, the rest of Manitoba, or anywhere else. The pages in your hands constitute the only general-purpose guidebook to the province, which is amazing, considering the number of travel tomes on the market. It's also surprising, considering the attractions Manitoba has to offer, including beaches without crowds, more lakes than non-mathematicians can quantify, a mix of urban culture and unspoiled wilderness, and a multifaceted ethnic mosaic where indigenous Canadians figure more prominently than anywhere else in the land.

But the mission behind *The Daytripper's Guide to Manitoba* is not to proselytize the masses who've never visited. Obviously, Thompson isn't Tahiti, Dauphin will never be Disneyland, and the Giant Golf ball of Gilbert Plains isn't destined to outshine the Great Wall of China any time soon.

The real motive for writing this book was to demystify the province for the people who finally make it here and want to know more.

Most Manitoba tourists actually live inside the province. Many more just happen to be passing through, either for business or as part of a cross-country jaunt along the Trans-Canada Highway. Others come here specifically to fish, shop, paddle, or head north to the province's sole well-developed tourist attraction, the eco-tourism Mecca of Churchill. This guidebook is intended to serve all of Manitoba travellers, from ecotourists to culture vultures. Don't be fooled by the title – this *Daytripper's Guide* is meant for long-term visitors and locals, too.

In the following chapters, you'll get the basic goods about natural and cultural attractions in every region of Manitoba, as well as in nearby northwestern Ontario. The vast majority of these places can be reached within a day's drive of Winnipeg.

On that note, if you want to see much of Manitoba, you're going to need a car. You're also going to need an energetic set of limbs, a sharp pair of eyes, and an adventurous palate. As flat as the land may seem, this is no place for the sedentary or the soft.

Just one word of warning, which is standard for any guidebook: It never hurts to inquire further about any destination you're thinking of visiting. This guidebook was rewritten in 2015. After this date, prices will go up, restaurants will close, and some undiscovered attractions will be trampled by visitors, possibly because of this very book.

This guidebook has been updated six times since it was first published in 2006. If you find any inaccuracies in this edition – or wish to add information for the next one – please e-mail info@greatplains.mb.ca.

Thanks in advance. Enjoy Manitoba!

And if you happen to be a parka-wearing grain farmer who drives a snowmobile to the local ice-fishing hole, my apologies. Thanks for buying the book, anyway.

Bartley Kives
Winnipeg
March 2015

Bartley Kives

A BRIEF HISTORY OF MANITOBA

The Earliest Inhabitants

Compared to almost any other chunk of earthbound real estate, Manitoba is one of the newest places on the planet. As recently as 13,000 years ago, a massive sheet of ice covered every square centimetre of the province. Plants, animals, and people only moved in after the glaciers melted, which means every single organism in Manitoba – every fish, mosquito, rodent, and corporate lawyer – is a recent arrival, in the grand geological scheme of things.

The great glaciers didn't melt all at once, but in a series of hiccups and spasms that allowed life to move first into the southwest corner of the province and then eventually spread north and east. The earliest humans arrived not long after the ice receded, likely following big game and offers of cheap real estate. Artifacts found near Boissevain, south of Brandon, suggest the first Manitobans moved in sometime between 12,000 and 10,000 BC and hunted mastodons and long-horned bison, both of which are now extinct.

Over the next 10,000 years, wave after wave of indigenous people migrated into the province and sometimes out again, as the climate fluctuated between temperate and mind-numbingly cold. From around 5,000 BC to around 200 BC, more technologically advanced toolmakers hunted elk and caribou but also fished, foraged for wild vegetables and berries, and began to cultivate wild rice. Then, from around 200 BC to AD 1100, a series of increasingly sophisticated semi-nomadic cultures developed seasonal but permanent villages throughout southern Manitoba, as well a complex network of trade routes with distant indigenous groups.

Five peoples – the Dene, Cree, Dakota, Anishinaabe and Oji-Cree – were firmly established in the province by the time Europeans arrived en masse to cause trouble for the locals.

The Dene and Cree have been in Manitoba for centuries, if not millennia. The Dene are Athapaskan-speaking hunter-gatherers whose numbers are now greater in Nunavut and the Northwest Territories. They once followed caribou across northwestern

PAM

The first people moved into southwestern Manitoba about 8,000 years ago. The forks of the Red and Assiniboine Rivers was first inhabited about 6,00 years ago and served as a historical trading spot for First Nations throughout the region.

Opposite: Seasonal agricultural workers during the fall harvest.

Manitoba, but are now largely confined to two remote communities: Tadoule Lake and Lac Brochet.

The Cree, whose language is in the Algonkian family, are the most populous indigenous group in Manitoba. The Cree fished and hunted along boreal forests, rivers, and lakes from Hudson Bay right down to the bottom of Lake Winnipeg. Forced to move west or settle, Cree communities are present in every part of the province, with the exception of the extreme north and southwest.

The Anishinaabe are another Algonkian-speaking group. They moved in (or back in) to Manitoba from Ontario in the 1700s, after leaving their traditional lands east of Lake Superior, where they came into conflict with the Iroquois as well as settlers from England and France. Today, Anishinaabe communities are concentrated in Manitoba's southeastern quadrant.

The Oji-Cree, who share cultural and linguistic ties with both Anishinaabe and Cree, are concentrated in the Island Lakes area.

The Dakota, the northernmost branch of the mostly American Sioux, are most commonly associated with Manitoba's southwestern plains, though Siouan-speaking Assiniboine – traditional allies with the Cree – used to hunt and fish as far north as the Saskatchewan River. That said, most of the Dakota who live in Manitoba moved into the southwest corner of the province from the United States, either to avoid conflict with the incoming Anishinaabe in the late 1700s, or fleeing from the US military in the late 1800s. Today, Manitoba's Dakota communities remain concentrated in a ribbon of land from Portage la Prairie to the Saskatchewan border.

Before the arrival of Europeans, indigenous peoples lived tough but independent lives, surviving the harsh climate by living off the land in relative harmony with nature. To describe the First Nations experience after 1492 as anything less than cultural genocide would be an irresponsible understatement. To many indigenous people, the entire continent of North America is a war crimes site – and Manitoba is no different, despite the fact roughly one in seven people in the province can claim some form of indigenous identity and one in two are believed to have some indigenous ancestry.

In retrospect, the story of indigenous/European contact in Manitoba is beyond regrettable. Manitoba's mostly nomadic First Nations were forced to settle on isolated reserves of marginal economic value as Canada's federal government pursued a policy of forced assimilation, epitomized by an inhumane residential-schools system. This effort at eradication failed, as a resilient indigenous population survived a brutal period from the 1850s to the 1990s with its identity intact in a handful of the more remote communities as well as in urban centres, including Winnipeg, the most indigenous city in Canada.

Over the past 25 years, a cultural reawakening has coincided with an improvement in living standards, though Manitoba's indigenous residents continue to be less healthy, wealthy, and gainfully employed than the provincial norm. But the future only bodes well, as a fast-growing indigenous population is uniquely positioned to take advantage of the province's stable economy and chronic shortage of skilled workers.

New Kids on the Block

The first white guy to see Manitoba was British seaman Thomas Button, who sailed into Hudson Bay and visited the mouth of the Nelson River in 1612. That said, the first European to really explore the province was Englishman Henry Kelsey, who paddled up the Churchill and Saskatchewan rivers and reached the edge of the Prairies as early as 1670, the same year the London, England-based Hudson's Bay Company was established to speed the flow of furs from the Canadian back-woods to the hat shops and coat racks of Europe.

PAM

Over the next century, British explorers and fur traders fanned out from forts at York Factory and later Churchill to make contact with Cree and Assiniboine trappers. At the beginning, trade was conducted by canoe. Eventually, much larger York boats were used to schlep European goods like gunpowder, flour, and booze up the Hayes River and down the length of Lake Winnipeg, eventually arriving at forts where furs would be collected for the return trip to Hudson Bay.

The Battle of Seven Oaks took place at what's now West Kildonan in Winnipeg, in 1816, when a simmering rivalry between fur-trading companies erupted into violence.

As the English explored from the north, the French moved in from the east. The first French Canadian to make his mark on Manitoba was Sieur Pierre Gaultier de la Vérendrye, a Quebec-born explorer who spent most of his life searching for a passage to the Pacific Ocean. After hearing tales of a great inland sea, he paddled west from Montreal, wound up in Lake Winnipeg, and got his feet muddy at the future site of the Manitoba capital in 1738. La Vérendrye established forts across southern Manitoba and northwestern Ontario. But the gig wasn't easy – he often ran out of provisions and became embroiled in a conflict between the Anishinaabe and Dakota.

Both factors contributed to the death of his son Jean-Baptiste, who was slaughtered in a Sioux ambush on Lake of the Woods while paddling east for supplies. (See *Massacre Island* in *Canadian Shield*). The elder La Vérendrye eventually made it as far west as the Missouri River near the North Dakota/Montana border, but died without ever glimpsing the West Coast.

Following in la Vérendrye's footsteps, the French-Canadian voyageurs of the Montreal-based North West Company – the

Hudson's Bay Company's bitter rival – plied small waterways from the east, paddling big-ass cargo canoes along a lake-and-river route now defined by the Ontario/Minnesota border. By 1810, the two fur-trading empires had erected 180 forts across what's now Manitoba, including rival posts at the forks of the Red and Assiniboine rivers. The intense competition finally ended with the amalgamation of the North West Company into the HBC in 1821.

By this time, the French and British in southern Manitoba co-existed with Scottish immigrants – who had established a settlement in the Red River Valley – and the semi-nomadic, bison-hunting Métis, people of mixed French and indigenous descent. Tensions between the newcomers and locals – especially the increasingly dispossessed Métis – eventually led to the creation of Manitoba.

Manitoba's Violent Birth

The first European settlers in the Red River Valley quickly learned it wasn't the greatest idea to build their new homes on a floodplain. Early Red River settlements were nearly destroyed by massive floods in 1826 and 1852.

But southern Manitoba was also wracked by periodic bloodshed, as territorial squabbles between the Métis and others erupted into battles. The Métis fought Scottish settlers at Seven Oaks — now in the West Kildonan area of Winnipeg — in 1816, and then the Dakota several times during buffalo hunts in southern Manitoba.

In the late 1860s, it was uncertain whether southern Manitoba would join an expansionist United States or become part of the newly established Dominion of Canada. Ontario-born Anglophones moving west favoured ties with Ottawa, but French-speaking Métis feared the loss of their already tenuous land rights. The matter came to a head in 1869, when the Hudson's Bay Company turned over its remaining lands to Canada and Ottawa sent land surveyors to the Red River region. That enraged the Métis, who had already begun to settle down on the same land.

Led by charismatic St. Boniface–born preacher Louis Riel, the Métis set up a provisional government, seized control of Upper Fort Garry, and petitioned Ottawa to negotiate Manitoba's entry into confederation.

But Riel's efforts were doomed by ethno-religious politics. Canadian Prime Minister Sir John A. Macdonald broke off negotiations in 1870 when he learned the French-speaking Catholic Riel ordered the execution of English-speaking Protestant rabble-rouser Thomas Scott.

Riel was charged with Scott's death and forced to flee in advance of an approaching Canadian army. But a tiny, "postage-stamp" sized Manitoba surrounding the Red River was granted provincehood, complete with language and religious rights for Francophones.

Remaining popular with local French-speakers, Riel went on to be elected to Parliament but was never allowed to sit. He spent years in exile in Montana before leading Saskatchewan Métis into one last military adventure: the Northwest Rebellion, which ended in defeat at Batoche, Saskatchewan, in 1885. Riel was captured, convicted of treason, and hanged.

It was only in the late 20th century that Riel was recognized as a defender of indigenous rights and acknowledged as the founder of Manitoba. His remains are buried on the grounds of the St. Boniface Cathedral (see *St. Boniface* in the *Winnipeg* chapter) and his memory is honoured on Riel Day, the February long-weekend provincial holiday.

Boom, Bust, and Decline

The creation of Manitoba was soon followed in 1871 by the signing of Treaty 1, which was supposed to secure the rights of First Nations in and around the Red River settlement in advance of an expected influx of European settlers. That didn't quite work out as intended.

Upon its founding in 1874, Winnipeg became the gateway for the settlement of western Canada. The century-long trickle of immigrants into Manitoba soon turned into a flood, as the completion of rail links to Minnesota and Ontario aided Ottawa's mission to populate the Canadian prairies with immigrants from across Europe.

Russian Mennonites arrived in southern Manitoba in 1874 and Icelandic settlers established a colony along Lake Winnipeg near Gimli in 1875 (see *Gimli* in *Beaches and the Interlake*). Over the next four decades, they were followed by Ukrainians, Poles, Germans, Jews, and other eastern Europeans, who helped swell Manitoba's population from about 25,000 in 1870 to almost 500,000 by the time the province's current boundaries were adopted in 1912.

Following the arrival of colonists from Europe, southern Manitoba's grasslands were replaced by farms. Initially, Manitoba exported more wheat than any other Canadian province.

While farming communities sprouted up all over southern Manitoba, many immigrants filtered back into Winnipeg, a roaring boomtown with colourful saloons, theatres, whorehouses, and a class of nouveau-riche merchants who made massive profits in real estate and warehousing.

From 1905 to 1912, Winnipeg was the fastest-growing city in North America outside Chicago, its railway-rich US counterpart. But the 1914 completion of the Panama Canal suddenly made shipping cheaper than rail transport, effectively ending Winnipeg's boom and setting

PAM

the city down a long course of relative decline that continued into the 1990s. Once Canada's third-largest city, Winnipeg now ranks eighth.

In 1919, Winnipeg was further pummelled by a general strike, the only workers' revolt ever to seize a Canadian or US city. Again, ethnic politics played a role, as English Protestant city leaders blamed the civil unrest on supposedly Bolshevik immigrants from Eastern Europe, though there was broad support for the strike among workers of many backgrounds, including returning First World War soldiers of British descent.

The combination of the Panama Canal, the First World War and the general strike hit Winnipeg particularly hard. Ironically, the city's arrested development in the 1920s and '30s protected its character, as many heritage buildings that might otherwise have been torn down still stand. A stunning collection of warehouse and office buildings constructed between 1880 and 1920 in downtown Winnipeg's Exchange District has been designated a National Historic Site (See *The Exchange* in the *Winnipeg* chapter).

But even through the Depression and into the postwar period, Winnipeg remained the economic engine for the rest of Manitoba and retained the finest cultural and intellectual life on the Prairies. Winnipeg established western Canada's first art gallery in 1912, the entire nation's first professional ballet company in 1939, and a symphony orchestra in 1946.

And as the Second World War loomed, the city cemented its reputation for independent thought when the *Winnipeg Free Press* was the lone Canadian voice editorializing against the growing Nazi threat and warning about the perils of appeasing Hitler.

Modern Manitoba

The latter half of the 20th century saw Manitoba develop an economy based on a humdrum but successful mix of manufacturing, mining, agribusiness, services and public administration. There are now grain farms and seed companies, hog barns and meat packers, aerospace and bus manufacturers, and insurance and investment companies. Much of the province's economic activity is centred in Winnipeg, with the notable exception of massive (and risky) public hydroelectric projects in the north and boom-and-bust private oil extraction in the southwest.

The biggest postwar undertaking, however, was more about protecting the economy than investing in it. In 1950, after another Red River flood devastated much of Winnipeg, Premier Duff Roblin ordered the creation of the Red River Floodway, a massive trench dug around the eastern side of Winnipeg. Originally, "Duff's Ditch" spawned ridicule. Yet nobody laughed in 1997 when the floodway allowed Winnipeg to escape the devastation of the Flood of the Century, which all but destroyed downtown Grand Forks, ND, and displaced 30,000 people in southern Manitoba.

The Floodway did not, however, protect farms and towns in the Red River Valley just south of the city, leading rural residents to charge that their homes were sacrificed for the well being of Winnipeg. The aftermath of the '97 flood only served to highlight the divide between the Manitoba capital and the rest of the province. A severe Assiniboine River Valley flood in 2011 only exacerbated this split.

PAM

With roughly 800,000 souls, metropolitan Winnipeg's population dominates a province of 1.3 million people. But there's a huge political and cultural chasm between the people who live inside and outside the Perimeter Highway, the road that loosely defines the city's limits.

Rural and small-town Manitoba retains a self-reliant spirit left over from the pioneer days. Farming is in decline, but other rural pursuits such as hunting, fishing, and snowmobiling remain a way of life. Rural voters typically support conservative parties in provincial and federal elections.

Winnipeggers, on the other hand, generally try to live the same suburban dream as residents of any mid-sized city in North America. But as an industrial town, Winnipeg's large number of unionized workers and diverse ethnic makeup leads to more support for the left-leaning NDP and centrist Liberals. Winnipeg voters are also a cosmopolitan lot, first electing the openly gay Glen Murray to the mayor's office in 1998 – when homophobia was still common – before welcoming his successor, Sam Katz, the city's first Jewish mayor, in 2004.

Current Winnipeg Mayor Brian Bowman, a Métis privacy lawyer elected in 2014, is the first indigenous mayor in the city's history.

Throughout the postwar period, the province experienced a second wave of immigration, as Italians, Greeks, Portuguese, Chinese, Filipinos, and Caribbeans joined eastern Europeans on the move to Canada in the 1950s and '60s. Later waves of immigration echoed political strife around the world, as Manitoba welcomed an influx of South Asians, Chileans and Vietnamese in the 1970s, Salvadorans in the '80s, Ethiopians and Somalis in the '90s, and Sudanese and Afghans in the early 21st century. Most of the immigrants settled in Winnipeg to join growing numbers of Cree and Anishinaabe. The city's diversity has become a source of pride to the locals and a pleasant surprise to visitors, who may be taken aback to learn Tagalog – not French – is the second-most-common mother tongue in Winnipeg.

But there's no disguising Manitoba's challenges: slow population growth, a shortage of skilled labour, and a capital city marred

The Red River Flood of 1950 inundated much of Winnipeg. The decision to build a city in the middle of a floodplain continues to have water-management implication for much of southern Manitoba.

11

by urban decay that began with the triple whammy of the canal, the war and the strike a century ago.

The hope for the future lies with Winnipeg's ongoing revitalization, the rising fortunes of the province's fast-growing indigenous population, and the stability provided by an economy that isn't solely dependent upon energy. Just don't expect to encounter this optimism in the form of unbridled boosterism. Manitobans are just as friendly as the slogan on the licence plate suggests, but also more cynical than your average North American.

Remember, this is the only Canadian province founded in an act of rebellion, while its capital is the only city in the US or Canada to witness a mass workers' uprising. Meanwhile, much of the indigenous community – 15 per cent of the overall population – doesn't fully recognize federal authority. Mistrust of power runs deep here, arguably deeper than in any other part of Canada.

But again, that rarely translates into personal mistrust, as Manitobans are incredibly helpful to people in need. Charitable donations exceed the national norm here, while few Manitoba motorists make it through a winter without a boost or a push from a fellow driver, usually a stranger.

If your car breaks down on the highway, this is the place you want to be. And hopefully, I'm going to encourage you to be out on the highway a lot — with a working vehicle, anyway.

Indian vs. Indigenous:
A Glossary of Terms
(or how to avoid insulting strangers in Manitoba):

Indigenous: A catch-all term for Canada's first inhabitants, which include the First Nations, Métis and Inuit.

Aboriginal: Means the same as indigenous, but is falling out of favour, especially because the term "aboriginals" – as opposed to "aboriginal people" – can be offensive.

First Nations: The Canadian equivalent to the US term "Native American" and the modern version of the usually offensive term "Indian." First Nations are indigenous Canadians who are neither Métis nor Inuit.

Inuit: The indigenous people of Canada's far north. Inuk is the singular form. The term replaces the archaic term Eskimos, now considered offensive.

Métis: Indigenous people of mixed European and First Nations ancestry; a distinct Métis identity was formed by the 1800s. The province of Manitoba was founded by Louis Riel, leader of the Red River Resistance, in 1870.

Native: A now-archaic and almost always offensive synonym for "aboriginal."

Indian: An archaic and usually offensive synonym for First Nations. First Nations people, however, may use the term with impunity.

Anishinaabe: Also known as Ojibway. An Algonkian speaking group of First Nations, located in Canada in Manitoba, Quebec, Ontario, Saskatchewan and Alberta. Also located in nine midwestern US states.

Cree: Another Algonkian-speaking group of First Nations, located in Manitoba, Quebec, Ontario, Saskatchewan and Alberta, generally but not always further north than the Anishinaabe.

Oji-Cree: An Algonkian-speaking group of First Nations in Manitoba and Ontario. The Oji-Cree identity emerged from intermarriage between Ojibway and Cree.

Dene: An Athabaskan-speaking group of First Nations located in northern Manitoba, as well as in Saskatchewan, Alberta, British Columbia, the Yukon, Northwest Territories and Nunavut.

Dakota: A Siouan-speaking group of First Nations found in Manitoba, as well as in Ontario, North and South Dakota, Montana and Saskatchewan.

Bryan Scott

Manitoba at a Glance

Size: 649,950 square kms, sixth among Canadian provinces.

Population (2015 estimate): 1.294 million, fifth among Canadian provinces.

Capital: Winnipeg. City pop. 717,100 (2015 estimate); Metropolitan pop. 792,100 (2015 estimate).

Ten other largest population centres (2011): Brandon (pop. 46,061), Steinbach (13,524), Portage la Prairie (12,996), Thompson (12,829), Winkler (10,670), Selkirk (9,834), Dauphin (8,251), Morden (7,812), The Pas (5,513) and Norway House First Nation (on-reserve pop. 5,395).

Five most commonly spoken languages (2011): English, German, French, Tagalog and Cree.

Five biggest ethnic groupings (2011): British, Slavic, German, indigenous and French.

Unemployment (November 2014): 5.1 per cent, third-lowest in Canada.

Gross domestic product (2013) $61.3 million, sixth among Canadian provinces.

Top five industries by GDP (2013): Manufacturing, public administration, health & social services, construction and mining.

Politics (2015): Governed by left-of-centre New Democratic Party, led by Premier Greg Selinger. Represented in Ottawa by 11 Conservative MPs, two NDP MPs and one Liberal MP.

Data sources: Statistics Canada, Manitoba Finance, City of Winnipeg.

Opposite: Night comes to Steep Rock, on the eastern shore of Lake Manitoba.

Manitoba

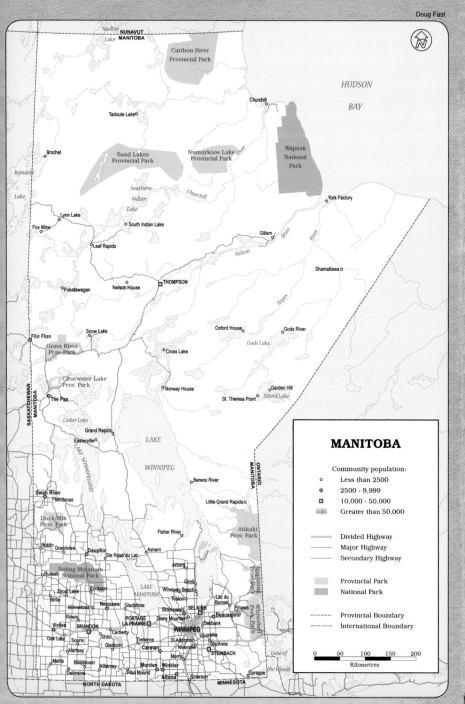

GETTING YOUR BEARINGS

2

The Geography of Manitoba

Drive down the Trans-Canada Highway and you might just believe Manitoba really is an endless expanse of grain fields punctuated by farmhouses and the occasional cow. But if you get off that ribbon of boredom, you'll find less than a third of the province conforms to the pancake-flat stereotype.

Most of Manitoba is a lush, wet, and surprisingly wild landscape of forests, rivers, and some of the largest lakes in the world. The diverse scenery ranges from treeless, sub-Arctic tundra along the coast of Hudson Bay to desert-like dunes in Spruce Woods Provincial Park at the opposite end of the province. There are dense coniferous forests in the rugged Canadian Shield to the east, scenic stretches of rolling prairie and aspen parkland in the west, sprawling wetlands all over the province, and even a few places where endangered tall grasses continue to grow on the rich, black prairie soil.

Rivers can be slow, meandering prairie ribbons, frenetic pool-and-drop whitewater routes, or massive hydroelectric-generating monsters like the Churchill and Nelson in the north. There are also more than 100,000 lakes, ranging from marshy, drainage-devoid Whitewater Lake, to deep, meteor-created West Hawk, to the massive but shallow inland oceans in the centre of the province: lakes Winnipeg, Winnipegosis, and Manitoba, the 11th, 22nd, and 27th-largest freshwater bodies in the world.

All of these features are a legacy of the glaciers that once covered the province and the water and debris left behind when the ice retreated. Simply put, Manitoba would not look anything like it does if it wasn't for the Ice Age.

Manitoba's Icy Origins

According to First Nations belief, water once covered the Earth. North America only emerged when a turtle – or, some nations say, a beaver – dove below the surface and brought back a wad of mud.

Judaeo-Christian cosmologists peg the planet's age at about 6,000 years. Modern science contends it's a little longer – more

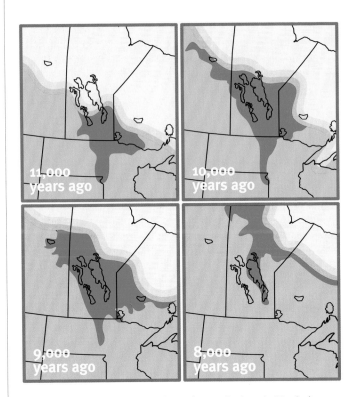

11,000 years ago

10,000 years ago

9,000 years ago

8,000 years ago

As shown in this series of maps, modern Manitoba was shaped by retreating glaciers and the resulting meltwater, whose remnants can still be seen in Manitoba's so-called great lakes.

like 4.6 billion years. But anything that took place in Manitoba before 12,000 BC is all but irrelevant, as there was nothing here but ice and snow. Glaciers more than a kilometre deep crawled across every square centimetre of the province, scraping soil and bedrock off the north and east regions and burying portions of the south and west in sediment known as glacial till. Only south-western Manitoba failed to be completely flattened by the ice, thanks to the Manitoba Escarpment, a deposit of relatively hard shale. Today, the escarpment's steep face runs southwest from the Porcupine Hills, across the eastern face of Duck and Riding mountains, and eventually down to the US border south-west of Winnipeg.

When the glaciers retreated, generally from southwest to northeast, the meltwater at first drained to the east through what's now Lake Superior. Most of it pooled into Lake Agassiz, a glacial lake that covered much of Manitoba before eventually draining into Hudson Bay when the rest of the ice sheet finally melted.

Manitoba's "great lakes" – Winnipeg, Manitoba, Winnipegosis, Cedar, and Dauphin – are the most obvious legacy of ancient Agassiz. But you can also find remnants of its sandy beaches in Spruce Woods, Sandilands Provincial Forest, and the Lauder Hills.

Long glacial-deposited ridges called end moraines mark places where the ice stopped moving forward and deposited all the debris it was carrying along a wide curve. One of the largest in the province begins as an isthmus between Lake Winnipegosis and Cedar Lake and extends east into Lake Winnipeg as Long Point. Other glacial ridges called eskers mark places where sand and gravel were carried along channels in the melting ice. Birds Hill Park, northeast of Winnipeg, is a good example.

The retreating ice also deposited massive boulders called glacial erratics, many of which can still be spotted in farmers' fields or along the southeast shore of Lake Winnipeg. Mighty torrents of glacial meltwater also carved out the Assiniboine, Shell, and Pembina valleys – wide spillways that dwarf the small rivers that now meander through the valley bottoms.

When the last of the ice melted, Manitoba was so compressed that the north side of the province – where the glaciers were thickest and heaviest – actually began to bounce back. In a process known as glacial-isotatic lift, rocks at the Hudson Bay shoreline have been rebounding at an average rate of roughly 1.3 metres per century. You can actually see this rebound in action during a visit to Churchill, as docking rings pounded into the rock to moor fur trade-era ships now sit metres south of the waterfront.

The retreating ice also gave plants and animals a chance to colonize an empty territory and create one of the newest ecosystems on earth. Again, this process took place from the southwest to the northeast, so it's no surprise there's less biodiversity in the northeastern lowlands than there is in the southwestern grasslands.

Today, Manitoba can be divided up into five loosely defined geographic regions: the Canadian Shield, the Manitoba Lowlands, the south-central prairies, the southwestern highlands, and a small strip of tundra along Hudson Bay.

The Regions of Manitoba

The Canadian Shield

The largest region of Manitoba, the Canadian Shield covers most of the northern half of the province as well as the eastern third. Coniferous forests, granite ridges, and thousands of cool, clear lakes and rivers of various sizes and lengths dominate this vast, sparsely populated area. The same bumpy, uneven landscape can be found in northeastern Alberta, northern Saskatchewan, northern Ontario, and western Quebec.

The Shield, named after the billion-year-old Precambrian rock uncovered by glaciers, is home to most of Manitoba's logging, mining, and trapping. Major centres include the nickel-mining city of Thompson in the

The red vein running through the granite along much of the Bloodvein River gives the Canadian Shield waterway its name.

Brenda Schritt

centre of the province and the copper-and-zinc town of Flin Flon at the Saskatchewan border.

Twenty Cree and two Dene communities are also scattered across the northern Shield, including some accessible only by winter ice road or by air. Unemployment is a major problem facing these remote communities, although some are negotiating for a piece of the profits from future hydroelectric projects.

The most significant rivers in the northern Shield are the high-volume but heavily dammed Churchill and Nelson rivers, and two heritage rivers, the Seal and the Hayes. All four drain east into Hudson Bay.

Rivers in the southeastern Shield, meanwhile, drain west into Lake Winnipeg. The Pigeon, Berens, and Bloodvein, prized by whitewater paddlers, are protected by Atikaki Provincial Wilderness Park. The less-remote Manigotagan River flows from Nopiming Provincial Park through a provincial-park river corridor established in 2004. The southernmost – and most-developed – protected area in the Shield is Whiteshell Provincial Park, home to thousands of cottage lots and dozens of lodges and resorts. The heaviest concentrations are at Falcon and West Hawk lakes.

The most common trees in the Shield are spruce, Jack pine, and fir. Large birds include bald eagles, great blue herons, osprey, great grey owls, and white pelicans, while wolves, moose, beavers, white-tailed deer, and black bears are common mammals. Less common are elk, wolves, woodland caribou, river otters, mink, lynxes, and wolverines, the latter only found in remote areas.

Bartley Kives

No, it's not the Mediterranean: Limestone cliffs at Steep Rock, on the east side of Lake Manitoba.

Manitoba Lowlands

On a big map, Manitoba's most dominant features are the wide, shallow "Great Lakes" that rank as some of the biggest puddles on the planet. Lakes Winnipeg, Manitoba, and Winnipegosis, and their smaller cousins, Dauphin and Cedar lakes – all remnants of glacial Lake Agassiz – sit in a completely flat basin in the centre of the province, surrounding an equally level expanse of boreal forest and wetlands known as the Interlake.

The main difference between the Lowlands and the Canadian Shield is geology. Instead of hard, Precambrian granite, Lowland bedrock is relatively soft, porous limestone, a sedimentary rock formed from the remains of ancient sea creatures. Erosion of this limestone leads to stunning natural features, like the cliffs at Sturgeon Gill Point on Lake Winnipeg and Steep Rock on Lake Manitoba, underground snake pits at Narcisse and a spring jetting out of the rock in Grass River Provincial Park. But much of the Lowlands is relatively featureless – and undeveloped, as human settlement is inhibited by poor drainage.

The chief economic activities in the Lowlands are tourism, logging, and commercial fishing. Lake Winnipeg's southern basin is lined by beaches and cottage communities, which serve as summer getaways for Winnipeggers. Lake Manitoba is the destination of choice for residents of Portage la Prairie.

Both lakes support large fisheries for walleye, a tasty, whitefleshed fish known in Manitoba as pickerel. Other commercially fished species include sauger (very similar to walleye), lake whitefish, yellow perch, northern pike and two species caught mainly to be shipped to US processors and ground up into gefilte fish – cisco (locally known as tulibee) and white sucker (locally known as mullet). Goldeye, a regional delicacy found in Manitoba and Saskatchewan, is only edible when smoked.

There are few large communities in the Lowlands, but plenty of small towns and First Nations. The largest centres in the Interlake are Gimli, a Lake Winnipeg fishing community and resort town founded by Icelandic immigrants, and Peguis, a series of Cree and Saulteaux towns that together comprise one of the largest reserves in Manitoba.

The largest community in the Lowlands is paper-mill town The Pas and neighbouring Opaskwayak Cree Nation in the northwestern corner of the region, on the Saskatchewan River.

Central Prairies

Charles Shilliday

In strict geographical terms, Manitoba's central Prairies are a southern extension of the Lowlands – the land is just as flat and the bedrock equally soft and porous. But 200 years of human settlement have seen most of the wetlands drained and replaced with farms, towns, and cities, the largest being Winnipeg, the sister cities of Morden and Winkler, Steinbach, Portage la Prairie and the steel-producing city of Selkirk.

Harvest time west of La Rivière, in Manitoba's Pembina Valley.

As the most densely populated region of Manitoba, the Prairies – located in the south-central portion of the province – have been altered to the point where little of the indigenous flora and fauna remains. Tall grasses and wildflowers that once covered the region have been all but eradicated. Only a handful of tallgrass prairie preserves near tiny Vita and Stuartburn protect rare plants such as the Western Fringed Prairie Orchid, which is unique in Canada to Manitoba. Large predators such as the plains grizzly were hunted out centuries ago, the passenger pigeon was shot to extinction by the 1920s and the indigenous mule deer have all but disappeared. Even the once-numerous plains bison is now restricted to captive populations on ranches and inside parks and nature preserves.

Surviving prairie fauna include coyotes, many species of raptors, and the remarkable great grey owl, Manitoba's provincial bird and one of the largest in the world. But the white-tailed deer thriving in record numbers across the prairies are actually migrants from the wooded east. Like rabbits in Australia, they seem to thrive off human settlement, living off farm stubble and even congregating around the big-box stores of southwestern Winnipeg.

Common crops in the Prairies include wheat, canola, barley, corn, and sunflowers, the latter most visible on farms near the US border in Manitoba's "Bible belt" – the fast-growing, mostly Mennonite communities of Altona, Winkler, and Morden. Marijuana grown both indoors and outside is believed to be one the province's biggest cash crops, much to the chagrin of local Mounties.

Along with the flat terrain, the most prominent feature of southern Manitoba is the gentle curve of meandering, flood-prone rivers such the eastward-flowing Assiniboine and the north-flowing Red.

Southwestern Uplands

The southwest corner of Manitoba rises subtly over the rest of the province, though you can only get a sense of the elevation if you stand right on the edge of the Manitoba Escarpment and look east. The Porcupine Hills, Duck Mountain Provincial Park, Riding Mountain National Park mark the eastern edge of Manitoba's very modest highlands, which also include islands of elevation such as Tiger Hills, Brandon Hills, and Turtle Mountain Provincial Park.

Aspen forests and open meadows within the parks protect habitat for moose, elk, beavers, deer, and, in Spruce Woods Provincial Park, Manitoba's only lizard, the northern prairie skink. But outside the parks, Manitoba's highlands look a lot like a western extension of the Prairies, with grain fields and cattle pastures dominating the undulating landscape.

Charles Shilliday

A prairie autumn sunset.

The largest communities in the southwest are Brandon, Manitoba's second-largest city, and Dauphin, which sits just north of Riding Mountain. The dominant rivers are the Assiniboine, Little Saskatchewan, Souris, and Pembina, which look like narrow ribbons compared to the massive glacial-meltwater-created valleys they follow throughout most of the region. Lakes are less prevalent here than elsewhere in Manitoba. The most notable are Clear Lake, inside Riding Mountain; the dam-created Lake of the Prairies in Asessippi Provincial Park; and Pelican Lake, a narrow ribbon near the Pembina River Valley. Whitewater Lake is also an important migratory bird staging ground.

The Southwest was settled following the earliest retreat of the glaciers. Arrowheads found near Boissevain date back 12,000 years and are among North America's earliest-known human artifacts.

Tundra

A narrow strip of tundra curves around the extreme northeast corner of the province at Hudson Bay, from Nunavut toward the Ontario border. This is a land of ice, snow, lichen, and permafrost, where trees are stunted or non-existent, and the frigid ground melts into impassable bogs during a brief but spectacular summer. It's also home to Manitoba's most famous ambassador – the polar bear – and, not coincidentally, the top ecotourist destination in the province, Churchill (pop. 813), the only settlement of any size in the region.

This may look and *feel* like the Arctic, but this is too warm to be a true Arctic environment. Still, you can experience a semblance of a Nunavut experience, given the spectacular Northern Lights, 22 hours of darkness in December (and corresponding daylight in June), and Churchill itself, which feels like an outpost on the edge of the world.

Vegetation in the extreme northeastern fringe of this region is restricted to lichen, sedges, grasses, dwarfish one-sided trees and wildflowers that bloom brilliantly during the summer. The fauna includes ptarmigans, tundra swans, Arctic foxes, wolves, barren-ground caribou, and a resident population of up to 900 polar bears, who spend all summer on land before venturing out on Hudson Bay ice to hunt for harbour seals during the winter. The bears' summer denning grounds are protected by Wapusk National Park, which is mostly off-limits to visitors. Beluga whales, meanwhile, congregate by the thousands each summer at the mouth of the Churchill and Seal rivers.

Between the tundra and the boreal forests of the Canadian Shield lies a transition zone known as the taiga, characterized by a mix of lichen, muskeg, and stunted stands of black spruce. Other than fly-in fishing camps and wilderness rivers, the taiga is too tough to reach to attract tourists.

Manitoba's Climate

Rummage through a Manitoban's closet and you'll find an unusual diversity of clothes. The province boasts a climate of extremes, as bitterly cold winters, warm, muggy summers, and bouts of sogginess during the spring and fall means everyone must own a parka, bathing suit, and every conceivable garment in between.

The only place in the world with more extreme temperature swings than the Canadian Prairies is Central Asia. In Winnipeg, there's an 89-degree spread between the all-time record high temperature, 41 C in 1949, and the record low of -45 C in 1960.

While those extremes are freakish, even a normal year in southern Manitoba usually sees a couple of 32 C days in July and a handful of February nights when the mercury dips below -35 C. Factor in the windchill – the effect of wind on exposed flesh in cold temperatures – and Manitoba can be a chilly place, indeed. Winnipeg is one of the coldest cities in the world in mid-winter, as the average January day peaks at -11 C and bottoms out at -21 C at night.

But averages fail to tell the entire climactic story. Winnipeg also has a slightly longer frost-free period than supposedly milder Calgary – the temperature stays above zero for 170 days a year in the Manitoba capital, vs. 169 in its oil-rich Alberta rival.

So what allows Winnipeg to be a tiny bit less frosty than Calgary, where Chinooks frequently cause mid-January thaws? The answer has to do with Manitoba's balmy summers.

July days in Winnipeg typically max out at 26 C and usually stay above 14 C at night, which is four to five degrees warmer than almost any town in Alberta.

Most of southern Manitoba experiences very similar weather, though areas around the big lakes tend to be more unpredictable. Generally speaking, southern Manitoba is a tiny bit warmer and wetter as you move from west to east. The US border town of Gretna and the southeast hamlet of Sprague are often Canadian hotspots during the summer.

Moving up into the Parkland, the Riding Mountain resort town of Wasagaming is usually colder than the rest of the region, partly due to its greater elevation. But just east of the national park sits the town of McCreary, which usually enjoys warmer temperatures than its neighbours because of air compression on the Manitoba Escarpment.

Northern Manitoba shivers through an even colder climate, as remote communities like Lynn Lake and Thompson experience extremely bitter winters. But late in the fall, even more remote Churchill may seem relatively mild, as the waters of Hudson Bay act as a moderating influence until they freeze. Precipitation varies much more than temperature from year to year. Over the past 25 years, southern Manitoba has experienced both flood and drought conditions.

Two blizzards during the winter of 1996-97 led to the Flood of the Century, which engorged the Red River and temporarily displaced about 30,000 people. Assiniboine and Souris River flooding during the spring of 2011 inundated land from the Saskatchewan border to Portage la Prairie and drove up water levels on Lake Manitoba. But the mild, dry winter of 1987-88 saw Winnipeg get less than three months of snow cover instead of the usual five. And the winter of 2002-03 was so dry across the province that Manitoba Hydro lost profits due to low water levels, which reduced generating capacity.

So how do you prepare for a trip to Manitoba? Basically, expect everything Mother Nature can throw at you. Summers are usually warm and winters are usually cold, but any day in the spring or fall could mean sun, rain, snow, or any combination of the above. In other words, expect the best but plan for the worst.

The following Environment Canada weather data will help you prepare for typical conditions — as long as you realize there isn't anything typical about Prairie weather.

JULY CONDITIONS

WINNIPEG
Average high: 26°C
Average low: 14°C
Monthly precipitation: 79.5 mm

BRANDON
Average high: 26°C
Average low: 12°C
Monthly precipitation: 68 mm

KENORA, ONT.
Average high: 24°C
Average low: 15°C
Monthly precipitation: 103 mm

WASAGAMING
Average high: 24°C
Average low: 10°C
Monthly precipitation: 67 mm

THOMPSON
Average high: 23°C
Average low: 9°C
Monthly precipitation: 81 mm

CHURCHILL
Average high: 18°C
Average low: 7°C
Monthly precipitation: 60 mm

JANUARY CONDITIONS

WINNIPEG
Average high: -11°C
Average low: -21°C
Monthly precipitation: 20 mm

BRANDON
Average high: -11°C
Average low: -22°C
Monthly precipitation: 18 mm

KENORA, ONT.
Average high: -11°C
Average low: -21°C
Monthly precipitation: 26 mm

WASAGAMING
Average high: -11°C
Average low: -24°C
Monthly precipitation: 19 mm

THOMPSON
Average high: -18°C
Average low: -29°C
Monthly precipitation: 20 mm

CHURCHILL
Average high: -22°C
Average low: -30°C
Monthly precipitation: 19 mm

Source: Environment Canada, Canadian Climate Normals, 1981–2010

Hucking the Jambusters:
A Glossary of Manitoban English

back lane *noun* alleyway.

bear box *noun* bear-proof storage device for food or garbage, usually metal.

beer bash *noun* an afternoon social at a university campus. See *social*.

boosters *noun* jumper cables.

booter *noun* the act of stepping through lake or river ice and getting your feet wet.

but it's a dry cold *retort* a commonly uttered lie.

DEET *noun* acronym for pesticide N, n diethyl-m-toluamide, the most effective means of keeping mosquitoes off your skin.

fall supper *noun* public dinner in a rural community or small town, usually in August, September and October. Originally "fowl supper," as the main course was goose, duck, or passenger pigeon, during early-settlement days.

fat boy *noun* fast-food burger, covered with "chilli" sauce, mayonnaise, lettuce and tomatoes.

feet James *unit of measurement* the height of the Red River above the normal winter ice level at James Avenue in Winnipeg. Anything above 15 feet James is a flood.

flying rats *noun* Canada geese, to farmers; herring gulls, to fishers.

Floodway *noun* The Red River Floodway, which diverts spring floodwaters around Winnipeg.

giv 'er *imperative command* enthusiatic form of encouragement to try something, as in "Giv 'er some juice and see if she starts."

goldeye *noun* a freshwater fish, *Hiodon alosoides*, found primarily in Manitoba and only edible when smoked.

Halloween apples *exclamation* Halloween greeting used in Manitoba instead of "Trick or treat."

honey dill sauce *noun* a dipping sauce for chicken fingers, unique to Winnipeg, made out of mayonnaise, liquid honey and dill, invented by accident at Mitzi's Chicken Fingers in the 1980s.

huck *tr. verb* throw or toss, usually without great regard for accuracy.

Hurry hard! *exclamation* curling-rink version of giv'er.

jambuster *noun* jelly doughnut, usually covered in icing sugar.

jam (out) *verb* to back out or otherwise renege on a commitment.

jammer (also **jam tart**) *noun* one who jams out.

Jeanne's Cake *noun (proprietary)* a bland but addictive layer cake with a cookie bottom.

kielkje *noun (pl.)* Mennonite noodles, usually served with *schmauntfatt*.

kubasa (or **kielbassa**) *noun* Garlic ham sausage.

LC *noun* government-owned liquor store, short for the agency formerly known as Manitoba Liquor Control Commission.

loogan *noun* hooligan or rowdy person.

lumpia *noun (pl.)* Filipino spring rolls.

meegwetch *greeting* literally, "thank you" in Anishinaabe.

MPI *noun* public auto insurance, or a place that sells it.

muskie *noun* the muskellunge (*Esox masquinongy*), a large, aggressive freshwater fish similar to the northern pike.

nip *noun* a hamburger, usually but not exclusively at Salisbury House restaurants.

Old Dutch *noun (proprietary)* a brand of potato chips found only on the Canadian and US prairies.

out East *noun, adverb* Toronto, southern Ontario, or any part of Canada east of Thunder Bay, Ont.

'Peg City (or **The 'Peg**) *noun* Winnipeg.

perogies *noun (pl.)* Ukrainian flour dumplings stuffed usu. with potato, cheddar, cottage cheese, or sauerkraut.

Perimeter Vision *noun* Inability of Winnipeggers to see, consider or understand the rest of Manitoba outside the Perimeter Highway.

pancit *noun* a Filipino dish of thin rice noodles, fried with soy sauce and citrus.

pickerel *noun* western Canadian term for a fish known elsewhere as walleye.

Bartley Kives

Some day you'll find it, the Portage Diversion: OK, so it isn't that exciting. This gate keeps part of the Assiniboine River's flow away from Winnipeg by sending it to Lake Manitoba.

Portage Diversion *noun* Floodway diverting Assiniboine River water to Lake Manitoba.

Sals *noun* a Salisbury House restaurant.

schmauntfatt *noun* Mennonite cream gravy, usually made with farmer's sausage

Sev *noun* a convenience store, usually 7-Eleven.

shmoo torte *noun* Jewish sponge cake flecked with hazelnuts and topped with whipping cream and caramel sauce.

smokie *noun* a fat, barbecue-friendly pork or beef sausage.

social *noun* boozy, informal fundraising party for charities, non-profit organizations, or couples trying to finance a wedding.

soft drinks *noun (pl.)* soda pop. Considered quaint or archaic elsewhere.

tansi *greeting* Cree equivalent of "Hi, how are you?"

'Toban *noun or adjective* Northwestern Ontario term for a Manitoban tourist, usually considered derogatory.

True North! *exclamation* expression of adoration for the Winnipeg Jets and/or its ownership group, True North Sports & Entertainment, shouted during Canada's national anthem.

vendor *noun* privately owned beer store attached to or adjacent to a hotel (as opposed to an *LC*).

vinarterta *noun* layered prune torte of Icelandic origin.

windchill *noun* measurement of the combined effect of wind and cold. Often exaggerated.

wrenijke (or **varenikes/vareniki**) *noun (pl.)* Mennonite/Russian variants of perogies.

Oversized Statues

When it comes to building monuments, small Prairie towns like to think big. Many of the communities in this book have erected large, colourful, and sometimes ridiculous statues of flora, fauna, and mythological figures in the hope that tourists will stop to take a snapshot.

Oddly enough, the gambit usually works. Here's a list of selected towns and their oversized *objets d'art*.

Altona: Van Gogh's *Sunflowers*; old tricycle
Arden: Crocuses
Ashern: Sharptail grouse
Austin: Tractor
Boissevain: Turtle
Dauphin: Beaver
Deloraine: Cookie jar
Dominion City: Sturgeon
Dunrea: Goose
Elm Creek: Fire hydrant
Emerson: Mountie
Erickson: Viking ship
Flin Flon: Flintabatty Flonitan
Gilbert Plains: Golf ball
Gimli: The Viking
Gladstone: The Happy Rock
Glenboro: Camel
Holland: Windmill
Inwood: Garter Snakes
Komarno: Mosquito
La Broquerie: Cow
La Rivière: Wild turkey
Lundar: Canada goose
McCreary: Alpine Archie
Meleb: Mushrooms
Melita: Banana
Minnedosa: Canvasback duck
Neepawa: Birdhouse
Oak Lake: Ox
Onanole: Elk
Petersfield: Mallard
Pinawa: Sundial
Poplarfield: King Buck
Portage la Prairie: cola can; grey owl

Roblin: Diamond
Roland: Pumpkin
Roseisle: Roses
Russell: Bull
St. Claude: Tobacco pipe
St. François Xavier: White Horse
St. Malo: Deer
Ste. Rose: White bull
Ste. Rose du Lac: Manipogo (lake monster)
Selkirk: Catfish
Sifton: Spinning wheel
Steinbach: Red Rolls-Royce
The Pas: Trapper
Thompson: King Miner
Transcona (Winnipeg): Hi Neighbour Sam
Virden: Oil derrick
Winnipeg Beach: Totem

Bigger is better: Boissevain's Tommy the Turtle and Minnedosa's Canvasback Duck.

Wilf Taylor

STUFF TO
SEE AND DO

3

Exploring Manitoba can be a yin-yang experience, as Winnipeg offers big-city culture while the rest of the province offers natural wonders and small-town charm.

First-time visitors to Winnipeg often marvel at the low cost of visiting art galleries and museums or taking in live theatre. The multitude of affordable cultural attractions is something Winnipeggers take for granted, as, unlike tourists, they expect their institutions to be cheap.

Winnipeg has never done a great job of trumpeting its assets, most of which don't translate well into the language of travel marketing. But the rest of Manitoba does an equally uneven job, and not just because the province fails to rival Hawaii and California as a holiday destination.

The deal is, most Manitoba tourists come from elsewhere in the province and often visit the same destination each year. Winnipeggers in particular are notorious for hitting the same provincial-park campground every July, August, and Labour Day long weekend, stubbornly refusing to try anywhere new. As a result, people who work in the fields of tourism and hospitality – from waiters and hotel front-desk staff all the way to park rangers – sometimes assume a degree of familiarity on the part of their visitors.

As well, small towns with no obvious tourist attractions fail to promote the things that do make them interesting. For example, the southeastern Manitoba hamlet of Piney, where some of the world's best mineral water is bottled, makes no effort to show off or sell its product to thirsty motorists zipping up and down Highway 12.

I'm not advocating that Manitoba become as tacky as South Florida, where every second trailer park offers phony "Indian" souvenirs and gasoline-powered airboat rides. But the absence of independent travel info is the main reason I've compiled this guidebook – and likely the only reason you decided to buy it.

So without any further ranting, here's what's great about Manitoba:

- Sandy, secluded beaches that rarely see more than several dozen visitors on summer weekdays.

Opposite: Each summer, hundreds of beluga whales congregate in the shallow waters of Hudson Bay near Churchill.

- More lakes and rivers than you could ever hope to fish or paddle.
- Thousands of square kilometres of mostly unvisited natural areas inside national and provincial parks, as well as on Crown land.
- No fewer than 382 species of birds frequenting more than 300,000 square kilometres of undeveloped forests and wetlands.
- The world's largest concentrations of polar bears and red-sided garter snakes, and some of the last forests where wolves and caribou still thrive.
- Four distinct seasons, including a winter with enough snow to actually look and feel like winter.
- Small towns that come alive each summer with an array of idiosyncratic celebrations.
- A large and increasingly vibrant indigenous community that's never forgotten its traditions.
- North America's second-largest fringe-theatre festival and one of its best folk-music festivals.
- And Winnipeg, arguably the weirdest city in North America that doesn't go by the name of Austin, Texas.

Manitoba's attractions vary from region to region. Most but not all cultural attractions are concentrated within Winnipeg, while the rest of Manitoba is the place to get outdoors. Here is a sample of what you can see and do – you'll find more detail in each chapter of this guidebook.

Cultural Attractions

Bryan Scott

The Winnipeg Art Gallery is renowned for its collection of Inuit art – the largest in the world.

Galleries

While few Inuit live in Manitoba, the province's location below the middle of Nunavut means you can find spectacular art from the Arctic in private and public galleries around the province. The Winnipeg Art Gallery boasts the world's largest collection of Inuit art and it's in the midst of building a new wing just to show it off. You can also see and usually buy soapstone and whalebone carvings at private galleries elsewhere in Winnipeg and in Churchill. Just beware of soapstone trinkets sold at tourist traps – they may have no closer connection to Inuit culture than an Eskimo Pie. When in doubt, inquire about the artist.

Cree and Anishinaabe art is just as stunning and even more widely available, especially in northern Manitoba towns. In Winnipeg, you can find a wide selection of indigenous art – from Inuit soapstone carvings to contemporary works – at galleries such as Wah-Sa and the artist-run Urban Shaman.

The Manitoba capital is also home to a wide array of conventional and contemporary art galleries, including the large and mainstream Winnipeg Art Gallery, the nearby the trail-blazing Plug In Gallery or private galleries such as Mayberry Fine Art in the Exchange.

Bryan Scott

Museums

Nearly every town in Manitoba operates some kind of museum. Set up inside abandoned rail stations, former churches, or old one-room schoolhouses, these usually document the pioneer history of the community in question, which is great, if you're fascinated by 100-year-old agricultural implements.

While even the most mundane small-town museum can provide a quirky diversion during a long drive, there are some genuine gems in rural Manitoba. If you're interested in early indigenous history, the best $2 you'll ever spend will be on the Moncur Gallery, a collection of archeological artifacts located in the basement of a public library in Boissevain. Dinosaur fans should check out the Mesozoic-era marine reptile skeletons at the Canadian Fossil Discovery Centre in Morden. And Second World War history buffs will enjoy a visit to Brandon's Commonwealth Air Training Plan Museum, which chronicles the training of Allied flyers from around the English-speaking world.

As the provincial capital, larger Winnipeg offers bigger and better-funded museums, such as the skyline-dominating Canadian Museum for Human Rights at The Forks, the Children's Museum, and the Manitoba Museum, a sort of history-of-everything that includes a life-size replica of a transatlantic sailing ship used during the fur trade.

The Canadian Museum for Human Rights, the first national museum commissioned outside the Ottawa area, opened in 2014 at a cost of $351 million. Here it's lit up red for Canada Day.

33

Festivals and Fairs

Bottled up indoors most of the winter, Manitobans let loose in the summer with a flurry of festivals packed into the short stretch of balmy weather between Victoria Day and Thanksgiving. These range in nature from relatively quaint summer fairs like Frog Follies in St. Pierre-Jolys (yes, they actually race frogs) and Morden's Corn and Apple Festival to big-budget music festivals attracting more than 12,000 fans, most notably Dauphin's Countryfest near Riding Mountain and the Winnipeg Folk Festival in Birds Hill Park. Other major rural events include Canada's National Ukrainian Festival at Dauphin; Gimli's Icelandic-themed Islendingadagurinn; and the Morris Stampede, the second-largest rodeo in western Canada.

In Winnipeg, the big three summer festivals are downtown's Jazz Winnipeg Festival, the Exchange-based Winnipeg Fringe Theatre Festival, and Folklorama, a cheesy but inexplicably popular celebration of multiculturalism. Wintertime events, meanwhile, include the Winnipeg Symphony Orchestra's New Music Festival; the Northern Manitoba Trappers' Festival in The Pas; and St. Boniface's Festival du Voyageur, commemorating the Francophone community's roots in the 17th-century fur trade.

You'll find a list of Manitoba festivals – and the weekends on which they usually occur – within this guidebook.

A love-hate relationship with Winnipeg: Literate indie-rock quartet The Weakerthans defined the cultural paradox at the heart of the city's psyche early in the last decade.

Live Music

Manitoba enjoys a reputation for producing decent music and there is some substance behind the hype. Back in the '60s, Neil Young and The Guess Who got their start playing Winnipeg community centres, pre-dating more recent made-in-Manitoba success stories such as thrash-punk band Propagandhi, indie-rock's The Weakerthans, Celtic musician Loreena McKennitt and classical violinist James Ehnes.

Bartley Kives

While recorded music's fortunes have waned, a live music scene based in Winnipeg remains vibrant. At the grassroots level, up-and-coming local acts play clubs and small theatres such as the West End Cultural Centre, The Park Theatre, Good Will Social Club and Times Change(d) High & Lonesome Club. A relatively large number of major touring acts also visit the city, thanks in large part to the success of MTS Centre, the downtown hockey arena.

Other significant Winnipeg concert venues include the Centennial Concert Hall and two fully restored heritage theatres, the Burton Cummings Theatre and the Pantages Playhouse. Live music venues in the rest of Manitoba include Brandon's Keystone Centre and the unusual Manitou Opera House in the heart of the Pembina Valley.

The best way to find out who's playing where in Winnipeg is to pick up the *Winnipeg Free Press* on Thursdays or peruse the listings at manitobamusic.com.

Performing Arts

Winnipeg's claim to fame as a cultural centre is due to presence of bricks-and-mortar institutions like the Winnipeg Symphony Orchestra, the Royal Winnipeg Ballet, Manitoba Opera, Winnipeg's Contemporary Dancers, and several professional theatre companies, most notably the Royal Manitoba Theatre Centre, Prairie Theatre Exchange, Rainbow Stage, Theatre Projects Manitoba, Shakespeare in the Ruins, and the Francophone Cercle Molière.

The WSO, RWB, and Manitoba Opera all perform at the Centennial Concert Hall but occasionally tour the rest of the province during the fall-to-spring performance season.

The MTC stages big dramatic productions at its John Hirsch Mainstage as well as an edgier series of plays in its smaller Tom Hendry Warehouse Theatre. PTE focuses on made-in-Manitoba productions, while the summertime Rainbow Stage concentrates on popular musicals. Theatre Projects Manitoba focuses on regional and political works, while SIR adapts the Bard's works to indoor and outdoor settings at the Trappist Monastery Park.

Indigenous Culture

Compared to insular First Nations such as the Puebloans of Arizona, Manitoba's indigenous communities are extremely outgoing. Visitors with an interest in First Nations culture are usually welcome at annual gatherings called powwows, though it's a good idea to check ahead: ceremonies differ from community to community. The more mainstream Manito Ahbee Festival, held in Winnipeg, is even more accessible.

You can also get a sense of Manitoba's millenias-old indigenous presence by visiting sacred sites like the petroforms of Whiteshell Provincial Park, and – if you're determined – pictographs at Tramping Lake near Snow Lake, Paimusk Creek east of Norway House, and along the Bloodvein River.

Made-in-Manitoba Food

The most rewarding aspect of travelling is tasting food unique to a particular region. No matter where you are, you can always discover regional delicacies if you resist the temptation of eating at fast-food franchises and corporate-owned restaurant chains, which specialize in serving up big, huge plates of humdrum.

In Winnipeg, don't turn up your nose at a *fat boy*, the gloriously messy local version of the fast-food burger, which comes slathered in mayo and a savoury brown meat sauce known as "chili" even though it bears no resemblance to US stew.

Manitoba's eastern European heritage means perogies pop up frequently, served as main course, side dish, or even breakfast

Bartley Kives

Cabbage rolls and coffee, indeed: The lowly cabbage plays an important role in Ukrainian cuisine, a staple of Manitoba socials and fall suppers.

item. When you have a choice, always order the dumplings boiled or pan-fried – the deep-fried variety should only be consumed at a roadside stand in a Lake Winnipeg beach community, and even then, only when you've been drinking.

Unfortunately for foodies, ethnic culinary traditions unique to Manitoba rarely make their way out of the home kitchen. If you're lucky, you might be able to sniff out hearty Mennonite fare like *kielkje* (noodles in cream gravy), dive into a traditional Franco-Manitoban tourtière – a baked pie of ground beef, pork and (rarely!) venison – or chow down on bannock, the Canadian term for the indigenous staple the Americans call frybread.

Compared to cooking styles, made-in-Manitoba ingredients are much more common on local menus. No trip to the province is complete without a taste of the sweet-fleshed freshwater pickerel, known elsewhere as walleye. Most of it comes straight from Manitoba lakes and is usually breaded lightly and then pan-fried. Pickerel cheeks are like freshwater scallops – small nuggets of sweet, meaty goodness. Northern pike and whitefish, if you can find either, are also excellent.

Commercial fishers also do wonders with smoked fish, the finest being goldeye, a tiny but tasty relative of the giant arapaima of the Amazon River. Smoked goldeye's rich flavour and delicate texture outshines smoked trout. Never, ever pass up an opportunity to try it.

Truly wild rice, only grown in eastern Manitoba and parts of Ontario and Minnesota, is oddly uncommon on local menus, as it's an expensive ingredient that's difficult to cook consistently. Wild rice is nonetheless cheaper here than anywhere else on Earth, so consider buying a packet as a travel memento or gift.

Other Manitoba foodstuffs to sample include bison (who can resist chowing down on the provincial symbol?), "Manitoba lamb" (which may actually come from northwestern Ontario) and saskatoons, which are blueberry-like fruit that are excellent in pies and jams. Winnipeg-style rye bread – light and fluffy, flecked with caraway – is also among the best in the world.

To wash it all down, the most popular local microbrews are bottled in Winnipeg by the Half Pints and Fort Garry breweries. Gimli is also the source of Crown Royal, Canadian whiskey that comes in the fuzzy purple bag, but it's actually processed elsewhere.

Restaurants

Yeah, I know – didn't we just talk about food? But there's a difference between a made-in-Manitoba cuisine and the food you actually find in restaurants.

In Winnipeg, you can chow down at a restaurant of almost any kind of ethnic cuisine you can possibly crave. Asian cuisine is a strong suit, as there are dozens of Vietnamese, Punjabi and Filipino joints to rival the usual mix of chain restaurants, pizza parlours, and Chinese-American buffets you'll find anywhere in North America.

Higher-end kitchens are on the upswing, as small plates and tasting menus have made their way on to the Prairies. At the other end of the scale, Winnipeg offers a huge number of homegrown burger joints that make life difficult for McDonald's, as well as the home-gown Salisbury House chain, which offers idiosyncratic burgers called "nips."

Outside Winnipeg, your restaurant options may be more limited, as small towns offer the basics, and the quality of highway roadhouses can be hit-and-miss. While there are a handful of high-end establishments in bedroom communities around Winnipeg, most rural fare tends to fall into the category of "more is better," with huge portions of short orders like perogies and hamburger steaks served up at reasonable prices.

When in doubt in rural Manitoba, ask a local for advice – or eat wherever you see a lot of cars on a Sunday evening.

Spectator Sports

When the National Hockey League's Winnipeg Jets left for Phoenix in 1996, it was like a knife was thrust into the Manitoba capital. The return of the Jets in 2011 sparked a spontaneous outpouring of joy akin to the end of a war.

The Jets play out of downtown Winnipeg's 15,300-seat MTS Centre, the smallest arena in the NHL. As a result, tickets can be hard to obtain as well as expensive, though some are always listed for re-sale online – or available through a hotel concierge. The atmosphere in the small arena is usually worth the admission price.

Equally beloved, albeit more grudgingly, are the Canadian Football League's Winnipeg Blue Bombers, one of the oldest clubs in North American professional sport. The Bombers turned 85 in 2015 but had not won a CFL championship in a full quarter-century. They play in 33,000-seat Investors Group Field, located on the

University of Manitoba's campus in the southern Winnipeg neighbourhood of Fort Garry.

Independent baseball's Winnipeg Goldeyes, meanwhile, play at downtown Winnipeg's 7,500-seat Shaw Park, a picturesque outdoor ball diamond north of The Forks.

Outside Winnipeg, the biggest sporting draw is the Western Hockey League's junior-aged Brandon Wheat Kings, who play at the 5,000-seat Keystone Centre. The OCN Blizzard of the Manitoba Junior Hockey League also has a rabid following in The Pas and neighbouring Opaskwayak Cree Nation.

For the ultimate Manitoba sporting experience, forgo hockey for a curling bonspiel, which can make national stars out of ordinary shmoes. A difficult game to master, curling is a religion on the Canadian prairies, partly because the players on the ice don't look much different than the hosers in the stands.

Shopping

A stereotypical list of Manitoba mementos would include indigenous crafts and non-perishable foodstuffs like wild rice and saskatoon jam.

This stuff is great, but you'll probably have more fun if you forget about knick-knacks and focus instead on vintage clothing, antiques, and second-hand books and music. Thanks to the relatively low population density, there's more great junk on the Prairies than anywhere else in Canada.

While Winnipeg boasts an abundance of vintage-clothing boutiques, small towns are often the best place to find the most interesting items, as university students in the city are notoriously quick to snap up all the best clothing and furniture in non-boutique stores like Value Village. The smaller the town, the better the chance of finding something weird, unique, or possibly even valuable. Just make sure you know what you're doing before you spend big bucks on a supposed antique.

If new consumer goods are what you're after, Winnipeg offers the same array of shopping-mall retail franchises you'll find anywhere else in Canada. Winnipeg's three largest malls are Polo Park in the west, St. Vital Centre in the southeast and downtown's Portage Place. Higher-end new clothing and consumer goods can be found in shops scattered along Winnipeg's Academy Road, Corydon Avenue, Osborne Street, and in the Exchange, in descending order of price.

Of course, not everyone wants to drop big bucks on designer clothing. If you prefer cheap tourist crap – and be honest, you probably do – the biggest concentration of useless doodads can be found at tourist-friendly retailers at The Forks.

Outdoor Activities:
Spring, summer and fall

Beaches

Given Manitoba's reputation for chilliness, the variety and quality
of beaches in the province is nothing less than shocking. Though
the sunbathing season is short, there are excellent strips of
sand along many of the province's lakes, a legacy of glacial Lake
Agassiz and 10,000 subsequent years of wind and wave action.
The most popular beaches include Grand, Victoria, Winnipeg, and
Gimli beaches on Lake Winnipeg. Cooler waters may be found at
Wasagaming Beach in Riding Mountain Park and West Hawk Lake
and Falcon Lake beaches in Whiteshell Provincial Park, while inexplicably popular artificial beaches exist at Birds Hill and St. Malo
provincial parks.

If you prefer solitude, Patricia Beach affords more privacy
and Beaconia tolerates nudists. But there are even more secluded
beaches accessible only from the water – Lake Winnipeg alone
has hundreds of kilometres of sand visited only by the occasional
kayak, sailboat, or motorboat.

Paddling

If you'll excuse the brutal pun, Manitoba is a paddler's wet dream.
Pool-and-drop rivers in the Canadian Shield beckon whitewater
paddlers; flatwater paddlers can find solitude on more than
100,000 lakes; and sea kayakers who can't afford to hit Baja
California can keep their skills sharp on wide-open Lake Winnipeg

Beaches abound
in the sub-Arctic:
The three-km-
long strip of sand
at Grand Beach
Provincial Park at
sunset, after the
dispersal of day-
time crowds that
sometimes exceed
10,000.

or take on the life-threatening tidal challenges of frigid, polar-bear-frequented Hudson Bay.

The remote Seal River, the historic Hayes River, and the relatively accessible Bloodvein River all belong on the life list of any serious paddler. But few people have the time or experience to take on monumental trips.

Brenda Schritt

A careful approach to a rapid on the Bloodvein River, which flows from Ontario through Atikaki Provincial Wilderness Park to Lake Winnipeg.

Experienced guides and outfitters can take you practically anywhere, for the right price. If you're a novice, start with a day paddle on a placid Prairie river such as the Seine or La Salle. Or if you have a little wilderness experience, consider a weekend trip in Whiteshell or Nopiming provincial park, both blessed with established flatwater routes and well-marked portages.

Even more experienced canoeists consider the Crown land east of Lake of the Woods as one of the best flatwater-paddling areas in North America. A portion of this region is known as the Experimental Lakes Area, where freshwater scientists conduct environmental research.

Kayakers and stand-up paddleboarders may prefer the portage-free maze of islands in Lake of the Woods itself, or head on to Lake Winnipeg to explore the islands of Hecla-Grindstone Provincial Park and the Kasakeemeemisekak Archipelago. Playboaters, on the other hand, congregate at easily accessible rapids on the Whitemouth River near Elma, or Sturgeon Falls on the Winnipeg River in Whiteshell Provincial Park.

If you're serious about a wilderness paddling trip, it's a good idea to flip through Hap Wilson and Stephanie Aykroyd's *Wilderness Rivers of Manitoba*, or the *Routes* page on Paddle Manitoba's website, paddle.mb.ca.

If you're interested in day paddles, you can rent a canoe, kayak, or playboat at most busy beaches during the summer, or at The Forks in downtown Winnipeg. Longer-term rentals are available from Winnipeg retailers The Wilderness Supply and Mountain Equipment Co-op.

Hiking and Backpacking

Given the absence of mountains, Manitoba is no place for hikers who thrive on altitude or get off on the long, lingering lactic-acid burn that comes with serious climbs. But there are many places in the province where the scenery makes a walk worthwhile, if not always challenging.

Whiteshell Provincial Park offers eight day-hikes through the rugged Canadian Shield landscape, the most popular being the 8.2-kilometre Pine Point Rapids trail. There's a little more elevation on the east face of Riding Mountain National Park, which rises 350 metres from the surrounding prairie.

Spruce Woods Provincial Park offers the most celebrated day-hike in the province in the Spirit Sands, a small patch of active sand dunes crisscrossed by a 10-kilometre trail system. Other short trails can be found in almost every other provincial park, including Birds Hill, located just 20 kms northeast of Winnipeg.

Backpacking options are more limited, as most parks lack trails of any considerable distance. Riding Mountain has an extensive trail system, but the wide, flat former roads are better suited to cycling and horseback riding. The two best backpacking trails are the easy, 22-kilometre overnight to northern Manitoba's Kwasitchewan Falls, the province's highest at 15 metres; and the biggest walk of them all – Mantario Trail, a relatively strenuous, 66-kilometre jaunt across the wildest section of the Whiteshell, traversable in three to five days.

It's also possible to cross the entire width of the province on Manitoba's 1,200-kilometre portion of the Trans Canada Trail (tctrail.ca), but I wouldn't advise it: Much of the route follows gravel roads, which doesn't make for enjoyable hiking.

For more ideas about rural walks, pick up *Hiking The Heartland*, a guidebook published by the Prairie Pathfinders, a non-profit walking club.

Cycling and Mountain Biking

On paper, flat land should translate into easy cycling. But high winds and a shortage of dedicated bike routes rarely make it easy for long-distance riders anywhere in southern Manitoba.

On the Trans-Canada Highway, semi-trailers are a constant menace. Cross-country cyclists traversing the province may want to consider slightly less dangerous Highways 2, 3 or 23.

Road cyclists looking for a shorter spin may be frustrated by Winnipeg, where there's little in the way of dedicated routes despite tens of millions in recent cycling-infrastructure investment. The best advice can be found in the *Cyclists Map of Winnipeg*, on sale at most Winnipeg bike shops as well as online. Bikes may also be rented at some sporting-good retailers.

Popular paved routes across the province include the Riverwalk in Brandon, the seven-kilometre Pine Ridge Bicycle Trail in Birds Hill Provincial Park, and the 13-kilometre South Whiteshell Trail, which runs from Falcon Lake to West Hawk Lake in Whiteshell Provincial Park. For other road cycling options, visit the Manitoba Cycling Association (MCA) at cycling.mb.ca.

Cycling through Beaudry Provincial Heritage Park, a small protected area just west of Winnipeg.

Charles Shilliday

Offroad cyclists have some options, thanks to cross-country ski trails that double as mountain-bike routes during the warmer months. Trail systems at Birds Hill Provincial Park, Sandilands Provincial Forest, and Grand Beach Provincial Park are suitable for novice mountain bikers, while the Brandon Hills, Birch Ski Area (open to MCA members only), and other areas of the Manitoba Escarpment feature more-challenging terrain. Both Turtle Mountain and Spruce Woods Provincial Parks offer the opportunity to ride a little longer on loops maxing out around 40 kilometres. One of the best daytrips in the province is the Epinette Creek-Newfoundland trail in Spruce Woods, a 42-kilometre single-track loop featuring many small hills but also enough sandy soil to cushion any spill.

Riding Mountain National Park is the only place where you can ride off-road for days without encountering a vehicle. In dry conditions, the 67-kilometre Central Trail, which bisects the west side of the park, is OK for a wildlife-watching overnight or leisurely long weekend. Watch for moose, bears, deer, and especially elk during the fall mating season. There are steeper day-use mountain-bike trails on the east side of the park.

Other off-road cycling destinations include sections of the Trans Canada Trail around Asessippi Provincial Park and Inglis; the Ontario border town of Ingolf; and the greenstone at Flin Flon, which the locals liken to the slickrock in Moab, Utah.

Charles Shilliday

Daytrips and longer journeys on horseback are possible in Riding Mountain National Park.

Horse Trails and Ranch Vacations

Riding Mountain National Park got its name for a reason: Early traders ditched their canoes to cross Manitoba's modest highlands on horseback.

Today, the best way to see wildlife in southern Manitoba's only national park is up in the saddle, which allows you to see above grasses and shrubs during the summer. The park has dozens of day-riding routes, plus equestrian campsites for longer rides. Other popular riding areas include Birds Hill, Spruce Woods, and Turtle Mountain provincial parks.

For a list of equestrian campsites and horse-friendly B&Bs – plus rural and farm vacation ideas – visit countryvacations.mb.ca.

Climbing

The highest point in Manitoba is Baldy Mountain, which stands a not-very-staggering 831 metres above sea level. It takes all of about 30 seconds to reach the summit from a parking lot just off the main road running through Duck Mountain Provincial Park. There is no actual climbing here.

For real rock-climbing, head east to the exposed granite of the Canadian Shield. There are at least 11 established, climbing areas in Whiteshell Provincial Park and northwestern Ontario. Some are road-accessible, but others can only be reached by canoe. They're all described on the resource page of the Manitoba Section of the Alpine Club of Canada at alpine-club.mb.ca.

In Winnipeg, you can climb in a controlled environment on indoor walls at Vertical Adventures (77 Paramount Rd. 204.632.5001, verticaladventures.ca) and Mountain Equipment Co-op (303 Portage Ave., 204.943.4202, mec.ca).

Wildlife Watching

Every October, an estimated 900 polar bears congregate on the Hudson Bay near Churchill, waiting for the ice to freeze. This unusual concentration of gigantic predators brings tourists from around the world to this northern Manitoba outpost, swelling both the town's population and the price of hotel rooms until the bears finally leave in early November.

Most of Churchill's visitors come to see the bears from safe vantage points in oversized vehicles called tundra buggies. But the town is also worth a visit during the summer, when white beluga whales and their charcoal-grey babies gather in amazing numbers in the Churchill River estuary.

Churchill is Manitoba's top ecotourist destination, but certainly not the only one. Riding Mountain National Park brings in visitors every fall to hear the elk bugle. Wolf fans head to the Whiteshell during full moons in the hopes of hearing howls. You also stand a decent chance of seeing moose, coyotes, black bear, and snapping turtles in a variety of parks.

If you're fascinated by cold-blooded creatures, about 70,000 red-sided garter snakes gather at limestone pits in the Narcisse Wildlife Management Area every spring and fall in the largest congregation of reptiles anywhere on Earth.

And if you have an interest in birds, you can spend a lifetime observing up to 382 species that either breed in Manitoba or pass through the province on annual migrations. Birding hotspots include Oak Hammock Marsh northwest of Winnipeg, Delta Marsh at the south end of Lake Manitoba, and Whitewater Lake just north of Turtle Mountain. But it's easy to spot some sort of interesting avian species anywhere there's a river, marsh, or lake – which is just about everywhere. Manitoba has large populations of dramatic species like white pelicans, cormorants, bald eagles, osprey, great grey owls, loons, great blue herons, and all manner of ducks, songbirds, and raptors. If you're lucky, you may also see sandhill cranes, ruby-throated hummingbirds, white-faced ibises and snowy egrets.

The definitive birdwatching bible is the Manitoba Naturalist Society's massive and remarkably complete *Birds of Manitoba*, but it's easier to tote around Andy Bezener and Ken De Smet's paperback field guide *Manitoba Birds*.

Patience is required for any wildlife-watching excursion, so put in plenty of trail time, and don't set unrealistic expectations. That said, it's easy to observe certain types of wildlife. At dusk and dawn, white-tailed deer pose a serious threat on Manitoba highways. During the spring and fall, Canada geese flock in such large numbers, light sleepers reach for earplugs. And anywhere towns encroach on forest, you could encounter human-habituated black bears, so it's extremely important to keep campsites and cottage areas clean.

Fishing

The biggest fish ever caught in Manitoba was a 185-kilogram lake sturgeon pulled out of the Roseau River in 1903. These ancient monsters have all but disappeared from Manitoban waterways,

Brenda Schritt

The essential ingredients of a Manitoba shore lunch: pickerel, a cast-iron frying pan, and an open fire.

but the province continues to teem with wonderfully tasty walleye – although we call them pickerel – as well as sport fish such as northern pike, lake trout, and massive channel catfish.

It might sound like a boast, but there really is nowhere in Manitoba where the fishing is lousy. There are more than 100,000 lakes in the province and an unquantifiable number of rivers and streams. Even the muddy, mildly polluted Red River supports a world-class catch-and-release catfish hotspot north of Lockport.

In total, Manitoba's inland waterways are home to 95 fish species, 83 of which are native to province. For more information about where to find them, peruse the fantastic *Freshwater Fishes of Manitoba*, an ichthyological tour-de-force by Kenneth Stewart and Douglas Watkinson.

Windsurfing, Kiteboarding and Sailing

Near-constant winds and open waters make Manitoba's big lakes ideal for racing around on windsurfers, catamarans, and sailboats. But extended touring is not as popular as you might guess, as lakes Winnipeg and Manitoba don't have enough ports of call to sustain the kind of sailing culture that flourishes in Lake Ontario, for example.

Sailboats frequently launch from marinas at Gimli and Gull Harbour on Lake Winnipeg. There are far more yachts plying the deeper waters of Lake of the Woods, where there's a multitude of islands as well as wealthy cottage-owners. Kenora, Ont. has an extensive marina.

Charles Shilliday

Boating and Cruises

Boating and fishing usually go hand-in-hand on most Manitoba lakes, but powerboats and other small pleasure craft are

Kite surfing on Lake Winnipeg near Gimli.

not uncommon summer sights, especially on the Red River near Winnipeg and on Lake of the Woods. Very few Manitoba lakes are off-limits to motorized craft. The main exceptions are designated wilderness areas inside provincial parks.

But you don't have to own a boat to hit the water. You can take day or evening cruises on Clear Lake in Riding Mountain National Park, on the Red River in Winnipeg, and the Souris River in Souris.

Lake of the Woods has more of a marine culture. You can rent or charter houseboats, powerboats, sailboats, powered yachts, and even tugs out of Kenora, Sioux Narrows, and Nestor Falls, Ont.

Hunting

One of Manitoba's most lucrative tourist draws is bear hunting, as it remains legal to bait the beasts in this province. Whether or not you consider this repugnant, Manitoba's black bear population is large enough to withstand the limited pressure of controlled hunting.

In southern Manitoba, there are bear-hunting seasons in the spring and fall. There are also seasons for white-tailed deer, moose, elk, wolves, ducks, geese, and upland birds, although seasons vary, and non-residents may be subject to restrictions. Woodland caribou, mule deer, polar bear, and all birds of prey are among species protected from hunting.

For more information about opportunities for killing all manner of furry and feathered things, pick up a copy of Manitoba Conservation's *Hunting Guide* at a local hardware or sporting store, or visit gov.mb.ca/conservation/wildlife/hunting/index.html.

To American visitors, Canadian firearm regulations can be complex and bizarre, so it's a good idea to read up ahead of time. Check out the Canadian Firearms Program website at rcmp-grc.gc.ca/cfp-pcaf/index-eng.htm to avoid a headache — or confiscated weaponry — at the border.

A warm, late-winter day at the Birch Ski Area, a cross-country ski-trail system on the Manitoba Escarpment, near Roseisle.

Outdoor Activities: Winter

Cross-country Skiing

One of the weirder facets of a Manitoba winter is cold doesn't guarantee snow. While the first white stuff usually falls by the second week in November, there often isn't enough to support skinny skis until Christmas – and even then, it may take another few weeks for river ice to freeze.

As a result, the cross-country ski season in Manitoba can seem excruciatingly short for people who enjoy one of the most balanced forms of cardiovascular exercise known to humankind. Given the province's flat topography, traditional Nordic skiing remains popular. But few Manitoban cross-country ski trails are completely flat.

Trail systems at Pinawa, Grand Beach, Falcon Lake, Birds Hill Park, Pumpkin Creek, Bittersweet and the Birch Ski Area offer enough hills to challenge novice skiers. There are also longer trails at Turtle Mountain, Spruce Woods, and Riding Mountain, the latter boasting an incredible 275 kms of traditional Nordic trails (prior to federal parks cutbacks) as well as a couple of routes groomed for skate-skiing. Frozen lakes and rivers also make for great skiing surfaces, as long as you avoid snowmobile routes. Most power-sled users are courteous to skiers, but the noise can be annoying.

Spring Hill Winter Park, on the outskirts of Winnipeg, makes use of an artificial trench dug for the Red River Floodway.

For a list of Manitoba ski trails and detailed directions, visit the Cross Country Ski Association of Manitoba at ccski.mb.ca.

Downhill Skiing and Snowboarding

When you don't have actual mountains, you make do with what you have. That's why three of Manitoba's most popular ski-and-snowboard areas are actually depressions in the ground.

Western Manitoba's Asessippi Provincial Park sits on the eroded banks of the Shell River Valley. La Rivière's Holiday Mountain runs down the Pembina Valley, while the Winnipeg-area Springhill Winter Park takes advantage of the oversized drainage ditch known as the Red River Floodway. Obviously, none of these places will ever host the Winter Olympics, but the modest elevation is fine for people learning to ski.

Other short downhill ski slopes can be found at Falcon Lake, Stony Mountain, Minnedosa, Thunder Hill west of Swan River, and Mystery Mountain, north of Thompson. If none of this works for you, it's time to save up for that trip to Whistler.

Snowshoeing

Forget those horrible childhood memories of lashing complex leather bindings to heavy wooden snowshoes and walking bow-legged through deep powder until your groin muscles ache. Modern, aluminum-frame snowshoes are light and ridiculously easy to use – if you can walk, you'll have no problem snowshoeing.

Bartley Kives

Along with a pair of winter boots, deerskin mukluks or waterproof, insulated hikers, snowshoes allow you to hit any hiking trail you like, no matter how deep the snow, and probably wind up with the trail all to yourself. And once January rolls around, you can also explore frozen rivers and streams.

Riding Mountain National Park offers three dedicated trails, but you can snowshoe almost anywhere you like in the province, provided you don't mess up cross-country ski trails.

Snowshoes are also great for winter camping, either as the primary means of moving along the trail, or in combination with cross-country skis. Some hikers also take a small pair along during late-season backpacking trips, just in case.

Don't be afraid of a little snow. While there is an element of risk in winter camping, a pair of snowshoes can make almost any trail traversible all year – even the frozen surface of Lake Winnipeg.

Winter Camping

As crazy as it sounds, winter camping in frigid Manitoba can be an amazing experience, provided you take the right gear and precautions.

On a still winter day, leafless forests and frozen lakes seem almost magically quiet. And in wilderness areas, the snow cover provides a record of all the wildlife in the area – snow makes it easy to identify the footprints of animals that leave no trace of their passage during the summer.

If the idea of sleeping in a tent in the middle of the winter still seems insane, there are backcountry cabins in Spruce Woods and Riding Mountain. You can also rent heated yurts at several provincial parks as well as at Minaki Yurt Adventures, north of Kenora, Ont.

If that still seems too rustic, you can always rent a cabin. Year-round accommodations ranging from rustic huts to luxury

Charles Shilliday

Winter kite surfing on Lake Winnipeg near Gimli – compare it to kite surfing on page 45!

lodges are concentrated in Whiteshell Provincial Park and, in western Manitoba, near Riding Mountain.

Ice Fishing

To people who make a living off pickerel, ice fishing is a way of life. For thousands of other Manitobans, it offers a chance to build elaborate temporary structures on lake and river ice and consume copious quantities of alcohol as long as the frigid weather holds.

The most lavish ice-fishing huts are decked out with portable heaters, couches, generators, stereos, and satellite TV. Hand augers have been replaced by gasoline-powered drills, which easily poke holes through any lake or river ice. If you've ever been to a sports bar on NFL Sunday, you pretty much know the atmosphere.

Still, it would be unwise to turn down an invitation to go ice fishing, as there are few more definitively Manitoban experiences. You just better be able to hold your rye, as heated Portapotties are never around when you need them.

Dog Sledding

In mid-January, "mush" refers to more than what happens to your brain when you're exposed to a northern Manitoba winter. Outfitters in Churchill and Thompson offer dog sled rides and sometimes even instruction.

In southern Manitoba, the Manitoba Dog Sledding Association maintains trails in Birds Hill Provincial Park, Mars Hills Wildlife Management Area, and Agassiz Provincial Forest.

Snowmobiling

An essential means of transportation for hunters and trappers up north, snowmobiles are extremely popular recreational vehicles in southern Manitoba. A 10,000-kilometre network of volunteer-maintained snowmobile trails criss-cross the province, making it possible to ride from town to town without having to use roadways.

Snowmobiles are noisy, but do a lot less damage to the environment than ATVs, as most riders stick to established trails. A map of Manitoba's snowmobile routes, as well as rules and regulations, is online at the Snowmobilers of Manitoba (Snoman) website at snoman.mb.ca.

In a nutshell, every snowmobile must be registered and insured, while drivers must wear helmets and pony up $125 for an annual Snopass from Snoman, which helps pay for trail maintenance. Tourists can buy a seven-day pass for $60.50. If you're caught on a trail without a pass, the ticket will set you back $400.

Top Ten Manitoba Attractions

BEST BIG-CITY NEIGHBOURHOOD:
Winnipeg's Exchange District

The draw: Neo-classical architecture from the turn of the 20th century, Winnipeg's heaviest concentration of clubs and restaurants, a good collection of independent art galleries and boutique retailers and most of the city's major performing arts venues. In the summer, the hypermodernist Cube stage at Old Market Square serves as ground zero for the Winnipeg International Jazz Festival, Winnipeg Fringe Theatre Festival and Manitoba Electronic Music Exhibition.

The duration: However long you like. Take a one-hour historical walking tour or hang out in the Exchange for days.

The damage: Free for window-shoppers on foot. Throw in admission to the Manitoba Museum admission, a concert, and a meal, and you can spend hundreds a day.

Winnipeg's Exchange District, filled with turn-of-the-twentieth-century architecture, often features in Hollywood films as a stand-in for American cities like Chicago or Kansas City. Many Winnipeggers credit our city fathers for maintaining this neighbourhood's heritage, but in fact, stagnation through most of the twentieth century allowed the city to protect the buildings.

BEST WILDLIFE-WATCHING SPOT:
Churchill and the Hudson Bay coast

The draw: The world's largest congregation of polar bears in the fall, amazing wildflowers in the spring, beluga whales and birds during the summer, and northern lights in midwinter.

The duration: Allow yourself at least two full days to explore everything Churchill has to offer, especially since it takes a long time to get here – 36 hours by train from Winnipeg, or 13 hours from Thompson following a seven-hour drive from Winnipeg. Flights from Winnipeg take two hours.

The damage: Anywhere from $1,000 to more than $5,000 a head, depending on your choice of transportation, accommodations, and tours.

CRAZIEST & MOST CONTROVERSIAL STRUCTURE: Canadian Museum for Human Rights, The Forks, Winnipeg

The draw: The first national museum in Canada commissioned outside of Ottawa, the CMHR is less a genocide memorial than it is a touchscreen-triggered spectacle of multimedia storytelling. The intention is to inspire – but you may just marvel at $351 million worth of alabaster, basalt, concrete, glass and steel. You must venture inside to get the full picture.

The duration: Give yourself at least two hours to stroll through the place. There's more than a kilometre of walkways connecting the exhibits.

The damage: $15 for adults, $12 for students and seniors or $7 for youths aged seven to 17. Free for kids six and under.

BEST EASY DAY HIKE: Spirit Sands, Spruce Woods Provincial Park

The draw: A 10-kilometre trail system encompassing active sand dunes that resemble desert, open meadows, aspen forest, and a rare colour-shifting pond called the Devil's Punchbowl.

The duration: Two to four hours, depending on how far you walk. Allow another 3.5 hours to drive from Winnipeg and back.

The damage: $5 per vehicle, or free with a $40 annual Manitoba provincial park pass.

BEST BACKPACKING ROUTE: Mantario Trail, Whiteshell Provincial Park

The draw: At 66 kilometres, Manitoba's longest and most rugged hiking trail, traversing granite ridges, wetlands, and lakes in a development-free patch of the Canadian Shield.

The duration: Three to five days.

The damage: Oddly, there are no trail fees, though vehicles parked at trailheads require a park pass. Spend whatever you like on food, which you must bring with you – there are no services along the trail.

BEST PLACE TO TAKE THE KIDS: Assiniboine Park Zoo, Winnipeg

The draw: Four polar bears and other Arctic animals are the star attractions at Journey To Churchill, the centerpiece of Winnipeg's partly remodelled Assiniboine Park Zoo, which reopened in 2014 after undergoing a $90-million facelift. The underwater viewing area for the bears is popular, so go early.

The duration: Give yourself at least 90 minutes.

The damage: $18.50 for adults, $14.81 for seniors and youths aged 13 to 17 or $10 for kids aged three to 12. Free for kids two and under.

BEST PLACE TO VEGETATE: Patricia Beach Provincial Park and Beaconia Beach, Lake Winnipeg

The draw: Kilometres of very fine sand and minimal crowds; even on summer weekends, both families and the musclehead/bikini crowd prefer Grand Beach and Winnipeg Beach.

The duration: One long, lazy day.

The damage: Half a tank of gas. You need a Manitoba parks pass for Patricia Beach, but diddlysquat for Beaconia.

BEST SUMMER FESTIVAL: Winnipeg Folk Festival, Birds Hill Provincial Park

The draw: Dozens of folk, roots, and global music peformers on eight outdoor stages, a glorious outdoor setting, and a wild campground resembling a miniature Burning Man Festival, all during the warmest weekend of the year.

The duration: Four days, if you can handle the stimulation.

The damage: Up to $68 for a day pass, $235 for a weekend pass, and $85 for camping, with discounts offered for early-bird purchasers – and breaks for students and seniors.

BEST WHITEWATER RIVER: Bloodvein River, Atikaki Provincial Wilderness Park

The draw: Dozens of runnable rapids along this riverine ribbon of Canadian Shield beauty – accessible by portage or floatplane only – suit wilderness trippers of all skill levels, thanks to well-maintained portage trails around almost every rapid. Bald eagles, river otters, and petroglyphs only sweeten the deal on this classic pool-and-drop river.

The duration: Seven to twelve days, depending how far east you start.

The damage: Nothing if you portage in, but flying in on a floatplane will set you back at least $500 per person. Fully outfitted trips cost in the thousands.

BEST RESORT TOWN: Wasagaming, Riding Mountain National Park

The draw: Rustic wooden buildings in the National Park style, the beach and marina at Clear Lake, a massive summer campground, and easy access to wilderness attractions throughout Riding Mountain, Manitoba's only road-accessible national park. Nearby Onanole, outside the park, gives you everything the Parks Canada does not allow.

The duration: A night or two in town, and perhaps longer in the backcountry.

The damage: One night at Elkhorn Lodge will set you back $190 during a summer weekend. Wasagaming Campground sites start at $27.40 a night. Popping in and out will only cost you a $7.80-a-head park admission fee.

Holiday and Festival Calendar

January

New Year's Day (Nationwide, Jan. 1): All retailers, government offices and banks, as well as most restaurants and many cultural attractions, are closed.

Assiniboine River skating trail and "Warming Huts" exhibition (Assiniboine River west of The Forks, Winnipeg, January and into February): Weather permitting, Canada's longest outdoor skating trail, lined with structures created by the winners of an international design competition.

Winnipeg Symphony Orchestra New Music Festival (Centennial Concert Hall and other venues, Winnipeg, late January or early February): Ten days of works by current and 20th-century composers.

February

Festival du Voyageur (St. Boniface, Winnipeg, mid-February): western Canada's largest winter festival: celebration of Francophone community and fur-trade-era history, with live music and snow sculptures.

Louis Riel Day (Province-wide, third Monday in February): Holiday commemorating Manitoba's founder. Provincial and municipal government offices and some are closed, along with some retailers.

Trappers Festival/Indian Days (The Pas and Opaskwayak Cree Nation, mid-February): Winter festival, with dog-sled races and skills competitions.

March

Freeze Frame (First week of March, Winnipeg): Children's film festival.

Royal Manitoba Winter Fair (Keystone Centre, Brandon, late March and early April): Week-long agricultural expo.

April

CBC Winnipeg Comedy Festival (Winnipeg, early April): Week-long stand-up comedy festival.

Good Friday (Province-wide, late March or early April): Banks and government offices are closed.

Sugaring-Off Festival (St.-Pierre-Jolys, mid-April): Maple-syrup-tapping festival.

Núna (Winnipeg, mid-April): Icelandic-Canadian arts festival.

May

Victoria Day (Nationwide, third weekend in May): Commonwealth-inspired holiday that amounts to the first long weekend of the summer, with fireworks held in most Manitoba communities on the Sunday or Monday night. Government offices, banks and most retailers are closed.

June

Back 40 Festival (Morden, first weekend in June): Folk and roots music.

Brandon Summer Fair (Brandon, first week of June): Rides, carnival food, and a circus.

Manitoba Paddlefest (FortWhyte Alive, Winnipeg, first weekend in June): Canoeing and kayaking expo.

Winnipeg International Children's Festival (The Forks, Winnipeg, first or second week in June): Children's performers and activities.

Pride Winnipeg Festival (Winnipeg, early June): LGBTQ festival.

Winnipeg International Jazz Festival (Downtown Winnipeg, mid-June): Ten-day jazz, pop, and urban-music festival. Free outdoor performances at Old Market Square and ticketed indoor performances.

National Aboriginal Day (Manitoba-wide, Summer Solstice): First Nations, Métis, and Inuit celebrations on June 20 or 21, including a concert at The Forks in Winnipeg.

Red River Exhibition (Exhibition Park, Winnipeg, late June): Two-week carnival with midway rides and free performances.

Nickel Days (Thompson, late June): Annual community festival.

July

Canada Day (Nationwide, July 1): National holiday, akin to US Fourth of July. Free performances and fireworks in most Manitoba communities. Banks, government offices and most retailers are closed.

Trout Festival (Flin Flon, Canada Day weekend): Fishing derby/fishfest.

Dauphin's Countryfest (Selo Ukraina Site near Dauphin, first weekend in July): Four-day country, rock and roots festival, with major international headliners; three outdoor stages, four campgrounds. Largest music festival in Manitoba.

Manitoba Highland Gathering (Selkirk, first Saturday in July): Scottish cultural festival.

Winnipeg Folk Festival (Birds Hill Park, second weekend in July): Four-day folk, roots, rock, and world-music festival, considered among North America's best; eight outdoor stages, two campgrounds.

Carman Country Fair (Carman, second weekend in July): Town fair.

Prairie Pioneer Days (Killarney, second weekend in July): Town fair.

Manitoba Stampede and Exhibition (Morris, mid-July): Manitoba's largest rodeo.

Winnipeg Fringe Theatre Festival (Exchange District, Winnipeg, late July): Short plays, sketch comedy, and experimental theatre in two dozen venues; it's the third-largest festival of its kind in the world.

Brandon Folk Music and Art Festival (Keystone Centre Grounds, late July): Two-day folk festival.

Gimli Film Festival (Gimli, late July): Film festival, with beachfront screenings.

Sunflower Festival (Altona, late July): Town fair.

Thresherman's Reunion and Stampede (Austin, last weekend in July): Agricultural festival, rodeo, and dance.

Rockin' The Fields of Minnedosa (Lake Minnedosa, late July or early August): Classic rock festival.

Kenora Harbourfest (Kenora, Ont., late July or early August): Three-day community festival.

August

Civic Holiday (Province-wide): First Monday in August, creating a three-day weekend locals call "the August Long." Banks and government offices closed.

Treaty & York Boat Days (Norway House Cree Nation, first week in August): Cree heritage celebration, with rowboat races and dances.

Islendingadagurinn (Gimli, first weekend in August): Town fair and Icelandic cultural festival.

Canada's National Ukrainian Festival (Selo Ukraina Site, Dauphin, first weekend in August): Ukrainian musical and cultural celebration.

Pioneer Days (Steinbach, first weekend in August): Town fair and Mennonite cultural expo.

Frog Follies (St. Pierre-Jolys, first weekend in August): Town fair, with frog races.

Métis Days (St. Laurent, first weekend in August): Town fair and Métis cultural celebration.

Folklorama (Winnipeg, first two weeks of August): Multicultural celebration with forty pavilions representing ethnic and national groups. Big with the bus-tour crowd.

Potato Fest (Portage la Prairie, second weekend in August): Community festival.

Great Woods Music Festival (Great Woods Park, Beausejour, second weekend in August): Blues and roots music.

Trout Forest Music Festival (Ear Falls, Ont., early August): Outdoor folk and roots festival, with campground.

Harvest Festival (Winkler, second weekend in August): Town fair.

Opaskwayak Indian Days (Opaskwayak Cree Nation, mid-August): First Nations cultural celebration.

Interstellar Rodeo (The Forks, Winnipeg, mid-August): Outdoor roots, rock and pop festival.

Manitoba Electronic Music Exhibition (Downtown Winnipeg, mid-August): Electronic dance music at The Cube in Old Market Square and elsewhere.

Harvest Sun Fest (Kelwood, mid-August): Outdoor roots and rock festival.

Rainbow Trout Music Festival (St. Malo, mid-August): Outdoor rock festival.

Quarry Days (Quarry Park, Stonewall, mid-August): Town fair.

Virden Indoor Rodeo & Wild West Daze (Virden, mid-August): Indoor rodeo and town fair.

Corn And Apple Festival (Morden, final weekend in August): Three-day town fair.

Cook's Creek Heritage Day (Cook's Creek, last Sunday in August): Community fair.

St. Malo Summer Festival (St. Malo, late August or early September): Town fair.

Ashern Rodeo (Ashern, late August or early September): Rodeo and town fair.

September

Labour Day (Nationwide): First Monday in September. Banks, government offices and most retailers closed.

Manito Ahbee (Winnipeg, second week in September): Indigenous music and cultural festival.

Honey, Garlic and Maple Syrup Festival (Manitou, second weekend in September): Town fair and culinary expo.

Winnipeg International Writers Festival (Winnipeg, late September): Week-long literary festival with public readings.

Harvest Moon Festival (Clearwater, late September): Outdoor folk and roots festival, with campground and sustainable-agriculture expo.

Nuit Blanche (Winnipeg, late September): All-night arts festival, encompassing various venues.

October

Roland Pumpkin Fair (Roland, first Saturday in October): Town fair and harvest festival.

Beef and Barley Festival (Russell, early October): Town fair.

Thanksgiving (Nationwide, second Monday in October): Harvest festival, held one month earlier than in US Banks, government offices and most retailers are closed.

Hoof and Holler (Ste. Rose du Lac, Thanksgiving long weekend): Cattle auction, rodeo, and dance.

November

Manitoba Livestock Expo (Brandon, early November): Music and moocows.

Remembrance Day (Nationwide, Nov. 11): Memorial day for Canadian war dead, with public ceremonies at 11 a.m. Banks and government offices closed. Retailers closed in morning.

December

Christmas Eve (Nationwide, Dec. 24) Business as usual during the day; Retailers and most restaurants close by 6 p.m.

Christmas Day (Nationwide, Dec. 25): Banks, government offices, restaurants, retailers and some cultural attractions are closed.

New Year's Eve (Nationwide, Dec. 31): Business as usual during the day; Retailers and government liquor stores close by 6 p.m.

Brenda Schnitt

STUFF
TO KNOW

4

Getting Around

Cars

You can live without a car in Winnipeg, but if you want to see a lot of Manitoba, you'll need a set of wheels. At 650,000 square kms, the province is twice the size of Norway, bigger than Ukraine, roughly the same size as Afghanistan, and slightly larger than the combined area of California and New York.

While most of the population is concentrated in the south, distances between cities, towns, parks, and other attractions remain immense. If you want to set your own agenda, you'll need a vehicle to get where you want to go, as bus service is inconvenient, railway destinations are limited, and passenger flights within the province tend to be prohibitively expensive.

If you don't own a car, daily rental rates start around $35, before taxes. You'll always pay less if you reserve ahead of time, especially if you book online. While 16-year-olds can drive in Manitoba, you need to be 21 – and in possession of a valid licence – to rent a car from most agencies.

Manitoba highways are well-marked and easy to navigate but not often in good condition. Watch out for potholes, even on some major highways. Winter conditions, meanwhile, will test the nerves of even the most experienced driver. While major highways are cleared of snow within hours of a heavy dump, some roads can remain slick for days, and blowing snow can reduce visibility to next to nothing, even during daylight hours. In open prairie, high winds can make it appear as if snow is falling sideways.

Even worse, the action of tires over packed snow occasionally creates a slippery surface known as black ice, all but impossible to spot. The best thing to do in winter is be sensible: give yourself plenty of time to travel long distances, stay off the road in lousy weather, and keep a mobile phone and warm clothes in the car in the unlikely event you spin out into a ditch and need to wait for a tow.

And at any time of year, don't get the behind the wheel when you've a few drinks. Manitoba has the toughest drunk-driving penalties in North America, with a variety of suspensions, fines, and vehicle seizures kicking in after your blood-alcohol percentage reaches a measly 0.05. For most people, that translates into a single drink.

Talking on your phone while driving in Manitoba will also net you a sizable fine, so use the Bluetooth or don't talk at all.

Buses and Shuttles

Unglamorous but reliable **Winnipeg Transit** (winnipegtransit.com) can take you anywhere you want to go in the Winnipeg except during the wee hours of the morning. Plug in your origin and destination at winnipegtransit.com/en/navigo or phone up Transit Tom at 311. A one-way fare costs $2.60.

Greyhound Canada (greyhound.ca) is the only bus company serving most Manitoba destinations. Sample one-way fares from Winnipeg in early 2015 were $34.20 to Kenora, Ont. $31.70 to Brandon and $72.20 to Thompson. Winnipeg's Greyhound station is located at Richardson International Airport.

For service between Brandon and Winnipeg's Richardson International Airport, you can also pre-book a van ride on **Brandon Air Shuttle** (brandonairshuttle.com, $52 one-way/$98 return). The same firm offers van service between Dauphin and Brandon ($45 one-way/$82 return).

Beaver Bus Lines (beaverbus.com) operates service between Winnipeg and Selkirk 11 times a day on weekdays and four times on Saturdays. One-way fares are $9 and return fares are $17, with lower fares offered for stops between the two cities. Beaver departs Winnipeg from Balmoral Street at Ellice Avenue and departs Selkirk at the Selkirk Bus Depot, Main Street at Dufferin Avenue.

Taxis, Limos, and Shuttles

For a city of 720,000, Winnipeg can be a tough place to hail a cab. The quickest way to snag one is to head to a higher-end downtown hotel, one of the city's two casinos, or the front of a busy nightclub. Otherwise, call Duffy's at 204.775.0101, Unicity at 204.925.3131, Blueline at 204.925.8888, or Spring at 204.774.8294.

From Richardson International Airport, expect to pay about $20 to get downtown by taxi. Limos might make sense for larger parties, while some downtown hotels offer free rides in shuttles. Winnipeg Transit's No. 15 (Mountain/Sargent) bus takes passengers from the airport to downtown, and vice versa, for $2.60.

Air Travel

If you're flying into Manitoba, there's direct service between Winnipeg's Richardson International Airport from 19 Canadian cities and eight US destinations. Some of those US flights are seasonal; **United** (united.com) offers year-round service between Winnipeg and US destinations through both Chicago and Denver,

Brenda Schritt

A floatplane is the only way to reach some remote paddling destinations in Manitoba.

while **Delta** (delta.com) connects Winnipeg to the US through Minneapolis-St. Paul.

Air Canada (aircanada.com) and **Westjet** (westjet.com) handle most of the flights between Winnipeg and larger Canadian destinations. Westjet also operates a flight between Brandon and Calgary.

Bearskin Airlines offers service between Winnipeg and northwestern Ontario cities. **Calm Air** (calmair.com), **Perimeter Aviation** (perimeter.ca) and **First Air** (firstair.ca) operate flights between Winnipeg and remote Manitoba and Arctic communities.

Sunwing (sunwing.ca) and **Air Transat** (airtransat.ca) offer seasonal service between Winnipeg and 19 Mexican and Caribbean destinations.

A handful of smaller airlines offer floatplane service to isolated First Nations, hunting and fishing lodges, or remote canoe areas. You will find a list of charter services online at travelmanitoba.com/huntfish/aircharters.html.

Trains

Go back 100 years and you could ride the rails almost anywhere in Manitoba. Now, passenger service is limited to a pair of **VIA Rail** routes: An east-west corridor between Ontario and Saskatchewan (part of a coast-to-coast line from Halifax to Vancouver), and a long, curving north-south jaunt between Winnipeg and Churchill.

Most tourists travel the east-west route as part of a cross-Canada jaunt. The trip up to Churchill takes at least 36 hours from Winnipeg – and often longer, due to poor track conditions – but many travellers take it anyway. It's faster to drive or take a bus to Thompson and then jump on the train for the final 13 or 20 hours to Hudson Bay.

Winnipeg's VIA Rail station is located in a handsome hall of a building on Main Street, near The Forks. VIA schedules and fares are online at viarail.ca.

Cycling

It's possible, if not optimally safe, to see southern Manitoba by bike. Avoid major highways to minimize contact with heavy trucks.

Bartley Kives

You may also follow the partly gravel, partly off-road Trans Canada Trail, if you have shocks on your bike and you're up to a bone-jarring challenge.

Popular bike daytrips from Winnipeg include short jaunts nearby to parks such as Beaudry and Birds Hill, or to bedroom communities such as Lockport and St. François Xavier. Make sure to keep an eye on your gear anywhere you go, especially in Winnipeg. While bike touring isn't big in Manitoba, bike theft is common.

It's never a bad idea to check trail conditions before you head out on your bike.

Hitchhiking

True to the slogan on the licence plates, Manitobans tend to be friendly to hitchhikers. But that doesn't mean it's safe to jump in a stranger's car. If you're broke and backpacking, there are always better transport options, such as negotiating a ride with someone you meet at a hostel or campground.

If you must hitchhike, travel in pairs for safety and set out early in the morning to show prospective drivers you're serious about reaching a destination. Carry some kind of baggage – if you don't have any gear, it looks like you're out to steal some.

The same rules apply if you're considering giving a stranger a ride. A lone, unencumbered hitchhiker at dusk is nothing but bad news.

Sleeping

Hotels

In small Manitoba towns, you'll find two kinds of hotels: cheap, 1950s-style row motels along the highway, and scarier, block-like 1920s structures in the middle of what passes for downtown. The row motels are almost always a better choice, but ask to see the room before you commit to a purchase. You can pay as little as $45 or as much as $90 for one of these spartan places, depending on the town and the time of year.

In slightly bigger centres, you'll also find modern chain hotels and larger, independently owned establishments. Expect to cough up $100 to $150 to stay at the chains.

In Winnipeg, you'll find all of the above, plus a handful of more luxurious hotels with dining rooms, high-end lounges, and, in some cases, spas. Expect to pay $150 to $250 for a room in the most-expensive Winnipeg establishments.

In resort towns such as Wasagaming, you'll pay a premium to stay in the summer. In Churchill, high season is the polar-bear-watching period in late October and early November. Counterintuitively, you may find the cheapest rates in downtown Winnipeg hotels during the summer, when business travel drops off. Use the usual online suspects to find the best deals.

Cabins, Lodges, and Resorts

Accommodations in parks and other wild areas range from rustic cabins to full-blown luxury lodges. Don't get hung up on terminology, because lodges, resorts, cabins, and even hotels tend to be interchangeable terms. For instance, some fishing lodges offer gourmet meals and guided excursions, while others are just a series of cottages in the woods. Cabins for rent can be loaded

Winnipeg's historic and allegedly haunted Fort Garry Hotel.

with satellite TV and saunas – or lack running water and electricity altogether. Resorts, meanwhile, can refer to anything from a trailer park to a full-service hotel.

In older holiday towns, such as Grand Marais and Ninette, small rustic cabins rent for as little as $300 a week. But you could easily pay $300 a night for a spacious, modern cabin in Riding Mountain or the Whiteshell. Fly-in fishing lodges in remote locations tend to be considerably more expensive.

To further confuse matters, some holiday accommodations are open year-round, while others only cater to summer crowds. Given the wide range of options, call before you book. Travel Manitoba maintains a searchable database of resorts at travelmanitoba.com/accomodations.

Bed and Breakfast

There are three things to consider when you opt for a bed and breakfast over a hotel room: price, personality, and privacy. B&Bs offer less of the first, more of the second, and almost none of the third.

Generally speaking, B&Bs offer more-interesting rooms at cheaper rates than conventional hotel chains, but there is a cost: you cannot help but interact with your hosts and fellow guests, which can be awkward if you're shy or antisocial. And don't even think about having sex in a room with paper-thin walls and a four-poster bed that squeaks like a tortured rodent if you dare to get a little frisky.

That said, B&B hosts usually prove to be excellent sources of travel advice and information. In 2015, bedandbreakfast.mb.ca listed 51 B&Bs in the province, including five in Winnipeg.

Campgrounds and Yurts

There are two types of campgrounds in Manitoba: Government-run sites in parks, and private campgrounds usually set up along highways or near recreational facilities in the middle of small towns.

Manitoba Conservation runs more than four dozen campgrounds in 41 different provincial parks, most open only from Victoria Day to Labour Day. Beginning in March, you can try to reserve a spot ahead online at prspub.gov.mb.ca or by calling 204.948.3333 in Winnipeg or 1.888.482.2267 from elsewhere. Reservations are a good idea, as the most-popular spots typically sell out of their summer weekend spots. Expect to pay $11.55 to $28.35 a night for a provincial campsite or $38.10 to $79.15 for a provincial-campground yurt.

Most provincial campgrounds offer spots for tents, RVs, and campers; firewood; electricity; showers; and, in some cases, interpretive programs. What they don't offer is any semblance of a wilderness experience, as campsites are packed together tightly enough to ensure you'll get to know your neighbours. Riding Mountain National Park has six campgrounds, but only accepts advance bookings for the most-popular one, Wasagaming (877.737.3783), beginning in April.

There are also dozens of private campgrounds spread out across Manitoba, including eleven on the Trans-Canada Highway alone. Information about nearly three dozen can be found at macap.ca.

Wilderness Camping

If you possess route-finding skills, you can pitch a tent anywhere you like on unregulated Crown land in Manitoba. Set up at least 100 metres away from any road, path, and waterway, practise leave-no-trace camping, and take particular care with fires.

A campsite – well, a tent, anyway – on Lake Winnipeg's southern basin, halfway between Winnipeg Beach and Grand Beach.

Bartley Kives

Backcountry camping is also possible within Manitoba provincial forests and wildlife management areas, provided you check ahead with Manitoba Conservation staff at the nearest district office. Some areas may be off-limits during hunting season, closed due to logging, or simply unsafe due to bear activity.

In most large provincial parks – namely Whiteshell, Nopiming, Spruce Woods, Turtle Mountain, Duck Mountain, and Paint Lake – wilderness camping is free but restricted to designated backcountry sites along established hiking and canoeing routes. You don't have to reserve sites ahead of time, but be prepared to share a camp at popular campsites on the Mantario Trail during summer weekends.

In Riding Mountain National Park, backcountry campsites cost $15.70 per night and must be reserved ahead of time at 204.848.7275 or at the park office in Wasagaming. Camping in Wapusk National Park is restricted to the Owl River in June, due to the polar-bear threat at other times.

Places where backcountry camping is not permitted include ecological preserves, private land within parks (usually well-marked), and provincial parks near Winnipeg, most notably Birds Hill and Grand Beach, which only offer car camping.

Avoiding Headaches

Small-town Sundays

If you're thinking about a Sunday drive, don't expect to find anything open in very small towns besides gas stations and the odd Chinese restaurant. Small towns in southern Manitoba still take the Christian day of rest very seriously, so you're in for a world of disappointment if you have your heart set on visiting museums or rummaging through second-hand stores. Visit rural Manitoba on a weekday or Saturday and reserve Sundays for parks or other natural attractions instead.

White-tailed Deer

From April to November, white-tailed pylons can be a menace on rural roads, especially in the fall, and at dusk and dawn. Manitoba's deer number about 200,000, and they live just about everywhere highways exist. Few drivers are killed by deer, but a collision will damage your car and possibly put you in the ditch.

Other highway obstacles include raccoons, skunks, porcupines, coyotes, and moose, the latter posing a serious threat on Highway 10 from Wasagaming to Flin Flon, and on Highway 6 from Lundar to Thompson.

Winter Driving

Highway driving during a Canadian winter should not be treated lightly. Always travel in a well-maintained car with enough gas and washer fluid to get from point A to B. In the event of a winter breakdown, stay in your car, where you'll remain safe and warm. This is especially important during a blizzard, as you can get completely disoriented in a whiteout and die from exposure.

If you're travelling any considerable distance during the winter, pack an emergency kit consisting of a candle, blanket or sleeping bag, high-carb snacks and a cellular phone. Also take a shovel, as low-clearance vehicles can get stuck in small snowdrifts.

Hypothermia and Frostbite

Hardy Manitobans tend to be comfortable until the temperature dips below −15 C. You don't need to be such a hero: take a toque, gloves, and warm winter coat along for any winter excursion, even if you don't intend to be outside.

Fashion is irrelevant when it comes to staying warm. When it's extremely cold – say, below −25 C – cover every inch of exposed skin with clothing to prevent frostbite and slather your lips in balm to ward off blisters.

For outdoor winter activities like cross-country skiing, you'll also need moisture-wicking socks and long underwear, waterproof-breathable outer layers, and a daypack to stow extra layers of clothing. Staying dry is your No. 1 priority in the bitter cold, so peel off layers as you warm up and consider sweat your mortal enemy.

Sunburn

Manitoba is one of the few places on Earth where frostbite and sunburn pose equal threats. As counterintuitive as it sounds, you may burn more quickly in Manitoba than you would in the southern US during the summer, thanks to high UV radiation caused by our slightly thinner ozone layer.

Let this be the only mosquito you ever encounter in Manitoba. Only the females bite.

It's easy to prevent sunburn by wearing a hat and using sunblock. SPF 30 is all you need; anything higher is a waste of cash.

In June and early July, the sun rises before 6 a.m. and sets after 10 p.m. in Winnipeg. UV levels are highest between 11 a.m. and 3 p.m.

Mosquitoes

Since much of Manitoba is wet, it's impossible to visit during the summer and not get eaten by mosquitoes. But the little critters aren't always a monstrous annoyance, as cool or dry spells during the middle of the summer tend to decimate their ranks.

In southern Manitoba, mosquitoes usually start buzzing in late May and multiply like mad until early August, when they gradually start to disappear. That's why May and September can be the best time to be outdoors. On the other hand, windy summer nights can be completely bug-free, while some summers simply aren't buggy at all.

The best way to avoid mosquito bites is to wear light-coloured long sleeves and pants on still, warm nights and apply bug spray that contains DEET to exposed areas like your neck and the back of your hand. When you do get bit, don't sweat it – little more than a handful of Manitoba's 1.3 million people contract West Nile Virus each summer.

If you're heading up north in the summer, definitely pack a bug hat, because black flies, deerflies, and no-see-ums are vicious enough to make mosquitoes seem like kittens.

Bears

For Manitobans and tourists alike, there's nothing more exciting than seeing a bear ... from a nice, safe distance. Up close, there's nothing cute about a 200-kilogram critter with razor-sharp claws.

Although most black bears are gentle scavengers who avoid contact with humans, they may act aggressive when cornered, surprised, or caring for their cubs. Make plenty of noise while walking along a trail in bear country to let the Yogis know you're on the way.

If you see a black bear, do not approach. Back away slowly and leave the area. If the bear sees you, speak to it loudly but calmly to let it know you're a human being. Don't worry if it stands on two legs and sniffs the air – it's just trying to figure out what you are.

In the unlikely event the bear charges, hold your ground, because the advance is probably a feint. But if it actually attacks, fight back with every fibre of your being, scratching and kicking at the eyes and nose, if you can. Black bears are only interested in easy meals and will likely give up if you become too much of a challenge.

To sleep safely in bear country, never bring food or fragrant cosmetics like soap and toothpaste into your tent. Store all food, toiletries, and garbage inside a car or a metal bear-box, when available, or hang it in a drybag from a long tree limb.

Black bears can be found almost anywhere in Manitoba, except in the extreme northeast, where bigger, stronger, and more-intelligent polar bears patrol the Hudson Bay coast. If you encounter a polar bear on foot, you're probably screwed – there's no more dangerous predator on Earth.

Crime

After 35 years of living in Manitoba, I've found most people polite, helpful, and considerate, if at times a little reserved. But there is a rough edge to the province that cannot be ignored, as the sometimes shocking chasm between rich and poor has created an environment where theft and property crime is far more common than visitors expect.

Your personal safety is not typically a problem, even in Winnipeg's roughest neighbourhoods. Your real concern should be the potential loss of personal property, as vehicle break-ins are common in Manitoba.

In Winnipeg, or any populated area, lock valuables in your trunk or take them with you when you park your car. Never, ever leave bags or boxes unattended inside a vehicle – opportunistic thieves view this as an invitation to break in. I am not exaggerating the threat: Many Winnipeggers endure some kind of vehicle break-in or act of vandalism *once every two years*.

Other than that, the only real dangers on Winnipeg's streets come in the form of the occasional aggressive panhandler on Portage Avenue; a polite but firm "no, sorry" is all you need to negotiate your way past that sort of obstacle.

Getting More Info

Tourism Info and Maps

If you need more information about any destination within Manitoba, **Travel Manitoba** (travelmanitoba.com) offers year-round tourism advice at the Explore Manitoba Centre at The Forks, and runs five highway information kiosks from mid-May to Labour Day:

- Canada-US border at Highway 75
- Canada-US border at Highway 10
- Manitoba-Ontario border at Highway 1
- Manitoba-Saskatchewan border at Highway 1
- Manitoba-Saskatchewan border at junction of Highways 16 and 83

As well, **Canadian Automobile Association** and AAA members can obtain maps and travel advice from CAA travel centres in Winnipeg (870 Empress, 2211 McPhillips, or 501 St. Anne's), Brandon (61 2nd Ave. NE), or Altona (1300 18th).

There are also municipal tourist information centres in almost every city and town. **Tourism Winnipeg** (tourismwinnipeg.com) dispenses advice in person (259 Portage Ave.) or by phone (204.943.1970 or toll-free at 855.734.2489) weekdays, 8 a.m. to 4 p.m.

Backcountry campers seeking topographical maps should head straight to Manitoba Conservation's **Canada Map Sales** office (1007 Century Ave.), which also sells a variety of guidebooks. Guidebooks and maps can also be purchased in Winnipeg at **Mountain Equipment Co-Op** (303 Portage Ave.), **The Wilderness Supply** (623 Ferry Rd. or 42 Speers Rd.) and **McNally Robinson Booksellers** (1120 Grant Ave.).

When To Go

Peak Seasons for Selected Activities

Beach-hopping
Season: June through August.
Best time to go: Weekdays in July.
Rationale: The hottest sun of the summer, without the crowds.

Cross-country skiing
Season: Late December to mid-March.
Best time to go: Late February and early March.
Rationale: Fully frozen waterways and deep snow, but slightly longer winter days and warmer temperatures.

Festival hopping
Season: All year.
Best time to go: Mid-June to early August.
Rationale: The biggest and best events are crammed into the early summer, including the Winnipeg International Jazz Festival, Dauphin's Countryfest, the Winnipeg Folk Festival and the Winnipeg Fringe Theatre Festival.

Flatwater Paddling
Season: Late May to early October.
Best time to go: Late August and early September.
Rationale: Warm water, less-crowded lakes, and fewer bugs.

Hiking/Backpacking
Season: Mid-May to mid-October.
Best time to go: Labour Day to Thanksgiving.
Rationale: Dry trails, cooler mid-day temperatures, spectacular foliage, more active wildlife, few mosquitoes, and even fewer crowds.

Mountain Biking
Season: May to October.
Best time to go: Late August and September.
Rationale: Dry trails, less oppressive heat, and, again, fewer crowds.

Performing Arts
Season: September to May.
Best time to go: September through November.
Rationale: There's more of a buzz surrounding early-season productions by the WSO, RWB, RMTC, and Manitoba Opera.

Whitewater Paddling
Season: May to early September.
Peak period: Middle of June.
Rationale: Go when there's still some big flows from the spring melt – yet before the summer bugs come.

Wildlife-Watching
Season: All year.
Best time to go: Late April and early May for garter snakes, June through August for pelicans, July for beluga whales, September for elk, late October and early November for polar bears, and winter for owls.
Rationale: You think animals have a rationale?

Driving Distances

Approximate driving distances from Winnipeg, in kilometres from the Perimeter Highway:

Altona – 98
Angle Inlet, Minn. – 185
Asessippi Provincial Park – 362
Baldy Mountain – 389
Beausejour – 46
Birds Hill Provincial Park – 15
Boissevain – 241
Brandon – 197
Carman – 62
Dauphin – 304
Emerson – 96
Falcon Lake – 126
Fargo, N.D. – 355
Flin Flon – 750
Fort Frances, Ont. – 399
Gillam – 1,034
Gimli – 76
Grand Beach – 87
Grand Forks, N.D. – 233
Grand Rapids – 408
Gull Harbour – 168
International Peace Gardens – 309
Kenora, Ont. – 205
Lac du Bonnet – 91
Lynn Lake – 1,066
Melita – 310
Manigotagan – 182
Mantario Trail, north trailhead – 149
Mantario Trail, south trailhead – 141
Minaki, Ont. – 250
Minneapolis–St. Paul, Minn. – 730
Minnedosa – 203
Morden –104
Morris – 52
Narcisse Wildlife Management Area – 98
Neepawa – 175

Nopiming Provincial Park, south entrance – 160
Oak Hammock Marsh – 27
Patricia Beach – 66
Pine Falls – 111
Pisew Falls – 635
Portage la Prairie – 70
Regina, Sask. – 570
Russell – 338
Selkirk – 21
Souris – 226
Spruce Woods Provincial Park, Spirit Sands trailhead – 177
Steep Rock – 217
Steinbach – 48
Stonewall – 24
Swan River – 476
The Pas – 602
Thompson – 738
Thunder Bay, Ont. – 700
Turtle Mountain Provincial Park, east entrance – 306
Virden – 277
Wasagaming – 253
West Hawk Lake – 140
Winkler – 102
Winnipeg Beach – 66

Opposite: The leopard frog is one of Manitoba's most common amphibians. There may be as many as 100 leopard frogs per hectare, provided there's a wetland nearby.

Bryan Scott

WINNIPEG

5

I f you're visiting Manitoba, you likely have no choice but to spend a few days in Winnipeg – and this is a good thing. Manitoba's capital and largest city is a paradoxically artsy/industrial centre that deserves to be considered one of North America's best-kept cultural secrets. No other mid-sized Canadian city has so much going for it – but so little clue how to sell itself.

On one hand, Winnipeg is a quirky and creative place, where a reasonable cost of living nurtures a vibrant visual arts community, excellent performing arts, and a celebrated music scene. First-time visitors marvel at the Exchange District architecture, rave about the friendly locals, and get taken aback by the summertime greenery. They need not be surprised, as the city of roughly 720,000 is large enough to boast most of the attractions of a major city, but folksy enough to remain uncrowded and ensure the cost of doing just about anything remains relatively modest.

On the other hand, 'Peg City suffers from a nasty reputation in the rest of Canada and a self-defeating inferiority complex at home. Winters are long and bitterly cold. Mosquitoes swarm by the trillions during the summer, industrial areas are immense, and socio-economic disparity gives the city many of the "urban doughnut" problems that plagued large American centres during the '70s, including rampant property crime.

But neither creativity nor ugliness is the city's defining feature. The real key to Winnipeg is a psychology of isolation, as the nearest larger centre, Minneapolis-St. Paul, is located eight hours and a border crossing away. When you have 720,000 souls surrounded by nothing, you end up with an extremely strong sense of regional identity. Locals often lament this as parochialism, but visitors will be delighted – you normally have to visit an outpost like St. John's, Nfld., or Iqaluit, Nunavut, to encounter such an idiosyncratic civic culture.

In other words, Winnipeg is weird, in the best possible way.

LEGEND

.... Underground Walkway

——— Second-level Walkway

▪▪▪▪ Riverwalk

+++ Railway tracks

Streets

Portage Avenue

Main Street

MAP OF
DOWNTOWN WINNIPEG

ELLEN

HARGRAVE

NOTRE DAME

ADELA

CUMBERLAND

CENTRAL PARK

QU'APPELLE

KENNEDY

EDMONTON

ELLICE

AIR CANADA BLDG.

AIR CANADA PARK

GLOBE

N.R.C.C

WEBB

THE PROMENADE

PRAIRIE THEATRE EXCHANGE

IMAX THEATRE

HARGRA

TO WEST END

SPENCE

BALMORAL

COLONY

VAUGHAN

YM/YWCA

PORTAGE PLACE

PORTAGE

MERCHANT PARK

DUCKWORTH CENTRE

ONE CANADA CENTRE

BUS DEPOT

UNIVERSITY OF WINNIPEG

TO WOLSELEY, MCV HOUSE, WINNIPEG INT'L AIRPORT

MEMORIAL

GOOD

COLONY

UNITED ARMY SURPLUS

THE BAY

POWER BLDG.

WINNIPEG ART GALLERY

KENNEDY

EDMONTON

CARLTON

LAW COURTS

WOODSWORTH BUILDING

KENNEDY

OSBORNE

MEMORIAL PARK

BROADWAY

SPENCE

BALMORAL

GREAT-WEST LIFE

TO OSBORNE VILLAGE & CORYDON AVENUE

MANITOBA LEGISLATIVE BUILDING

GOVERNMENT

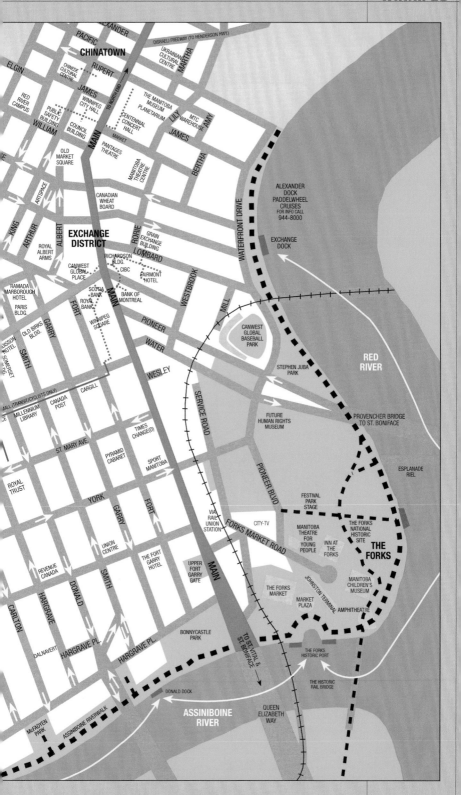

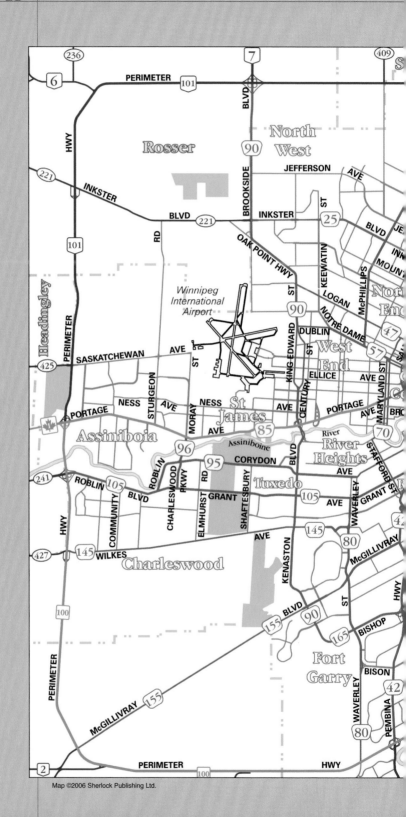

Map ©2006 Sherlock Publishing Ltd.

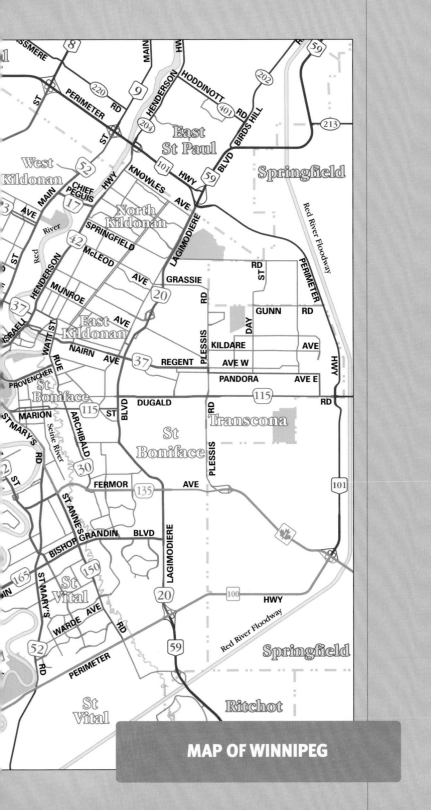

MAP OF WINNIPEG

A Little History

For centuries, Cree, Assiniboine and other indigenous peoples had the confluence of the Red and Assiniboine Rivers to themselves. This situation ended in 1738, when Quebec explorer la Vérendrye was the first of many Europeans to find his way here to (a) sell useless stuff to the Indians, (b) colonize their land, and (c) find out the joke was on them the first time a spring flood deluged their brand-new homesteads and spawned an armada of mosquitoes.

Thousands of ethnic British, French, Scandinavians, and Métis lived in the area by the time the City of Winnipeg was founded in 1874. They were joined by hundreds of thousands of eastern European settlers as the Canadian Pacific Railway opened up the Prairies.

At the turn of the twentieth century, Winnipeg was a boomtown, a fast-growing transport-and-warehousing centre rivalled only by Chicago in North America. This period saw the construction of the stunning cut-stone and terra cotta buildings that still stand in the Exchange District and other parts of downtown.

The exponential growth ended in 1914, when the start of the First World War and the completion of the Panama Canal killed the railway boom. Five years later, the only general strike ever undertaken in Canada and the US hastened the Depression. In the aftermath, Winnipeg would grapple with a perceived feeling of decline for the rest of the century. The city went from being Canada's third-largest metropolitan area in the 1950s – after Toronto and Montreal – to the eighth today, after Vancouver, Ottawa, Edmonton, Calgary, and Quebec City. But the long decline was more a matter of perception than reality: Winnipeg simply took a long time to accept its status as a slow-growth city, which is not such a bad thing.

This self-consciousness ended at the turn of the 21st century, when the city began to grow comfortable within its own idiosyncratic, creative-but-gritty skin. It's safe to say Winnipeg is more confident today than at any other time since 1914.

Winnipeg's Main Street, looking north, ca. 1875, before the advent of paved streets.

Getting Around

If you're only spending a few days in Winnipeg and don't plan to leave the inner city, you don't need a car. Many bus routes converge downtown, and most places of interest are within walking distance. If you have time to explore the entire city or plan to see the rest of Manitoba, you definitely need a vehicle.

An aerial view of Portage & Main, Winnipeg's busiest and most infamous intersection. Pedestrians aren't allowed to cross on foot, thanks to a deal struck to create underground walkways in the 1970s.

Cabs are expensive and difficult to hail if you're not in front of a major hotel. **Winnipeg Transit** buses, while cheap at $2.60 a ride, are inconvenient for cross-town travel, especially during off-peak hours (schedules: winnipegtransit.com/navigo).

In the summer, the **Splash Dash Water Bus** (see *The Forks*) is a fun way to cruise between downtown, Osborne Village, and the Corydon area, but service can be sporadic due to fluctuating water levels on the Red and Assiniboine rivers.

If you drive, nab a city map or use your GPS. Hastily planned in what seems like 11 minutes in 1905, the city lacks any semblance of a grid pattern. Streets that abut each other at 45-degree angles and wind around the curves of meandering creeks and rivers occasionally confuse lifelong Winnipeggers. Even worse, some long streets change names every couple of blocks. The most annoying is a single, heinous route that starts off in the north as Salter Street before becoming Isabel, Balmoral, Colony, Memorial, Osborne, Dunkirk, and finally Dakota before it dead-ends at the Red River Floodway.

Still, finding your way around is nowhere near as difficult as navigating a European capital. Winnipeg's wide major arteries, which used to be muddy ox-cart trails back in the settler days, loosely parallel the north-south Red River and the east-west Assiniboine River, which converge downtown at The Forks. The busiest east-west routes are Portage Avenue, Nairn/Regent, and Roblin/Grant, while Main Street, Henderson Highway, Pembina Highway, and St. Mary's Road are the primary north-south streets. An outer ring road called the Perimeter Highway encircles the city and an interior ring road of sorts is being cobbled together in stages.

Other major features of the city include the massive Canadian Pacific Railway yard that divides downtown from the North End; the Seine River in the southeast; the Assiniboine Park and Forest in the southwest; and Richardson International Airport, precariously placed next to a residential area called St. James as well as the city's busiest shopping area, a big-box retail wasteland known as Polo Park. Luckily, it's easy to land a plane on the flat prairie.

A fun way to see the city is to paddle the rivers – or walk on them in the winter. The Red, Assiniboine, and La Salle are navigable to canoes and kayaks as soon as the ice disappears, and usually stay that way until the fall, when water levels drop dramatically. The Seine River is usually navigable until late June, while the lower portion of Sturgeon Creek makes for good playboating during the spring snowmelt. Water levels fluctuate, so check before you head out on to the water – boat rentals are available at **Wilderness Supply** (Mon-Sat, 623 Ferry Rd., 204.783.9555), **Mountain Equipment Co-op** (daily, 303 Portage Ave., 204.943.4202) and at the marina at The Forks (see *The Forks*).

The Red, Assiniboine, Seine, and La Salle usually freeze solid by January, making it safe to snowshoe and cross-country ski. If ice conditions are good, The Forks also grooms an ice-skating path on the Red River and up the Assiniboine to Osborne Village.

Road cycling in Winnipeg can be annoying, as drivers on major arteries can be less than courteous to people on bikes. Over the past decade, the city has expanded its network of commuter-bike paths; designated bike routes include Scotia Street, Wolseley Avenue, and Wellington Crescent, which are closed to vehicle traffic on Sundays and holidays between Victoria Day and Thanksgiving. There are now separated lanes on Assiniboine Avenue downtown and Sherbrook Street in West Broadway.

Where to go

The Forks

First-time visitors to Winnipeg often head straight for **The Forks** (open all year, theforks.com) a riverside retail-and-entertainment complex built on a reclaimed industrial site that itself was built over a 6,000-year-old, on-again, off-again human habitation.

Located at the confluence of the Red and the Assiniboine, The Forks is the most convenient place to pick up cheesy souvenirs

and tourism information, the latter at Travel Manitoba's **Explore Manitoba Centre** (Daily, 9 a.m. to 6 p.m. mid-May to Labour Day/ 9 a.m. to 5 p.m. Labour Day to mid-May). There are dozens of shops in two main retail structures – **The Forks Market** building and **Johnston Terminal**. The Forks also features restaurants, food stalls, outdoor patios facing the Assiniboine, a national historic site with occasional programming, an outdoor stage, a hotel, several museums, a kids' theatre, an outdoor skating rink and the **Plaza Skatepark**, one of the best-designed skateboarding and BMX parks in Canada.

There's also a marina where – if the rivers aren't bulging over their banks – you can catch a ride on the **Splash Dash Water Bus** (splashdash.ca, one-way fares $3.50, day passes $15), a river taxi that stops at eight inner-city docks and doubles as a sight-seeing cruise boat (tours $11 adults, $9 students/seniors). Splash Dash also offers **canoe rentals** ($10 half hour/$18 per hour/$40 a day).

In the summer, it's possible to walk to and from The Forks along the **Assiniboine Riverwalk**, a riverside trail. Unfortunately, the riverwalk is often submerged due to spring and summer flooding.

From late December to late February, if the weather is sufficiently cold, The Forks also serves as the main access point for the **Red River Mutual Trail,** a skating and walking path that during some winters breaks the world record for the longest skating path.

The acclaimed skatepark at The Forks, with downtown Winnipeg in the background.

MUST SEE:
The Forks
Shops and restaurants at the confluence of the Red and Assiniboine rivers, plus winter ice skating, summer skateboarding at a site inhabited on and off for the past 6,000 years.

If ice conditions are favourable, the skating and walking trail on the Red River can extend for kilometres during the winter.

The trail is packed with thousands of skaters and pedestrians on winter weekends and hosts occasional pick-up hockey games, curling competitions and in February, an ice-bike race. It's also lined with the winning designs from the international **Warming Huts** competition (warminghuts.com), which offers architects a chance to get creative with structures that generally are not warm at all.

One of the structures, however, is the fully enclosed **Raw: Almond** restaurant (raw-almond.com), which operates on the river ice near The Forks for two weeks in late January and early February. Chefs from higher-end restaurants in Winnipeg and elsewhere in Canada offer $130-a-head *prix fixe* menus; tickets usually sell out in days in December.

A much more accessible place to chow down at The Forks is the inexpensive, multi-ethnic **food court** in the Forks Market, where Caribbean stall **Bindy's Caribbean Delights** (204.942.8409) makes a decent roti and **Tall Grass Prairie Bread Co.** (daily, 204.957.5097), a satellite of a fantastic Wolseley-neighbourhood bakery, offers organic breads, amazing cinnamon buns, and Folk Fest cookies.

For a more leisurely meal at The Forks, your best options among sit-down restaurants are **The Original Pancake House** (daily, Forks Market, 204.957.5077), a chain famous for its oversized apple pancakes, and **Smith** (daily, 204.944.2445), a carnivore-friendly, small-plates restaurant at Inn At The Forks.

The lounge at Smith, with bench seating decorated in a Hudson's Bay-blanket motif, is the most stylish place to grab a drink at The Forks. If you prefer a pub, try **F.M. Local's** (daily, Johnston Terminal, 204.944.8118). You can also sit outdoors along the river during the summer at patios belonging to both **Muddy Waters Smokehouse** (daily, 204.947.6653) and **The Beachcomber** (daily, Forks Market, 204.948.0020).

Of the many shops at The Forks, do not miss **Wah-sa Gallery** (daily, Johnston Terminal, 204.942.5121), which has specialized in Woodland School indigenous art since the likes of Norval Morrisseau and Daphne Odjig contemporized the style in 1976. Can't afford one of the fantastic prints? Buy some postcards.

During the summer, interpretive programs at **The Forks National Historic Site** and **Oodena Celebration Circle** drive home the point people have been meeting at The Forks for millennia. The Forks site is home to **Winnipeg International Children's Festival** (kidsfest.ca) in June, **National Aboriginal Day** on Summer Solstice and **Interstellar Rodeo** (interstellarrodeo.com), a rock and roots music festival in mid-August.

Year-round Forks attractions include the **Manitoba Children's Museum** ($10 admission, 9:30 a.m. to 4:30 p.m. Sun-Thurs; 9:30 a.m. to 6 p.m. Friday & Saturday; Closed Christmas Eve, Christmas Day and four days following Labour Day, 204.924.4000 childrensmuseum.com) the **Manitoba Theatre For Young People** (showtimes and tickets, mtyp.ca 204.942-8898) and the massive **Canadian Museum for Human Rights** (10 a.m. to 5 p.m. Tues, Thurs-Sun;

MUST SEE: Canadian Museum of Museum Rights
Come for the architectural hubris. Stay for the stunning interior design at the first federal museum commissioned outside the National Capital Region.

10 a.m. to 8 p.m. Wed; Closed Mondays, holidays and the week after Christmas, 204.289.2000 humanrights.ca).

The human-rights museum, which opened in 2014, is Canada's first national museum commissioned outside the Ottawa area. The $351-million structure, designed by New Mexico architect Antoine Predock, was intended to be a piece of destination architecture as well a flagship tourist attraction in Winnipeg. Built with a mix of private and public money, the museum proved controversial even before it opened due to cost overruns, construction delays and squabbles over content among ethnic groups who feared their stories would receive too little attention – and allegations of federal interference with the content.

Most of the content in the CMHR's 11 permanent galleries, however, is entirely electronic and reprogrammable, as touchscreens and videos make up the majority of the visitor experience. The interior itself is a mind-blowing expanse of steel, concrete, glass, basalt and Tyndall stone; there's more than a kilometre of alabaster-lined walkways inside carrying visitors up to the **Tower of Hope**, which offers a panoramic view of The Forks and much of Winnipeg. Admission is $18 for adults, $12 for seniors/students and $7 for kids aged seven to 17 – and free for indigenous Canadians. Guided tours, which are helpful considering the scale of the place, are an extra $5 for adults, $4 for students and seniors and $3 for kids aged seven to 17. If you need a drink or some sustenance after trekking through the museum, **Era Bistro** (Tues-Sun, 204.289.2190) offers regional fare such as bannock and pickerel cheeks.

Backlit alabaster walkways are among the stunning interior features of the architecturally ambitious Canadian Museum for Human Rights.

To the east of the CMHR, a pedestrian bridge called **Esplanade Riel** connects The Forks to St. Boniface. Initially criticized as a wasteful extravagance, the bridge has become a symbol for the city. Unfortunately, a restaurant space offering south-facing views of the Red sits vacant; it may have reopened by the time you read this.

North of the museum, you'll find **Shaw Park**, a 7,300-seat baseball stadium used by the Northern League of Baseball's **Winnipeg Goldeyes** (goldeyes.com) from May through August. The baseball stadium is one of the nicest in minor-league ball, with civilized concessions and fully stocked bars. Goldeyes tickets range from $9 to $20 at 204.780.3333 or ticketmaster.ca and can usually be purchased on short notice.

Esplanade Riel, a pedestrian bridge linking The Forks to St. Boniface, is a downtown Winnipeg icon.

The stadium also sports one of four Winnipeg locations of the local **Clay Oven** chain (Mon-Sat as well as game days, 204.982.7426), which serves flavourful South Asian food.

The only place to stay within The Forks neighbourhood is a good option: **Inn at The Forks** (75 Forks Market Rd., 204.942.6555, innforks.com, rooms $168-$213) is located within stumbling distance of Johnston Terminal, The Forks Market and the CMHR and also has a spa. If you don't like crowds, avoid it on Canada Day on July 1 and during Insterstellar Rodeo in mid-August.

Once you've had your fill of The Forks, you can make your way on foot to four interesting neighbourhoods: The Exchange District to the northwest, Downtown to the west, old St. Boniface across the Red River to the east, and Osborne Village, accessible by strolling west along the riverwalk past the Legislature then taking the Osborne Bridge south across the Assiniboine.

The Exchange District

The most visually attractive stretch of downtown Winnipeg is the Exchange District, a great collection of late-19th and early-20th-century office and warehouse buildings that escaped the wrecking ball. The area is now protected as a National Historic Site – economic stagnation has its benefits!

The neo-classical architecture, as well as a series of modernist public buildings erected in the 1960s and '70s, demands a walking tour, either of the guided variety or on your own. The streets with the most impressive architecture are Princess Street, King Street, and Main Street, the latter featuring a collection of majestic former financial institutions such as the **Millennium Centre** (389 Main St.), **Bank of Hamilton** (395 Main St), **Confederation Life Building** (457 Main St.), and the **Union Bank Tower** (Main and William), the oldest surviving skyscraper in western Canada, now part of Red River College's downtown campus. Also don't miss the brutalist **Public Safety Building** (151 Princess St.), a decommissioned police headquarters that looks like a Stalinist fever dream and makes up part of an ensemble of similarly stark municipal structures that also includes the bunker-like **City Hall** (510 Main St.).

From late May through the end of August, the **Exchange District BIZ** offers daily 90-minute **walking tours** ($6-$8, hours vary, 204.942.6716, exchangedistrict.org) of both the East and West Exchange, as well as a series of specialty tours: Death & Debauchery, Newspaper Row, The 1919 General Strike and "Devour the District," a culinary tour. Most leave from Old Market Square and you'll need to book the specialty tours in advance.

If you prefer self-guided tours, the **Winnipeg Architecture Foundation** (weekday afternoons, 266 McDermot Ave., 204.960.8097, winnipegarchitecture.ca) offers a QR code tour, a downloadable terra cotta tour and a $15 brutalist tour guidebook, as well as tours for structures located outside the Exchange.

The west side of the Exchange – the area west of Main Street and North of Notre Dame Avenue – is also where you'll find the largest concentration of art galleries, clubs, restaurants, curio shops, vintage clothing boutiques and second-hand stores, most notably vinyl emporium **Into The Music** (daily, 245 McDermot Ave., 204.287.8279).

No fewer than a dozen good art galleries are located within striding if not stumbling distance of each other. Artist-run, non-profit galleries scattered about the vicinity of McDermot Avenue and Albert Street include the indigenous-focused **Urban Shaman** (233 McDermot Ave. 204.942.2674), **Platform Centre for Photographic + Digital Arts** (Tues-Sat, 121-100 Arthur St., 204.942.8183), **Ace Art** (Tues-Sat, 290 McDermot Ave. 204.944.9763) and **RAW Gallery of Architecture & Design** (Wed-Sat, 290 McDermot Ave.). Commercial galleries in this cluster include upscale **Mayberry Fine Art** (Tues-Sat, 212 McDermot Ave., 204.255.5690), affordable **Warehouse Artworks** (Tues-Sat, 222 McDermot Ave., 204.943.1681), contemporary specialists **Gurevich Fine Art** (Mon-Sat, 62 Albert St., 204.488.0662), frame shop and vendor **Fleet Galleries** (65 Albert St., 204.942.8026) and the Winnipeg-centric **Lisa Kehler Art & Projects** (171 McDermot Ave).

The West Exchange is also home to **Old Market Square** and the hypermodernist **Cube** stage, which hosts free noon-hour concerts on most summer weekdays and serves as a home base for three summer festivals. Much like any piece of recent Winnipeg architecture, the Cube is both beloved and reviled; its audacious design has won awards but has also been condemned for its functional impracticality. It cost $1.2 million to build and features aluminum "chain mail" curtains too heavy to retract more than once per summer, so they remain open the entire performance season. It still looks pretty cool illuminated at night.

Early-twentieth-century architecture on Main Street. Neoclassical columns define the building style of what was once the financial centre of western Canada.

Charles Shilliday

Nonetheless, the Cube is the place to be in late June, during the free opening-weekend concerts of the 10-day **Winnipeg International Jazz Festival** (jazzwinnipeg.com), which offers a program of jazz, funk, rock, and electronic music at a dozen downtown locales.

In mid-July, the **Winnipeg Fringe Theatre Festival** (winnipegfringe.com) uses Old Market Square as a home base. Over 12 days, you can check out more than 100 short plays and comedy sketches in dozens of small, mostly makeshift venues, all within walking distance of Old Market Square, rarely paying more than $10. You'll need to drop a few loonies on a Fringe program to navigate your way through the selection, or pick up the *Winnipeg Free Press*'s daily Fringe Guide – anything that gets four or more stars is bound to sell out.

In August, the Cube is home to a festival that actually matches the stage's esthetic – the **Manitoba Electronic Music Exhibition** (memetic.ca), or MEME, which also runs paid events featuring DJs in other venues.

Due south of Old Market Square, **Cinematheque** (100 Arthur St., 204.925.3456 winnipegfilmgroup.com/cinematheque) serves as Winnipeg's only indie cinema. Tickets to most films are $9 for non-members. East of the square, the **Rachel Browne Theatre** (211 Bannatyne Ave.) serves as a venue for most performances by **Theatre Projects Manitoba** (theatreprojectsmanitoba.ca), which focuses on works by local playwrights.

If you need fuel in the West Exchange, **Parlour Coffee** (Mon-Sat, 468 Main St.) is the first and finest of Winnipeg's artisanal coffee shops. More substantial sustenance can be found nearby at **Shawarma Khan** (Mon-Sat, 225 McDermot Ave., 204.504.0453), run by former Blue Bomber lineman Obby Khan; the **White Star Diner** (Mon-Fri daytime only, 58 Albert St., 204.947.6930), a tiny cubbyhole that makes an excellent burger; **King and Bannatyne** (Mon-Sat, 4-100 King St., 204.691.9757), a sandwich shop that slices up brilliant porchetta and brisket; and **Underground Café** (weekdays, 70 Arthur St., 204.956.1925), where the vegetarian sun burger is the main attraction.

For a more upscale meal in the West Exchange, your best bets are the quasi-French bistro **Peasant Cookery** (daily, 283 Bannatyne Ave. 204.989.7700) or **Deer + Almond** (daily, 85 Princess St. 204.504.8562), a hipster-friendly small-plates joint.

The lounge at Peasant boasts the nicest bartop in Winnipeg as well as a good wine list. If that's too upscale, try the **King's Head Pub** (daily, 120 King St., 204.957.7710), where Red River College students, cops and city hall suits co-mingle over two levels. And if that sounds too crusty, try **Whiskey Dix** (Fri-Sat nights, 436 Main St., 204.944.7539), a dance bar/pickup joint with a young clientele.

Immediately north of the West Exchange sits Winnipeg's dilapidated Chinatown, which is outside the protection of the Exchange National Historic Site and has suffered horribly from

Bryan Scott

wanton building demolition as a result. The main attraction is a handful of restaurants, most notably the sprawling **Kum Koon Garden** (daily, 257 King St. 204.943.4655), the best dim sum parlour in town, and hole-in-the-wall **Noodle Express** (daily, 107-180 King St., 204.943.9760), a Hong Kong-style diner.

On the east side of the Exchange – that is, east of Main Street – you'll find many of Manitoba's big cultural institutions. Sprawling along an entire city block, the **Manitoba Museum, Planetarium, and Science Gallery** (190 Rupert Ave., 204.956.2830, manitobamuseum.ca) occupy a modernist complex created as a downtown-revitalization megaproject in the 1960s. The museum has natural-history exhibits and galleries representing all of Manitoba's eco-systems and a life-sized recreation of the *Nonsuch*, an ocean-going fur trade sailing ship. The stuffed bison at the museum entrance is a provincial icon. The Planetarium, located below the museum, offers astronomy shows, while the Science Gallery features an interactive exhibit about Lake Winnipeg's environmental challenges. Admission to any of the three attractions is $9 for adults, $7.50 for teens, students and seniors and $6.50 for kids aged 3 to 11, with discounts offered for visits to more than one. The complex is open 10 a.m. to 4 p.m. Tues-Friday and 11 a.m. to 5 p.m. weekends and holidays.

Alongside the museum complex, the 2,300-seat **Centennial Concert Hall** serves as a home for three performing-arts institutions: the Royal Winnipeg Ballet, Manitoba Opera, and the Winnipeg Symphony Orchestra.

The Royal Winnipeg Ballet (204.926.2792, rwb.org) was Canada's first professional ballet company. It usually presents four productions during the fall-to-spring season. Tickets range from $107 to $29 a

A not-quite-frozen Red River, with downtown Winnipeg in the background

MUST SEE:
Manitoba Museum
A life-size replica of an HBC sailing vessel, prehistoric fossils, and recent artifacts illustrate the natural and human history of Manitoba.

pop. **Manitoba Opera** (204.944.8824, manitobaopera.mb.ca) presents two full productions and one concert each season, with individual seats ranging for $129 to $29.

The 67-member **Winnipeg Symphony Orchestra** (204.949.3999 or wso.ca) presents a bewildering array of concerts from September to May, offering up a fantastic program of challenging modern works at its midwinter **New Music Festival** (late January or early February), conventional classical music all season and also artistically suspect pops concerts. For better and for worse, this is an orchestra for all tastes. Individual seats for most concerts sell for $106 to $22; New Music Festival seats are a steal at $30 to $14 each.

The other big cultural institution in the East Exchange is the **Royal Manitoba Theatre Centre** (204.942.6537, mtc.mb.ca), which presents six sometimes-stodgy plays per season at its **John Hirsch Mainstage** (174 Market Ave., tickets $77 to $21) and four edgier offerings at the smaller Tom Hendry Warehouse (140 Rupert Ave, tickets $40 to $17). RMTC also runs the city's most-exciting summer festival, the Winnipeg Fringe Theatre Festival (see *Old Market Square*), which completely energizes the entire Exchange in late July.

The Exchange also boasts two fully restored heritage theatres that date back to the Vaudeville era. The 1,640-seat **Burton Cummings Theatre** (364 Smith St.), named after the mustachioed and still-quite-alive Guess Who singer, is usually used as a venue for rock concerts. Snag a seat on the floor, because the view from the upper balcony will induce vertigo. The 1,400-seat **Pantages Playhouse Theatre** (180 Market Ave.) is more often used for folk and middle-of-the-road performers. Both theatres were used as backdrops for the Brad Pitt film *The Assassination of Jesse James*.

The eastern edge of the Exchange, a once-sketchy area along the Red River, is now gentrifying. The boutique **Mere Hotel** (333 Waterfront Drive, 204.594.0333, merehotel.com, rooms $159-$199,) has brightened up the waterfront; its satellite restaurant, **Cibo Waterfront Cafe** (daily, 204.594.0339) occupies a former harbourmaster's station right on the river. The ambience surpasses the food, but it's worth a visit. Nearby, Brazilian barbecue **Carnaval** (daily, 270 Waterfront Drive, 204.505.0945) offers unlimited skewers of flesh for a flat rate, while sister establishment **Corrientes** (Mon-Sat, 137 Bannatyne Ave., 204.219.5398) offers empanadas and Argentine-style pizza.

Further north along the waterfront, **Alexander Docks** is the departure point for **River Rouge Cruise Line** (May-October, 204.774.7009, msrouge.com), which offers afternoon sight-seeing cruises ($18.95) and sunset dinner-dance cruises ($19.95) along the Red River and day-long jaunts downstream to Lower Fort Garry ($69.95). There are also occasional party cruises ($15) and Winnipeg Blue Bomber tailgate cruises ($25) that include transportation to and from Investors Group Field.

At the northeast edge of the Exchange, in downtown Winnipeg's roughest area, you'll find a few more cultural gems:

Ukrainian cultural centre **Oseredok** (Mon-Sat, 184 Alexander Ave. East, ukrainianwinnipeg.ca/oseredok), indigenous spiritual centre **Thunderbird House** (rarely open, Higgins & Main), the **Canadian Plains Gallery**, in the basement of the Aboriginal Centre (181 Higgins Ave., 204.943.4972) and **Martha Street Studio** (Mon-Sat, 11 Martha St., 204.779.6253), an artist-run gallery with good exhibitions.

Downtown Commercial Core

West of The Forks and south of the Exchange District, the remainder of Winnipeg's sprawling downtown is still recovering from a century of incompetent planning and uninspired civic leadership.

Toward the end of the railway boom, when most of the inner city's economic activity was concentrated along Main Street, hubris-afflicted retailers Eaton's and The Bay had the bright idea of erecting massive department stores on Portage Avenue. The construction of these edifices stretched out downtown into a needlessly large dogleg of an urban core that could easily serve a city the size of Philadelphia.

Charles Shilliday

Thanks to Winnipeg's slow population growth over the past century, downtown has never been able to reach critical mass. Generations of entrepreneurs and politicians have tried to "save" downtown with megaprojects such The Forks, the Manitoba Museum/Centennial Concert Hall complex, Portage Place mall, and hockey arena MTS Centre.

A view of downtown Winnipeg, with the office tower 201 Portage Ave. in the centre

Today, there are signs of life in the city's core, though visitors still complain of feeling unsafe due to empty streets and aggressive panhandlers. Their beefs are legitimate, but let's get a grip – downtown Winnipeg is a Garden of Eden compared to heroin-ravaged East Vancouver or the inner core of practically any American Rust Belt city.

The first place Canadian tourists often head is the corner of **Portage & Main**, arguably Canada's most famous intersection and easily one of the windiest in North America. Unfortunately, there's nothing to see here beyond the majestic Corinthian columns of the **Bank of Montreal building** – pedestrians haven't been allowed to cross Portage & Main since the 1970s, when an underground walkway was built to speed the flow of motor-vehicle traffic.

If you insist on visiting the intersection, take note of the two tallest office buildings, each representing the fortunes of two powerful Winnipeg families. On the northeast corner sits the **Richardson Building**, a 30-storey tower created by financiers James

Richardson & Sons. Standing 9.5 metres higher, on the northwest corner, is **201 Portage Ave.**, the former headquarters for the Asper family's media holdings. The old-money Richardsons, worth $4.5 billion in 2013, avoid publicity; the more flamboyant, *nouveau-riche* Aspers are no longer counted among Canada's wealthiest 100 families, though late patriarch Izzy and daughter Gail managed to get the Canadian Museum for Human Rights built through sheer force of will.

As far as most Winnipeggers are concerned, the biggest downtown attraction is the city's hockey arena, **MTS Centre**, home of the National Hockey League's **Winnipeg Jets**. Originally a controversial project – it was built on the site of the former Eaton's department store – the 15,300-seat facility is now beloved as the structure that made it possible for the NHL to return to Winnipeg in 2011 after a 15-year absence. The team's owners, True North Sports & Entertainment, are so popular, Jets fans shout "True North" during the Canadian national anthem. Jets tickets are not easy to obtain; visit Ticketmaster (ticketmaster.ca) to access the small number of seats that don't belong to season-ticket holders. The NHL season runs from October to April and seats range in price from $210 to $45.

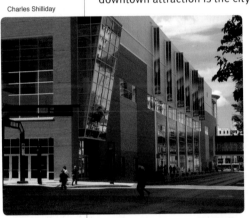

Charles Shilliday

Downtown Winnipeg's MTS Centre, a hockey arena and concert venue, was built on the site of the former Eaton's department store.

Public walkways on the second floor of the arena act as a museum of sorts; a statue of Eaton's founder Timothy Eaton, which used to adorn the old department store, is perched in front of a window overlooking Portage Avenue. The second-floor pedestrian area is part of an elaborate system of **weather-protected walkways** that connects much of Winnipeg's downtown, affording protection from the winter windchill. The walkways run from the Richardson Building northeast of Portage and Main; continue underground through Winnipeg Square mall; and head aboveground through the new Winnipeg police headquarters, the Millennium Library, and Cityplace mall before continuing west through MTS Centre to Portage Place and the Bay.

On the most frigid winter days, so many pedestrians use the temperature-controlled walkways that downtown streets appear deserted. Unfortunately, you can't use this system to get around late at night, so bar-hoppers must rely on cabs or sensible clothing.

Compared to the Exchange District's uniformly neo-classical architecture, the southwestern expanse of downtown Winnipeg is a canine's croissant of post-modern monstrosities and more thoughtful design. Arguably the ugliest structure is **Portage Place**, an imposing inner-city mall that occupies three blocks of Portage Avenue. It nonetheless houses one significant cultural institution on its third and uppermost level: **Prairie Theatre Exchange** (204.942.5483, pte.mb.ca, tickets $29-$49), a Canadian-centric company that stages six productions during an October-to-April season. Immediately across the street from the mall sits the sleek and innovative **Manitoba Hydro Place** (360 Portage Ave.), a wonder of environmental design, whose most prominent feature is a 119-metre-tall "solar chimney" that helps cool the office building during the summer and heat it during the winter.

Other downtown structures worth visiting for the architecture alone include the 1911 **Via Rail Station** (Main Street at Broadway), the sole remaining stone gate of 19th-century fur-trading post **Upper Fort Garry** (100 Main St.) and the **Millennium Library** (daily, 251 Donald St.) as well as its adjacent park, home to the city's most ambitious piece of public art: *emptyful*, an illuminated metal "container of nothing" that epitomizes Winnipeggers' love-hate relationship with their city.

Also visit the **Manitoba Legislature** (450 Broadway), a fascinating structure adorned with references to Greek, Roman, Assyrian, Babylonian and Egyptian mythology, as well as Hebrew and Christian scripture. It was completed in 1920, after numerous delays resulting from the First World War, labour shortages and even the theft of construction materials by the contractor. Kids will just marvel at the pair of bronze, life-sized bison at the foot of a grand staircase in the north-facing front lobby. The interior is open daily, 8 a.m. to 8 p.m. **Guided tours** take place on the hour from Canada Day to Labour Day – or by appointment (204.945.5813) from September to June. Experts in the building's occult symbolism offer well-regarded **Hermetic Code Tours** of the Legislature from April through October ($39.30 through Heartland

MUST SEE: Manitoba Legislature Stately neoclassical architecture and mysterious occult symbology – open to the public all year.

The neoclassical Manitoba Legislative Building, with the statue of The Golden Boy on top. Designer Frank Worthington Simon was a student of the *Beaux-Arts* school and you see the influence in the triangular pediment above the front columns.

Travel Manitoba

Travel, 204.989.9630, heartlandtravel.ca). On the south side of the Legislature, facing the banks of the Assiniboine, stands a sterile **statue of Louis Riel**, Manitoba's controversial founder. This bland image of Riel as a dignified statesman was installed in 1994 to replace a much more fascinating piece by Étienne Gaboury – one of Winnipeg's most celebrated architects – and sculptor Marcien Lemay. They cast Riel as a naked, twisted and tortured soul, but Métis leaders didn't like looking at the great man's genitals and demanded the statue switcheroo. The Gaboury/Lemay version now stands across the Red River on the grounds of St. Boniface College. Visit both to see why politicians should never be allowed to make artistic decisions.

On the north side of the Legislature, a green space called **Memorial Park** – home to war memorials and impromptu summer soccer games – stretches toward Portage Avenue. Keep heading north and you'll come to the **Hudson's Bay** department store, one of the last vestiges of that seventeenth-century fur-trading empire, the HBC. It is a glorious structure, eerily devoid of shoppers and awaiting an uncertain fate.

MUST SEE: Winnipeg Art Gallery + Plug In ICA
The world's largest permanent collection of Inuit art in Manitoba's largest gallery – plus contemporary exhibits at the gallery right next door.

Across Memorial, it's impossible to miss the monolithic facade of the **Winnipeg Art Gallery** – the largest gallery in the province, the oldest in western Canada, and home to the most extensive permanent collection of Inuit art in the world. A new wing to house more Inuit art is in its planning stages; in the meantime, some of this collection is usually on display. The WAG (Tues-Sun, 300 Memorial Blvd., 204.786.6641, wag.ca) typically houses three temporary exhibits at a time. Admission is $18 adults, $14 seniors/students.

Across Colony Street from the WAG, the **Plug-In Institute of Contemporary Art** (Tues-Sun, 1-460 Portage Ave., 204.942.1043, plugin.org) occupies the main floor of the Buhler Centre, a structure shared with the **University of Winnipeg** as part of its expanding downtown campus. Here you'll find more experimental visual and multimedia art. Admission is free. The Buhler Centre also houses the most stylish of six restaurants belonging to a Winnipeg restaurant chain known as **Stella's** (daily, 204.772.1596), which specializes in breakfasts and seems irresistible to anyone with neo-hippie tendencies.

Another strong breakfast option downtown is **The Don Restaurant** (daily, 120 Donald St., 204.947.6644) offers a handful of Mennonite items, such as the cottage-cheese pancakes known as gloms kuak.

At lunch, head across the street to **V.J.'s Drive Inn** (daily, 170 Main, 204.943.2655), a tiny shack where you'll find the finest fat boy – that is, a gloriously messy, Winnipeg-style burger – in the entire city. There's nowhere to eat inside, so sit on the benches in the summer or sit in your car. **Mitzi's Chicken Finger Restaurant** (Mon-Sat, 250 St. Mary Ave., 204.943.9770) is equally legendary as the creator of honey-dill sauce, a uniquely Winnipeg condiment that's supposed to be applied to – what else? – your chicken fingers, which come with a side of Chinese-Canadian stir-fried veggies. Yes, this is a real place.

Too bland? Head to **Famena's Famous Roti & Curry** (Mon-Sat, 295 Garry St., 204.414.9040), a Guyanese diner crammed into the main floor of a circular parkade, or sample the buffet at **East India Company** (daily, 349 York Ave., 204.947.3097). There's also vegetarian Chinese at **Affinity** (Mon-Sat, 208 Edmonton St., 204.943.0251) and fantastically ungreasy wings at **Carbone Coal Fired Pizza** (daily, 260 St. Mary Ave., 204.691.2213).

Notable downtown watering holes south of Portage Avenue include the tiny, bourbon-soaked roots club **Times Change(d) High & Lonesome Club** (Fri-Sun and Tuesdays, 234 Main St., 204.957.0982), corporate but handsome pub **The Pint** (daily, 274 Garry St., 204.942.3069) and the no-frills beverage room at the **Windsor Hotel** (daily, 187 Garry St., 204.942.7528), a former dive bar that's become a vital indie-rock venue. The old-school **Palm Lounge** at the Fort Garry Hotel, meanwhile, is a place to see but not be seen.

Of all of Winnipeg's hotels, the **Fort Garry** (222 Broadway, 204.942.8251, fortgarryhotel.com) has the most character. The rooms, some ornate and other hilariously small, date back to the completion of the establishment as a railway stopover in 1913. Other attractions include the luxurious **Ten Spa**, which includes a Turkish *hamam* steam room, allegedly haunted floors and the Palm Lounge. Rooms will set you back $127 to $251.

Elsewhere in the commercial downtown core, you'll be staying in chain hotels, such as the upscale **Fairmont** (2 Lombard Place, 204.957.1350, fairmont.com/winnipeg, rooms $161 to $349) or the convention-centre-connected **Delta Winnipeg** (350 St. Mary Ave., 204.942.0551 deltahotels.com, rooms $179 to $234), destined to become a Marriott property in 2015. The boutique **Alt Hotel Winnipeg** (310 Donald St., winnipegalthotels.ca, rooms $149) is slated to open across from MTS Centre in 2015.

St. Boniface

Winnipeggers are fond of claiming their city has the largest Francophone population of any Canadian city west of Ottawa. It's a nice idea, but it's complete and utter bullshit, as Toronto, Vancouver, Calgary, and Edmonton sport larger numbers of ethnic French-Canadians, as well as more people who actually speak French, according to Statistics Canada.

What makes Winnipeg *appear* more Francophone is many of the city's 77,000 French speakers are concentrated in St. Boniface, a central neighbourhood that was a proud and separate city until 1974, when Winnipeg swallowed up most of its suburbs.

On foot from The Forks, you can wander across Esplanade Riel pedestrian bridge and stroll down Taché Boulevard parallel to the Red River – where you can have the best views of downtown – and then return to The Forks via Queen Elizabeth Way. As a diversion, you can stop in cafés on Provencher Boulevard, as well as the

MUST SEE: St. Boniface Cathedral The ruins of the Basilica, Louis Riel's grave, and a bold statue of Manitoba's colourful founder.

Charles Shilliday

The remains of the basilica at St. Boniface Cathedral: a majestic facade now enclosing a new church by celebrated architect Étienne Gaboury.

stunning **St. Boniface Cathedral** (daily, 190 Avenue de la Cathédrale), which is actually the fifth incarnation in a series of Catholic churches dating back to 1818. The fourth basilica, completed in 1906, burned down in 1968. Architect Etienne Gaboury incorporated its west-facing façade into a modern structure completed in 1972. This facade, which often appears on postcards, is stunning after dark. The surprisingly modest **grave of Louis Riel**, Manitoba's founder, sits on the grounds of the cathedral, facing Avenue de la Cathédrale between the façade and Taché Boulevard.

A short walk east, on the Aulneau Street side of St. Boniface College, you'll find Gaboury and Marcien Lemay's brilliant, tortured **statue of Riel**. To the south of the cathedral, **St. Boniface Museum** (daily, 494 Taché Blvd., 204.237.4500, msbm.mb.ca) is packed with Riel artifacts, and chronicles the history of Winnipeg's Francophone community. Admission is $6 for adults, $5 for seniors/students and $4 for youths.

To see real, live Franco-Manitobans, visit St. Boniface in mid-February during **Festival du Voyageur** (festivalvoyageur.mb.ca), a 10-day celebration of Winnipeg's Francophone heritage and fur-trade history. The main festival site at **Whittier Park** (St. Joseph at Messager) has outdoor snow sculptures, French-Canadian folk, Celtic, and Cajun music inside heated tents; plus a recreation of the wooden **Fort Gibraltar** fur-trading post. More music is scattered around a dozen "trading post" locations around St. Boniface. Try the traditional taffy on snow, mashed potatoes topped with toutière, pea soup or the fortified wine known as caribou, the latter served at an open-air ice bar. The festival also adjudicates a beard-growing competition, which is fun if utterly redundant following the mainstreaming of hipster fashion. Day passes are $17 for adults, $11 for youths and $9 for children.

Moving to the south, there's one more St. Boniface building worth a pilgrimage for the architecture alone. **Precious Blood Parish** (200 Kenny St.), also designed by Gaboury, is a conical Catholic church that resembles a massive wooden teepee. Daytime visitors are welcome, provided you don't mess with mass.

The main drag for pedestrians in St. Boniface is **Provencher Boulevard**, lined by a few shops on the blocks east of Esplanade Riel as well as the former **St. Boniface City Hall** (219 Provencher Blvd.), which is now a francophone tourism bureau. Stop in for good coffee at **Café Postal** (daily, 202 Provencher Blvd., 204.414.3654), pickerel fingers and a beer at **Le Garage** (Mon-Sat, 160 Provencher Blvd., 204.237.0737) or excellent artisanal chocolate at **Constance Popp** (Mon-Sat, 180 Provencher Blvd.,

204.897.0689). Popp's red beet truffle with caraway seed is the most Manitoban confection ever made.

On block north of Provencher, there's decent Jamaican at **Purple Hibiscus** (Tues-Sun, 171 Dumoulin St., 204.233.0670). Elsewhere in St. Boniface, try bistro fare on the rarely crowded patio at **In Ferno's** (Mon-Sat, 312 Rue des Meurons, 204.262.7400), bison chili at **Marion Street Eatery** (daily, 393 Marion St., 204.233.2843), pulled pork at **Lovey's BBQ & Smokehouse** (Wed-Sun, 208 Marion St., 204.233.7427) or excellent pastries at **Le Croissant** (Wed-Sat, 276 Taché Ave., 204.237.3536), which fulfills the French stereotype for buttery decadence.

Osborne Village and Fort Rouge

While downtown Winnipeg boasts most of the city's tourist attractions, the population density in the centre of the city is fairly low. To find people on the streets, you have to head southwest.

On the south side of the Assiniboine River, **Osborne Village** is one of the few legitimate pedestrian areas in car-crazy Winnipeg. Here you'll find university students, street punks, club kids and well-groomed seniors who live in the neighbourhood's high-rise condos, all coexisting somewhat happily. Dozens of funky retailers and restaurants are packed into a six-square-block area of the Village, concentrated around Osborne Street from River Avenue to Confusion Corner, the intersection of Osborne, Corydon Avenue and Pembina Highway. Come during the day to shop or at night to go barhopping.

Start with a coffee at **Little Sister** (daily, 470 River Ave.), peruse the vinyl at **Music Trader** (daily, 97 Osborne St., 204.477.5566) and consider lunch at **Nu Burger** (daily, 472 Stradbrook Ave., 204.888.1001), the potato-beet latkes at **Osborne Village Cafe** (Mon-Sat, 160 Osborne St., 204.452.9888) or an Ethiopian platter (and often a lengthy wait) at **Massawa** (Tues-Sun, 200-121 Osborne St., 204.284.3194). For a higher-end meal, the Spanish and North African small plates at **Segovia** (Wed-Mon, 484 Stradbrook Ave., 204.477.6500) consistently rank among the best restaurant fare in Winnipeg; reservations aren't accepted, so show up promptly at 5 p.m. or leave your name and go for a drink elsewhere in the Village while a table becomes available.

Toad In The Hole (daily, 112 Osborne St., 204.284.7201) is the best spot for a pint before it fills up late with wasted refugees from other establishments; the adjoining whisky bar has an impressive hooch selection and doesn't allow entry to anyone under 25. Why? Neighbouring, ultra-popular dance club **Green Room** (Thurs-Sat, 2-108 Osborne St., 204.421.9164) attracts lengthy lineups. To avoid all pretense, no one at the mellow, faux-Mexican **Carlos & Murphy's** (daily, 129 Osborne St., 204.284.3510) cares if you dress terribly, order wings and drink a non-craft beer.

Several blocks of Osborne Street shut down for days during Canada Day for a multi-day street festival that sends many Village residents fleeing to the lake. On the plus side, there's free live music. The other main cultural draw is the **Gas Station Theatre** (445 River Ave., gsac.ca), most prominently used as a venue for the **Winnipeg Comedy Festival** (winnipegcomedyfestival.com), usually held in April.

Also consider hopping in a cab or take a No. 16 bus further south down Osborne to Fort Rouge, where the **Park Theatre** (698 Osborne St., parktheatrecafe.com) hosts live music and **Deseo Bistro** (Mon-Sat, 696 Osborne St., 204.452,2561) serves boldly seasoned, Spanish-influenced small plates.

Crescentwood and River Heights

A few minutes on foot from the Village lies another rare Winnipeg pedestrian neighbourhood: Crescentwood, dominated by the **Corydon Avenue strip**. Patios along a five-block stretch of Corydon between Daly and Wentworth streets go into operation as soon as night-time temperatures climb above 10°C. During summer weekends, the strip is packed.

The most popular patios are crammed into a single block between Hugo and Cockburn, where you'll find the inexplicably popular **Saffron's** (Mon-Sat, 681 Corydon Ave., 204.284.2602), the smaller and hipper **Teo's** (Mon-Sat, 691 Corydon Ave., 204.414.6305) and the coffee-bar-by-day, hip-hop-club-by-night **Bar Italia** (daily, 737 Corydon Ave., 204.452.1929), which has the most Italian cred in a supposed Little Italy where sushi is more common than pasta.

A little off the strip, steakhouse **529 Wellington** (daily, 529 Wellington Cresc., 204.487.8325) positions itself as Winnipeg's most expensive restaurant and caters to the business-expense crowd. A more democratic atmosphere can be found at **The Grove** (daily, 164 Stafford St., 204.415.3262), a neighbourhood local with plenty of taps and better-than-average pub food.

Continuing west on Corydon Avenue into affluent River Heights, **Eva's** (daily, 1001 Corydon Ave., 204.452.3827) serves the best gelato in Winnipeg and Israeli-Canadian diner **Falafel Place & Deli** (daily, 1101 Corydon Ave., 204.489.5811) happily serves both vegan breakfasts and chicken soup with matzo balls. Jump into a vehicle and head even further west for the borscht and house-made corned beef at **Bernstein's** (daily, 1700 Corydon Ave., 204.488.4552), excellent traditional Japanese at Yujiro (daily, 1822 Grant Ave., 204.489.9254), high-end pizza at **Pizzeria Gusto** (Mon-Sat, 404 Academy Rd., 204.944.8786) or small plates at **Enoteca** (Tues-Sun, 1670 Corydon Ave., 204.487.1529), one of the city's best restaurants.

Crescentwood and River Heights are also fertile shopping territory, with clusters of gift shops, clothing boutiques and knick-knack retailers on the Corydon strip, Lilac Street and Academy Road. Retailers of note include Inuit art gallery **Nunavut** (Mon-Sat, 603 Corydon Ave., 204.478.4233), upscale clothing boutique **Moulé** (daily, 443 Academy Rd., 204.488.1891) and Canada's largest independent bookstore, **McNally Robinson Booksellers** (daily, 1120 Grant Ave. in Grant Park mall, 204.475.0484).

West Broadway, Wolseley and the West End

Due west of Winnipeg's downtown, gentrifying **West Broadway** is Winnipeg's answer to Toronto's Ossington: a once-sketchy neighbourhood that was colonized first by artists, then students and eventually hipsters. Do not let that scare you, because you're only coming here to eat or drink.

Thom Bargen (daily, 64 Sherbrook St., 204. 234.5678) is the requisite hipster coffee shop. Line up for the brisket and fried chicken at **Tallest Poppy** (Tues-Sun, 103 Sherbrook St.), order a soy, nut or veggie patty at **Boon Burger** (daily, 79 Sherbrook St., 204.415.1391) or cram into **The Nook** (daily, 43 Sherbrook St., 204. 774.0818) for eggs Benedict on avocado and polenta. Shell out for high-end sushi at **Wasabi On Broadway** (daily, 588 Broadway, 204.774.4328) or enjoy cheap drinks while slumming with the university students at **Handsome Daughter** (evenings, 61 Sherbrook St., 204. 615.2977) or **Cousins** (daily, 55 Sherbrook St., 204.783.4695).

While West Broadway sports an urbanist-punk esthetic, neighbouring **Wolseley** is gentler, more gentrified and ... way more hippie-ish. On the edge of West Broadway, you'll find Manitoba's longest-running hostel, **Backpackers International** (168 Maryland St., 204.772.1272, backpackerswinnipeg.com, rooms $60 to $30). Wander further into Wolseley for a cinnamon bun from **Tall Grass Bakery** (Mon-Sat, 859 Westminster Ave., 204.783.5097), a pioneering organic institution in Winnipeg, or cram into a communal table for lunchtime pasta in the restaurant upstairs from the grocery floor of **De Luca's** (Mon-Sat, 960 Portage Ave., 204.774.7617).

North of Portage Avenue sits a collection of ethnically diverse neighbourhoods collectively known as the **West End**. Here you'll find the widest array of inexpensive restaurants and groceries in Winnipeg, concentrated along Sargent and Ellice avenues. Locals may tell you this 'hood is sketchy, but do your best to ignore them; the eating here is great and nothing bad is going to happen to you during daylight hours.

Food from every continent except unpopulated Antarctica is represented along Ellice and Sargent, so wander around and take your pick, though Vietnamese establishments dominate. Grab a fresh-fruit bubble tea at snack shop **Asia City** (daily, 519 Sargent Ave., 204.783.8118), sit down to a bowl of classic pho at **Pho Kim Tuong** (Thurs-Tues, 856 Ellice Ave., 204.661.8888) or try the beef sate soup at **Thanh Huong** (daily, 534 Sargent Ave., 204.774.8888). Pick up Portuguese egg-custard tarts and water bread at **Lisbon Bakery** (Mon-Sat, 717 Sargent Ave., 204.775.7612) or a pork-on-a-bun bifana from **Viena do Castelo** (Mon-Sat, 819 Sargent Ave., 204.415.4615). There's also perfect baba ghanouj at **Shawarma Time** (Mon-Sat, 616 Ellice Ave., 204.774.2109), jerk chicken at the Caribbean-run Greek restaurant **Juliana Pizza** (daily, 678 Ellice Ave., 204.775.2925) and some of the best Filipino food in town at **Rice Bowl** (Tues-Sun, 641 Sargent Ave., 204.779.2777).

The West End also boasts one of Canada's best live-music venues in the **West End Cultural Centre** (586 Ellice Ave., 204.783.6918, wecc.ca), a folk and roots club in a former United Church. On the edge of West Broadway, **Good Will Social Club** (daily, 625 Portage Ave., thegoodwill.ca) serves as a live music venue, espresso stop and pizza-by-the-slice joint.

Northeast of the West End, in the central Centennial neighbourhood, there are two more restaurants worth checking out, both in the same strip mall. **Kyu Bistro** (Tues-Sun, I85 Isabel St., 204.504.8999) serves up ramen and izakaya fare, while **Kimbaek** (Tues-Sun, 193 Isabel St., 204.942.1833) is a good spot for Korean standards like bibimbap.

The North End and West Kildonan

Go back a century, and Winnipeg's sprawling **North End** was the most vibrant immigrant community in western Canada, a place where Ukrainian, Polish, Russian, German, and Yiddish were heard more often than English in the streets. Cut off from the rest of the city by the sprawling Canadian Pacific rail yards, the North End developed a distinctive culture of its own centred around bustling Selkirk Avenue.

Unfortunately, the latter half of the twentieth century wasn't kind to the North End, and upwardly mobile folks moved out. After decades of decline, the region is turning the corner, although it remains one of the largest economically depressed areas in Canada.

One sign of the North End's renaissance is **Neechi Foods Co-Op** (daily, 865 Main St.), an indigenous-run complex featuring a grocer where you can pick up wild rice at a decent price and fresh-baked bannock. As well, you can still taste the Slavic influence in the North End, the best place in Canada to sample various varieties of eastern European sausage, especially kubassa, the garlicky Polish-Ukrainian ham coil. North End butcher shops are legendary: Visit **Tenderloin Meat & Sausage** (Tues-Sat, 1483 Main St., 204.582.2280) for coarse-ground kubassa, **Karpaty** (Tues-Sat, 536 Bannerman Ave., 204.586.1395) for smoky barbecue sausage, and **European Meats** (Tues-Sat, 533 Burrows Ave., 204.586.2728) for gloriously hot, paprika-infused Hungarian sausage.

If you're looking for smoked goldeye, **Gimli Fish** (Mon-Sat, 596 Dufferin Ave., 204. 589.3474), is the next best thing to driving north to the Interlake. Scarf it down with crispy lavash or bagels from **Gunn's Bakery** (Mon-Sat, 247 Selkirk Ave., 204.582.2364), a North End institution, which also makes fantastic knishes and other Jewish pastries.

Beyond the hearty grub, the big attraction of the North End is its colourful past – represented by surviving structures. The **Ukrainian Labour Temple** (591 Pritchard Ave.), headquarters for Winnipeg trade unions during the 1919 General Strike, and **St. John's Cathedral** (135 Anderson Ave.), site of the first Anglican Church in western Canada and home to a graveyard first used by

Red River settlers in 1812. **Holy Trinity Ukrainian Orthodox Metropolitan Cathedral** (1175 Main St.) also demands a look-see, given the way it dominates Main Street.

Farther north, in residential West Kildonan, you'll find **Kildonan Park**, which houses a modest set of gardens, an outdoor skating rink, and a covered outdoor theatre called **Rainbow Stage**, which usually produces musicals but may be closed for good by the time you read this due to financial difficulties.

Also in West Kildonan, **Seven Oaks House Museum** (115 Rupertsland Ave., 204.339.7429) offers history about the Red River Settlement, including the 1821 Battle of Seven Oaks, which saw Métis face off against colonists. The free museum is open Victoria Day to Labour Day, 10 a.m. to 5 p.m.

The North End's Holy Trinity Ukrainian Orthodox Cathedral overlooks the Red River at Main Street and Mountain.

Polo Park and St. James

Polo Park, the busiest shopping district in Winnipeg is a maze of big-box stores, airport-vicinity hotels and parking lots in a concrete no-man's land that divides the West End from residential neighbourhood **St. James**. The area takes its name from the **Polo Park** shopping centre (1485 Portage Ave.), which in turns takes its name from an old racetrack.

The quirky attraction here, just north of boring big boxes, is **Westview Park**, a former landfill that's now the highest point in Winnipeg. You can drive to the top of "Garbage Hill" between dawn and dusk from a park gate at Wellington Avenue, just east of Empress Street. In the summer, park on Wellington Avenue before dawn and walk up the hill to watch the sun rise over downtown Winnipeg. In the winter, the slope at the northern part of the park makes for a great toboggan ride.

Just west of Polo Park, on the edge of Richardson International Airport, the **Western Canada Aviation Museum** (Mon-Fri 9:30-4:30, Sat 10-5, Sun noon-5 p.m., 958 Ferry Rd., 204.786.5503, wcam.ca) offers airplane buffs the chance to check out vintage military and civilian aircraft. Admission is $7.50 for adults, $5 for students/seniors and $3 for kids.

Polo Park also boasts two Winnipeg eateries with decades of tradition behind them. The **Original Pancake House** (daily, 1445 Portage Ave. in the Clarion Hotel, 204.775.9035) is famous for its giant apple pancakes, while **Rae & Jerry's Steakhouse** (daily, 1405 Portage Ave., 204.783.6155) is the genuine old-school article, with red leather chairs, dark oak panelling, and properly mixed martinis. This place was retro before retro existed — take a seat in the lounge and order an open-faced steak sandwich.

Deeper into St. James, you'll find the **Living Prairie Museum** (2795 Ness Ave., 204.832.0167), a tall-grass prairie preserve. This 12-hectare patch of vegetation protects 160 species of indigenous grasses and other plants indigenous to the tall-grass prairie ecosystem, more than 99 per cent of which has been eradicated from North America. Admission to the grounds and a small interpretive centre is free. It's open 10 a.m. to 5 p.m. on Sundays in May and June and daily in July and August.

MUST SEE:
Assiniboine Park
Riverside footpaths, indoor and outdoor gardens, and Assiniboine Park Zoo, home to the polar bears of the Journey To Churchill exhibit.

Assiniboine Park and Forest

Occupying 440 hectares of southwest Winnipeg, **Assiniboine Park** and its wilder neighbour, Assiniboine Forest, make up the largest patch of vegetation in the city. Nestled between Corydon Avenue and the Assiniboine River, the park is home to **Assiniboine Park Zoo**, **Assiniboine Park Conservatory**, outdoor **English gardens**, the **Leo Mol Sculpture Garden**, a duck pond, the outdoor **Lyric theatre**, and a Tudor-style pavilion housing the **Tavern in the Park** restaurant (Tues-Sun, 55 Pavilion Cresc., 204.938.7275) and two floors of art exhibitions, including works by Ivan Eyre and a painting of Winnie the Pooh, the A. A. Milne character named after the City of Winnipeg.

The park is in the midst of a $180-million renovation. Half that sum has been spent on its zoo (assiniboineparkzoo.ca), which is dominated by a sub-Arctic exhibit called **Journey To Churchill**. In 2015, there were five polar bears in the exhibit, which includes an underwater viewing area. Arrive early to avoid large throngs of children and avoid visits on warm summer days, when animals adapted to northern climates are inactive. Zoo hours are 9:30 a.m. to 4:30 p.m. from April Fool's Day to Thanksgiving and close one hour earlier the rest of the year. Zoo admission is $18.50 for adults, $14.81 for seniors/youths and $10 for kids three to 12.

Admission to the Assiniboine Park Conservatory, which houses native and non-native plants, is free. The Lyric Theatre offers occasional free performances during the summer. Admission to outdoor gardens is also free.

Assiniboine Park is accessible from gates at Corydon Avenue and at the end of Wellington Crescent at Park Boulevard. A footbridge over the Assiniboine River offers pedestrian access from Portage Avenue and an ice-cream joint called **Sargent Sundae** (daily, 2053 Portage Ave., 204. 832-5021), famous for its pumpkin-pie soft serve in the fall.

South of the park, relatively undeveloped **Assiniboine Forest**, one of the largest natural areas within the bounds of a Canadian city, occupies two parcels of land alongside Corydon and Grant Avenues. The northern section is bisected by a paved walkway for joggers, cyclists, and rollerbladers. The section south of Grant has eight km of wood-chip paths, plus a single, short paved walkway that provides access to a marsh. The south end of Assiniboine Forest connects to the Harte Trail, a flat footpath that runs west through Charleswood and across the Perimeter Highway into Headingley, eventually connecting to Beaudry Provincial Heritage Park.

Southern Suburbs

Winnipeg's fast-growing southern suburbs are generally bland and well … suburban. The main attraction in southeastern **St. Vital** is the city's most popular shopping mall, **St. Vital Centre** (Bishop Grandin Boulevard at St. Mary's Road). The big driver of traffic to the southwest are corporate retail stores along Kenaston Boulevard, including an **IKEA**-anchored complex called **Seasons of Tuxedo** (Sterling Lyon Parkway at Kenaston Boulevard) and a big-box shopping wasteland known as **Kenaston Common** (Bishop Grandin Boulevard at Kenaston Boulevard).

There are some signs of life in Winnipeg's south, however. St. Vital, which sits east of the Red River, is worth a summertime visit for **Riel House National Historic Site** (330 River Rd., 204.785.6050), Manitoba founder Louis Riel's family home. Thanks to Parks Canada cuts, the interior is only open Canada Day to Labour Day from 10 a.m. to 6 p.m. Admission is $3.90 for adults, $3.40 for seniors and $1.90 youths.

During wintertime in **Windsor Park**, the best place to try out skinny skis is **Windsor Park Nordic Centre** (10 Des Meurons, windsorparknordic.ca), where the Manitoba Cross-Country Ski Association maintains 15 kilometres of trails lit for night-time skiing. Day passes are $5 for adults, $4 for seniors/students and $3 for kids. You can rent skis, boots and poles for $10 for two hours or $15 for a day.

In **Southdale**, another southeastern suburb, you'll see the handsomely modernist, Étienne Gaboury–designed **Royal Canadian Mint** (Tues-Sat, 520 Lagimodière Blvd., 204.983.6429, mint.ca), in which hard currency has been produced for 75 countries. Guided tours are offered run from 9 a.m. to 4 p.m. and it's a good idea to reserve. Weekday admission is $6 for adults, $5 for seniors and $3 for kids and youths. That drops to $4.50, $3.75 and $2.25 on Saturdays.

If you have little kids in tow, continue east down Fermor Road to **Springfield**, where you'll find amusement park **Tinkertown** (621 Murdock Rd., tinkertown.mb.ca, mid-May to mid-September, $15 for unlimited rides,) and **Fun Mountain Waterslide Park** (804 Murdock Rd., funmountain.ca, mid-June to Labour Day, admission $17 to $26).

On the other side of the Red River, southwestern suburb **Fort Garry** is best known as the home of the **University of Manitoba**'s main campus, which includes **Investors Group Field**, the

33,500-seat home for the Canadian Football League's **Winnipeg Blue Bombers**. Tickets to see the Bombers are easier to obtain than NHL seats and summer-evening games in the open-air stadium are fantastic. Individual seats range from $180 to $30 at Ticketmaster, ticketmaster.ca or 855.985.5000. From downtown, the easiest way to reach the stadium is by jumping on a No. 160 or 161 transit bus, which will take you right to the gate.

Fort Garry is also the de facto home of Winnipeg's unofficial new Chinatown, as the city's most innovative Chinese restaurants are located along Pembina Highway. Try **Sun Fortune** (daily, 2077 Pembina Hwy., 204.269.6868) for northern Chinese hot pot or **Golden Loong** (daily, 2237 Pembina Hwy., 204.504.6766) for fiery, Xian-style dishes from China's northwest.

The newest attraction in Fort Garry is **Thermëa Winnipeg** (775 Crescent Drive, 204.284.9595, thermea.ca), a Nordic spa with outdoor baths, at Crescent Drive Park. Access to the baths is $45-$60; spa treatments, $95-$249.

Near the city's southwestern edge, non-profit environmental-education centre **FortWhyte Alive** (daily, 1961 McCreary Rd., 204.989.8355, fortwhyte.org), boasts a herd of plains bison, several man-made lakes with year-round fishing, a small forest frequented by white-tailed deer, and an interpretive centre housing indigenous waterfowl and a freshwater-fish aquarium. In the winter, FortWhyte is open 9-5 p.m. Mon-Fri and 10-5 weekends/holidays; with later Thurs-Sat hours during the summer. Admission is $7 for adults, $6 for seniors, $5 for students/kids or free if you bike to the centre. By car, take McGillivray Boulevard southwest to McCreary Road, turn right and the entrance is clearly marked 200 metres to the north.

St. Norbert, Winnipeg's southernmost 'hood, is worth a visit on its own. **St. Norbert Farmers Market** (3514 Pembina, stnorbertfarmersmarket.ca) is the finest in the city, offering up fresh produce, preserves, baked goods, and some excellent food carts. It's open 8-3 Saturdays from early June to late October and also 1-7 Wednesdays in July and August. If you need to work off what you eat, the 3.5-km **St. Norbert Dike Trail** starts just east of the market site and loops along a bend in the Red River and back through a residential neighbourhood where wild turkeys wander the streets.

To the south, bald eagles, white pelicans and snapping turtles congregate at the mouth of La Salle River, which enters the Red at **St. Norbert**

MUST SEE: FortWhyte Alive
A herd of bison, native waterfowl, and a freshwater-fish aquarium at an environmental education centre.

The ruins of the Trappist monastery at St. Norbert: Goth kids come at night, but the caretakers prefer that you visit by day. The monks have since relocated to Holland, Manitoba.

Travel Manitoba

Provincial Heritage Park (40 Turnbull Drive), home to a trio of restored pioneer dwellings and a one-km interpretive walking trail. On the west side of Pembina Highway, **Trappist Monastery Provincial Heritage Park** (100 Rue des Ruines du Monastere, 204.269.0564) protects the ruins of a – yes, you guessed it – Trappist Monastery destroyed by fire in 1983. Theatre company **Shakespeare In The Ruins** (shakespeareintheruins.com) holds outdoor performances of The Bard's work at the site in June; bring mosquito repellent and you'll have a blast.

At the extreme south end of this city limits – technically, right outside it – **La Barriere Park** offers canoe access to the placid La Salle River during the summer and a network of cross-country ski trails during the winter. Access is from Waverley Street.

Gambling

Official Winnipeg tourism literature promotes Winnipeg's two casinos, **McPhillips Street Station** (daily, 484 McPhillips St., mcphillipsstation.com) in the North End, and **Club Regent Casino** (daily, 1425 Regent Ave., clubregent.com) in Transcona, an eastern suburb. While gamblers visit by the busload, people accustomed to Vegas glitz may find these government-run ventures sad and depressing. Club Regent does have an interesting walk-through aquarium, and both gambling emporiums offer live entertainment, usually by fading country stars and aging classic-rock bands.

A more old-school way to gamble is to visit **Assiniboia Downs** (3975 Portage Ave., assiniboiadowns.com), home to thoroughbred races from May to September. Admission is free.

Charles Shilliday

RED RIVER VALLEY & AROUND

6

More than two-thirds of Manitoba's population is concentrated in Winnipeg and the surrounding area, an agricultural region dotted by dozens of towns and five cities with more than 5,000 people: Portage la Prairie, Selkirk, Steinbach, Winkler, and Morden. This is the most developed part of the province, despite the fact much of the region is prone to flooding every spring — and winter commuter travel can be scarier than an amusement ride operated by intoxicated carnies.

Most of the municipalities immediately outside Winnipeg are booming, thanks to a combination of low taxes and land-use rules that allow the sort of gargantuan housing lots the city no longer sanctions. You can also sense prosperity in Steinbach and the "Bible belt" towns of Morden, Winkler, and Altona. Long-term changes in the agricultural economy, however, means many smaller towns are actually shrinking.

Long before this region turned into a big bedroom community for Winnipeg, most of its natural features were eradicated. Before European settlers showed up, the 100-km-wide Red River Valley was made up of marshes and tall-grass prairie, while areas to the east of what's now Winnipeg were heavily forested. Today, most of the marshes have been drained, only a tiny fraction of the tall-grass prairie remains and forests have been reduced to a few sizable parks, including Beaudry and Birds Hill, on the outskirts of Winnipeg. As a result, most of the attractions described in this chapter are historical and cultural as opposed to natural. That makes them perfect for daytrips, as almost all the destinations in this chapter can be reached within a 90-minute drive from the provincial capital.

Opposite: Old-growth tree at Beaudry Provincial Heritage Park, just west of Winnipeg.

Red River Valley North

The banks of the Red between Winnipeg and Selkirk look a lot more like Quebec than the rest of Manitoba. Like French colonists on the St. Lawrence River, the original Red River

Near Edrans, MB.

settlers plotted out homesteads along the water, subdividing lots into narrower and narrower strips as generations passed.

Today, this slender band of land is home to some of the ritziest suburban dwellings in Manitoba, many of them *nouveau riche* monstrosities built within the past two decades. The influx of wealth has breathed a lot of life into this once-pastoral strip.

You can zip through most of the area in a couple of hours along a loop from north Winnipeg. From the Perimeter, take Highway 9 – an extension of Main Street – north to River Road, also known as Provincial Road 238. Turn right and follow the scenic drive up to Lockport, detouring around flooded-out areas in the spring. Cross the Red at Highway 44 and return south along Henderson Highway, also known as PR 204.

This route also makes a decent bike trip, although you will share the road with plenty of motor vehicles. You can also get a spectacular view at some of the homes in the area from the water – take a boat cruise (see *Winnipeg: Exchange District*) or paddle a canoe.

Winnipeg to Lockport

The 20-km trip from Winnipeg to Lockport is one of the most popular recreational drives in the province. If you head up the west side of the Red River, take River Road to gawk at the homes across the river and stop at a handful of historical sites.

St. Andrews on the Red Anglican Church (3 St. Andrews Rd., standrewsonthered.ca) is the oldest stone church in western Canada, with a graveyard that reads like a history of the settlement. The church and rectory across the way date back to 1830, and comprise a national historic site open Victoria Day to Labour Day.

Captain Kennedy House (417 River Road) is the former home of William Kennedy, a Métis entrepreneur who campaigned for Canadian annexation of the area in the 1800s. The site houses the **Maple Grove Tea Room** (Tues-Sun, May through October, 204.334.2498), which serves high tea.

Henderson Highway, on the east side of the Red, doesn't offer as many views of the river. Henderson and River Road both converge on **Lockport** and **St. Andrews Lock & Dam**, which spans the river. The fully operational lock and dam, completed in 1910, raise the water levels upstream on the Red and cause fish to congregate just below; the massive channel catfish here are prized by anglers from around the world. It's all catch-and-release, so don't be alarmed by the numbers of fishers. Outfitter **Cats On The Red** (669 River Rd., 204.757.9876) can set you up for a day of fishing or more.

The fish also attract a flock of white pelicans that station themselves below the locks from late May until early September. If you can't see them at the locks, head farther north to the outflow of the **Red River Floodway** – it's rare to visit during the summer without seeing at least a dozen pelicans.

Bryan Scott

Lockport Provincial Heritage Park (north side of Highway 44), on the peninsula between the river and the floodway, is a significant archeological site; **Kenosewun Visitor Centre and Museum** (Victoria Day to Labour Day) houses artifacts dating back 3,000 years. Caches of squash, maize and beans found in this area show indigenous farmers – possibly relatives of today's Mandan and Hidatsa – were practising agriculture along the river in the 1400s, in what may be the northernmost reach of Mississippian farming technology, if not culture.

Two hotdog restaurants compete for the business of all the anglers and daytrippers who visit Lockport. On the west side of the river, **Skinners** (daily, 608 River Rd., 204.757.2951) is packed with hockey memorabilia and photos dating back to the restaurant's establishment in 1929. Its east-side rival is **Half Moon** (daily, 6860 Henderson Hwy., 204.757.2517) established in 1940. Don't expect high-end charcuterie: You're getting a hotdog.

In Lockport, hot-dog purveyors Skinner's and Half Moon compete for tube-steak supremacy.

Bryan Scott

Lower Fort Garry

When the great flood of 1826 turned Upper Fort Garry – the modern site of Winnipeg – into an aquatic theme park, the Hudson's Bay Company decided to rebuild farther north. **Lower Fort Garry National Historic Site** (5925 Highway 9, 204.785.6050, parkscanada.gc.ca/garry), originally known as the Stone Fort, was a supply post in the nineteenth century, serving York-boat crews heading back and forth from Hudson Bay, as well as pioneer farmers and local Métis, Cree, and Anishinaabe.

Today, the stone-walled fort is the last of its kind on the Canadian prairies. In summer, Parks Canada interpreters don

MUST SEE:
Lower Fort Garry and Lockport
The only fur-trading stone fort still standing on the Prairies, just north of an odd-ball town where pelicans and humans spend their summers trying to catch channel catfish.

period costume in an attempt to recreate life at the tail end of the fur-trade era. This is kitschy, but worth a stop if you care about history at least a smidge.

Lower Fort Garry is open 9:30 a.m. to 5 p.m. from mid-May to Labour Day. Admission is $7.80 for adults, $6.55 for seniors and $3.90 for youths. It's possible to wander the grounds at off hours —security guards won't eject people who are just nosing around respectfully.

Selkirk

Manitoba's seventh-largest community, **Selkirk** (pop. 9,834), takes its name from the Scottish earl who founded the Red River Settlement. Originally a river port, Selkirk now has an economy based on steel, and bills itself the "catfish capital of North America," thanks to the super-sized siluriforms that swim in the Red between Lockport and Selkirk.

Bryan Scott

Most visitors come to try to catch the cats, launching boats at the marina or building ice-fishing shacks on the Red in the middle of the winter. **Chuck the Channel Cat**, an 11-metre fibreglass statue, greets Main Street motorists from a perch at the front of Smitty's Restaurant – a chain franchise. Family restaurant **Barney Gargles** (daily, 185 Main St., 204.785.8663) and **Roxi's Uptown Café** (219 Manitoba Ave, 204.482.1903) are your best bets for a made-from-scratch meal.

The other chief point of interest is the outdoor **Marine Museum of Manitoba** (490 Eveline St., 204.482.7761, marine-museum.ca), where six retired river and lake steamships, freighters, and tugs sit along the river, near the entrance to

Chuck the Channel Cat, the piscine saint of Selkirk

Selkirk Park. The museum is open from the May long weekend to Labour Day. Admission is $6.50 for adults, $5 for seniors and $3.50 for kids.

Selkirk also sports a **Community Arts Centre** (250 Manitoba Ave.), which houses the **Gwen Fox Gallery** and a gift shop, both featuring local crafts, open Tues-Sat, 11 a.m.-4 p.m.

St. Peter's

On the east side of the Red River you'll find testament to one of the most important figures in indigenous-settler relations – who was ultimately betrayed for his diplomacy. North of East Selkirk sits **St. Peter's Dynevor Anglican Church** (8 Old Stone Church Rd.), the centre of a formerly all-Aboriginal parish, and the final resting place of Saulteaux Chief Peguis.

In the late 1700s, Peguis moved his people – Anishinaabe from the eastern shores of Lake Superior – to the Netley Marsh region at the bottom of Lake Winnipeg. After befriending Red River settlers, he signed a treaty with Lord Selkirk and granted the land around the Red and Assiniboine rivers to the British colonists.

Peguis died a respected man in 1864. The Canadian government repaid his generosity by forcing his descendants off their land in 1907 and relocating them to the site of the current Peguis First Nation, in the northern Interlake region.

To reach St. Peter's Dynevor, drive five kms north of East Selkirk on PR 508 and follow the signs to the church.

Northeast of Winnipeg

Heading east from Winnipeg, only 50 kms of farmland separate the city from the forests that mark the transition toward the Canadian Shield. This section deals with a chunk of plains northeast of Winnipeg, between Highway 44 and the Trans-Canada Highway.

Springhill

Where do people in the flattest place on Earth go skiing? In a hole in the ground, of course! **Springhill Winter Sports Park** (Oasis Road at Highway 59, 204.224.3051, springhillwinterpark.com) is built on the east slope of the Red River Floodway, a channel dug into the prairie. Weather permitting, it's open December through March on Tues-Fri from 6:30 -9:30 p.m. and weekends 10 a.m. to 5 p.m. Lift tickets are $32 adults, $27 students and $22 senior/kids 13 and under. Ski rentals are available.

Five minutes south, **Oasis Resort** (64123 Oasis Rd., theoasis. ca) is a private campground surrounding an artificial lake. There's no public access, so you'll need an invitation. Try Birds Hill Park instead if you're really desperate to swim in an unnatural pond.

Birds Hill Provincial Park

When the flood of 1826 deluged the Red River Settlement, freaked-out homesteaders dragged their oxcarts to higher ground. On the flat prairie, one of the few options was Pine Ridge, a series of sandy eskers east of river lots owned by a retired Hudson's Bay Company officer named James Bird.

Over the next 150 years, the modest upland subsequently known as **Birds Hill Park** would see Ukrainian, Polish, and German settlers clear land to farm rye and potatoes. Later, loggers cleared some of the pines and construction crews removed millions of tonnes of gravel and sand to build roads. The exploitation ended in 1964, when Birds Hill Provincial Park was established to protect 35 square kilometres of forest, prairie, and wetlands, creating a natural playground for nearby Winnipeg.

Bartley Kives

Pine Ridge Cemetery, the final resting place for Polish and Ukrainian settlers who cleared what's now Birds Hill Provincial Park.

Bartley Kives

Today, the park's main attractions are two seasonal campgrounds (May-Thanksgiving, $17.85-$25.20), a shallow artificial lake with a pair of popular beaches, and best of all, 16 trails for walking, cross-country skiing, horseback riding, rollerblading, and mountain-biking.

Short walking routes include the one-km **Bur Oak** and 3.5-km **Cedar Bog** trails, both located near the park's West Gate at Highway 59, plus the 1.5-km **White-Tailed-Deer** and 2.4-km (return) Pine Ridge trails near the south campground and the two-km **Nimowin** trail at the end of the road to the park's stables. You can pick up interpretive pamphlets at all five trailheads.

The trails in Birds Hill Park were initially designed for cross-country skiers and horses but have expanded for in-line skating and mountain bikes.

Off-road cycling routes include the 14-km **Bluestem trail**, which circumnavigates the north campground, and imaginatively named **Mountain Bike Trails** looping around Nimowin. Road bikes and rollerbladers prefer the seven-km Pine Ridge bike route, which zips around the artificial lake.

The best cross-country ski routes are the easy Chickadee and Aspen trails (four and 6.5 kms, respectively) and the slightly more challenging Esker, Lime Kiln, Tamarack, and Bluestem trails (six, eight, 12, and 14 kms, respectively). The Hazelnut, Bridlepath, and Carriageway trails are used almost exclusively by horses and horse-drawn carriages.

At the east end of the park, an artificial mound of earth called **Pope's Hill** marks the spot where Pope John Paul II held a mass in 1984. Other points of interests include the Manitoba Horse Council's Equestrian Centre, home to polo games during the summer, and the Pine Ridge cemetery, where some of the park's early settlers are buried.

Birds Hill Park also plays a starring role as the setting for Manitoba's premiere outdoor musical event, the **Winnipeg Folk Festival** (winnipegfolkfestival.ca) which takes over the east side of the park on the second weekend of July. About 80 folk, roots, rock, and world-music acts perform on seven outdoor stages over four days at the festival, one of the largest in North America, attracting crowds averaging around 12,000 people a day. Headliners have included Elvis Costello, Emmylou Harris, Ani DiFranco, Bonnie Raitt, and Steve Earle. About half the audience spends the weekend in the hard-partying Festival Campground, a sprawling tent city with an anarchic, Burning Man-like vibe. Attendance in this campground is capped at 6,000 people, but the more-distant Quiet Campground can hold another 1,200. The festival also sports a neo-hippie craft village, and food concessions that produce amazingly little garbage, thanks to a reusable-plate policy. Don't worry – the hippies wash the plates. Folk Fest weekend passes to range from $235 to $115, depending on your age and how early you reserve, while day passes range from $88 to $43. Camping will add up to another $75. Tickets are on sale at Ticketmaster (ticketmaster.ca or 888.655.6354) or at the Folk Fest Music Store in Winnipeg's Exchange District (Tues-Sat, 211 Bannatyne Ave., 204.231.1377).

To reach Birds Hill Park by car, take Highway 59 northeast from Winnipeg to enter at the West Gate. To enter at the East Gate, take 59 north, head east on PR 213 – also known as Garven Road – and then turn north on PR 206 until you reach the gate. Winnipeg Transit buses run between downtown and the park during the Winnipeg Folk Festival. Park admission is $5 per vehicle per day or $12 per vehicle for three consecutive days.

Around Birds Hill Park

East of Birds Hill Park, you'll find one of the most unusual struc-tures in Manitoba, the onion-domed **Immaculate Conception Ukrainian Greek Catholic Church**
(68003 PR 212, 204.444.2748) and the
adjoining and quite unlikely **Grotto of
Our Lady of Lourdes**. The parishioner-
built church is an impressive structure
on its own, but the grotto is an unusual
sight in the middle of the prairie:
two ramps and an elevated platform
enclose a large artificial cave that contains plaster-cast renditions of the 12
Stations of the Cross. It's like a theme
park, but the faithful take it seriously,

Bryan Scott

so please be respectful if you visit. To reach the Church and Grotto, take Garven Road east to PR 212 and turn north to the Zora Road intersection. The grounds and grotto are open to the public in July and August from noon to 8 p.m. The church requests a small dona-tion per visitor and offers weekend tours (noon to 6 p.m., Victoria Day to early October).

Farther north on PR 212, in the village of **Cooks Creek**, the **Cooks Creek Heritage Museum** (Weds-Sun, mid-May to end of August, 68148 PR 212, 204.444.4448) offers the usual assortment of pioneer artifacts and displays. It's worth a visit on Cooks Creek Heritage Day, usually the last Sunday in August, when local arti-sans sell crafts, honey, preserves, and baked goods. Otherwise, admission is $4 for adults and $2 for kids.

Beausejour and Vicinity

Branching off Highway 59 northeast of Birds Hill Park, Manitoba Highway 44 is the most direct route from Winnipeg to the north-ern Whiteshell. Stop in **Garson**, the first village along the way, for a meal at the **Harvest Moon Café** (Wed-Sun, 180 Garson Rd., 204.268.4554), a superior country diner with homemade soups, good burgers, and fried pickerel. Don't be discouraged by the exterior. The town also boasts **Garson Pond**, a privately owned

MUST SEE:
*Immaculate
Conception
Ukrainian
Greek Catholic
Church
A lavishly deco-
rated Eastern
church in the
middle of the
prairies — with
a larger-than-
life outdoor
recreation of
the 12 stations
of the cross.*

sport-fishing park in a former quarry. Garson is the source of Manitoba's famous Tyndall stone – the cream-coloured limestone used in Canada's Parliament Buildings, the Manitoba Legislature, and Lower Fort Garry. Three kilometres east lies the town of Tyndall, which lends the stone its name.

Continuing east on Highway 44, **Beausejour** (pop. 3,126) is best known as the home of the **Canadian Power Toboggan Championships** (cptcracing.com), a snowmobile-racing competition held in early March. Admission to the CPTC Raceplex (PR 302, 1.5 kms south of Highway 44) and its 1,300-seat grandstand, is $15 for adults.

Beausejour also sports the requisite **Pioneer Village Museum** (July and August, 7th Street North and Park Avenue), the remains of the Manitoba Glass Works, and an endearing greasy spoon in **Vickie's Snack Bar** (719 Park Ave., 204.2681922), a gloriously untrendy diner with an inexpensive bison burger.

Northeast of Beausejour, along the Brokenhead River, **Great Woods Park and Campground** (greatwoodspark.com) hosts the three-day **Great Woods Music Festival** ($125 adults, $50 youths) in early August. The park is east at the junction of highways 44 and 12 – if you're driving east on the 44, keep going straight until you hit the river.

Southeast of Winnipeg

Heading southeast from Winnipeg toward the US border, the fertile Red River Valley farmland gives way to rockier soil and the beginnings of the scrubby forests that mark the transition to the Canadian Shield.

In the late 1800s, French-Canadian, Mennonite, and Ukrainian settlers cleared most of the land in this area, which has retained its rural European character, if not its original flora and fauna. A small patchwork of ecologically rare tall-grass prairie still exists just north of the border, near the towns of Tolstoi and Stuartburn.

Steinbach

The largest city in southeast Manitoba, **Steinbach** (pop. 13,524) is also the centre of Manitoba's Mennonite community, a pacifist ethno-religious group with origins in Russia, Germany, and the Netherlands. The city, located 35 minutes southeast of Winnipeg on Highway 12, has a reputation for social conservatism that largely (and now, unjustly) stems from a prohibition on alcohol sales that lasted until 2003.

The end of Prohibition did not transform this prosperous little city into a snow-swept Sodom and Gomorrah. The main attraction is **Mennonite Heritage Village** (231 Highway 12 North, 204.326.9661), a model pioneer community with a functioning windmill, early-twentieth-century buildings, a petting zoo, and a restaurant called the Livery Barn, which serves up Mennonite

Bartley Kives

Bison cows and calves along Highway 12, southeast of Steinbach.

specialties like kjielke and pluma mousse. Costumed interpreters are only present on Canada Day (July 1) and Pioneer Days (the first weekend in August). As a result, the grounds are underwhelming compared to the Village Centre's indoor museum exhibit, which chronicles the history of the Mennonites from their origins as a persecuted religious minority in Europe to their successful colonization of the Prairies. Mennonite Heritage Village is open in July and August on Mon-Sat 10-6 and Sundays noon-6; May, June, and September hours are Mon-Sat 10-5 and Sundays noon-5; October-April hours (museum only) are weekdays only 10-4. Admission is $10 for adults, $8 for students/seniors and $4 for kids.

If you don't eat at the Livery Barn, **MJ's Kafe** (Tues-Sat, 408 Main St., 204.326.2224) is the spot for Mennonite food, **Niakwa Pizza** (daily, 197C Main St., 204.320.9955) offers Menno-style farmer's sausage as a topping and **Main Bread & Butter Company** (Mon-Sat., 235 Main St., 204.326.6108) is the recommended sandwich joint. On Thursdays from June through October, also try the **Steinbach Farmers Market** on the grounds of Clearspring Village Mall (Highway 12 North, across from Mennonite Heritage Village).

Around Steinbach

Ste. Anne (pop. 1,626) marks the start of a nice drive down picturesque Provincial Road 210, which snakes southwest through at the Francophone towns of Giroux, La Broquerie, and Marchand on its way to Sandilands Provincial Forest. From June to September, make a detour at PR 311 to **Giroux** to check out **Philip's Magical Paradise** (weekends, 1-6 p.m.), a museum of magic built in an old United Church.

West of Steinbach, on PR 216 near the junction of PR 311, the tiny town of **New Bothwell** is the home of **Bothwell Cheese** (Mon-Sat, 61 Main St., 204.388.466), a source of the ubiquitous cheddar cubes found at Manitoba socials, good cheese curds and dozens of other varieties; the retail shop has them all.

Farther south on PR 216, the even tinier town of **Kleefeld** bills itself as Manitoba's honey capital. During daylight hours in the late summer, stop in at any farm along the road that advertises honey for sale.

St-Pierre-Jolys and St. Malo

About 50 kms south of Winnipeg on Highway 59, the partly Francophone town of **St-Pierre-Jolys** (pop. 1,099) is the home of two extremely quaint rural festivals. The **Sugaring-Off Festival** (usually early April) is all about Manitoba maple syrup, which tastes different from the condensed sap from sugar maples found in Quebec and Vermont. As soon as temperatures allow, maple producers get busy with their taps and start boiling sap into a syrup you can try at the Sugar Shack on the grounds of the **Musée**

Bartley Kives

de St-Pierre-Jolys (423 Joubert St., 204.433.7002), a former convent. The museum itself is open only in July and August, Wed-Sun, 11-5. Admission is $2.

During the August long weekend, St-Pierre-Jolys' **Frog Follies** (frogfollies.com) would be a run-of-the-mill rural fair if it weren't for the main attraction: frog-jumping contests usually held on the Saturday afternoon. No amphibians are harmed during the event – not even at area restaurants, which unfortunately do not offer *cuisses de grenouilles* on their menus.

Sixteen kms south of St.-Pierre-Jolys, **St. Malo** (pop. 1,148) sports a free **pioneer museum** (July to September, 10-7) and the **St. Malo Grotto**, a reproduction of the Grotto in Lourdes. But the main attraction is **St. Malo Provincial Park**, a recreation area along a stretch of the Rat River widened by a dam and spill-

Fall supper in southeastern Manitoba means a Ukrainian buffet, usually inside a church.

way. On summer weekends, the park's campgrounds and beaches are packed with families from Morris, Winnipeg, and Steinbach. Wander away from them along a 5.5-km hiking trail that arches around the northeast corner of the park. You can also rent paddle-boats and canoes on the lake. Park admission is $5 per vehicle per day or $12 per vehicle for three consecutive days.

St. Malo also marks the start of **Actif Epica** (actifepi.ca), a 130-km winter bike race that terminates at The Forks in Winnipeg. Usually held the first Saturday of Festival du Voyageur in February, it's part of a cold-weather cycling triple crown that also includes ultramarathons in Minnesota and Wisconsin.

Roseau River

While most prairie rivers make for a meandering paddle, **Roseau River** attracts whitewater canoeists and kayakers in April and May. A popular post-snowmelt daytrip takes paddlers down the west-flowing river from the town of Roseau River, underneath the Senkiw Suspension Bridge and through Roseau Rapids at the east block of Roseau River First Nation to a takeout at PR 218. This 15-km trip can be extended by an additional 40 kms by putting in at the beginning of the Gardenton Floodway, south of the town of Vita. Do not try this without whitewater skills and equipment. Flows are only high enough following the snowmelt; later in spring, you'll be scraping along rock gardens.

Manitoba Tall-Grass Prairie Preserve

Between St. Malo and the US border, cattle ranches and forests begin to replace farmland alongside Highway 59. Thanks to the relatively poor quality of the soil in this corner of the province, more natural vegetation has been left undisturbed, most notably at the **Manitoba Tall Grass Prairie Preserve**, a 30-square-km patchwork of indigenous vegetation protected around the towns of Stuartburn, Tolstoi, Gardenton, and Vita.

No ecosystem in North America has been devastated more than tall-grass prairie, which once stretched from Saskatchewan to Texas. The natural vegetation disappeared in the 1800s, when settlers ploughed up the grasses and all but killed off the bison that lived off these plants and kept their growth in check. Today, less than one-tenth of one per cent of Manitoba's tall-grass habitat remains intact, though bison have bounced back from the brink of extinction as captive ranch animals.

For a double shot of tall grass, visit both the **Prairie Shore Trail** (PR 209, about four kms east of Tolstoi) in the south block of the preserve, and the newer **Agassiz Interpretive Trail** (just north of PR 201, 1.5 kms east of the junction with PR 209) in the north block. The Agassiz trail is the only place in Canada where you can find the endangered western fringed prairie orchid, a

MUST SEE:
Manitoba Tall-Grass Prairie Preserve
A rare patch of undisturbed tall-grass prairie, home to endangered plants like the western fringed prairie orchid and small white lady's slipper.

Yeah, so the wild rose is Alberta's official flower. But you'll find rosebushes growing anywhere remotely wet along the Red River Valley.

Bartley Kives

Bartley Kives

Orchids unfurling in the spring along the Agassiz Interpretive Trail at the Manitoba Tall-Grass Prairie Preserve.

single-stalked plant with wispy white flowers that bloom spectacularly in July. The south block, meanwhile, is home to the almost-as-rare small white lady's slipper, which blooms briefly in May.

The entire preserve protects 300 species of plants, as well as animals such as the 70-gram least weasel (which you won't see) and the awe-inspiring sandhill crane (which you can't miss, if they happen to be in the region).

Between the north and south block, stop at the **Gardenton Ukrainian Museum** (Victoria Day to Labour Day, 9-5) if you're interested in the cultural history of the region. There are seven Ukrainian Orthodox, Russian Orthodox, and Ukrainian Greek Orthodox churches in this corner of the province, most notably **St. Michael's** (two kms west of Gardenton), completed in 1899.

Services are scarce in this area – for gas and groceries, drive east on PR 201 to Vita.

Red River Valley South

In the spring of 1997, almost the entire Red River Valley between Winnipeg and the US border turned into a temporary lake during the snowmelt-induced Flood of the Century, which swallowed up more than 1,800 square kilometres in Canada alone. More than 30,000 people were evacuated from a dozen communities along the Red, all of which were completely surrounded – if not submerged – by frigid waters by the time the river crested in early May.

The flood devastated the Winnipeg suburb of Grande Pointe, swamped the Franco-Manitoban town of Ste. Agathe, and threatened to sneak into Winnipeg via La Salle River before the Canadian military used bulldozers, old school buses, dirt and whatever else they could find to hastily erect a 22-km-long barrier called the Brunkild Z-Dike.

When the waters receded, angry Red River Valley residents complained their communities and farms were sacrificed to protect Winnipeg, as the Red River Floodway backed up the floodwaters. After a nasty debate, the federal and provincial governments decided to expand the floodway to prepare for an even greater flood – the Great Flood of 1826, for example, saw 50 per cent more water flow through the valley than the 1997 deluge had.

Today, a ring dike surrounds every community along the Red, while many farmhouses sit on elevated mounds of earth. Barely a spring goes by without Valley residents worrying about the snowmelt, despite the fact the lazy, meandering Red is placid most of the time.

The main route through the southern portion of the Red River Valley is the dull, four-lane Highway 75, on the west side of the Red. Provincial Roads 200 and 246 have more character.

St. Adolphe and Ste. Agathe

Heading south from Winnipeg on PR 200 – an extension of St. Mary's Road – the first town of any size is the Francophone village of **St. Adolphe,** home of **A Maze in Corn** (daily, August through Halloween, 1351 PR 200, cornmaze.ca), a seasonal corn maze that changes configuration every year to confound regulars. There's also a petting zoo, pony rides and a pumpkin barn. Admission is $10.50 for adults and $8.50 for kids. At the same site, **Amazing Zip Lines** (June to Halloween) offers high-wire tours for $20 to $70. Book in advance at 204.883.2048.

Charles Shilliday

    Continuing south on PR 200 to PR 305, cross the Red River to visit **Ste. Agathe**, a village that became the symbol for the destruction wrought by the Flood of the Century. As the Red River rose, the floodwaters made an end run around the community's dikes and rushed in from behind at Highway 75. The most enduring image of the deluge is a snapshot of the town's Catholic church, gleaming in the sunlight reflected off the floodwaters. At **Cartier Park** (Highway 75 at PR 305), the **Red River Valley Floods Interpretive Centre** (mid-May to mid-October, 1-9 p.m., 204.882.2696) chronicles the destruction and recovery efforts that remain ongoing. Admission is $5 for adults.

Morris

An island during the Flood of the Century, Morris (pop. 1,797) is best known as the home of Manitoba's only professional rodeo and the second-largest rodeo in western Canada, the **Morris Stampede and Exhibition** (manitobastampede.ca), usually held during the third weekend of July. Bull riding, steer wrestling, and other cowboy contests are held in front of a 6,000-seat grandstand. Admission is $25 for adults.

The church at Ste. Agathe, the only Red River Valley town to succumb to the 1997 "Flood of the Century." The town has largely recovered.

    If you find yourself in town at any other time of year, you can wrestle yourself some cow at the steak pit in **Burke's Roadhouse on 75** (355 Main St. South, 204.746.2222). The usual assortment of pioneer artifacts – plus a small collection of pre-colonial First Nations arrowheads – is on display at the **Morris and District Centennial Museum** (June-August, 2-8 p.m., Highway 75 at Highway 23. Admission is free.

Emerson

If any Red River Valley community should have been obliterated in '97, it was the border town of **Emerson** (pop. 655), whose streets were an astounding *nine metres* below the floodwaters when the crest of the Red lapped at the top of a ring dike, which was extended at the last minute by the Canadian Forces. Somehow, the all-but-evacuated town remained dry.

    Most travellers visit Emerson as the last Canadian stop before a visit to North Dakota. The nearby US border post at Pembina,

North Dakota, is open 24 hours, while a secondary crossing at Noyes, Minnesota, is open 10 a.m. to 6 p.m.

Things were a little livelier 120 years ago, when Emerson was a Prairie boomtown that profited off steamship traffic from the United States. But the town's fate was sealed when the Canadian Pacific Railway decided to cross the Red River at archrival Winnipeg instead.

Today, you can see a semblance of Emerson's boomtown past in a handful of stately nineteenth-century buildings. You can also walk a portion of the Trans Canada Trail up the west side of the Red River. Three kilometres up is **Fort Dufferin**, an 1872 Boundary Commission post later used as a staging ground for North-West Mounted Police heading west in an attempt to tame the Canadian frontier.

Charles Shilliday

Near Altona, where the town fair celebrates the addictive sunflower seed.

Altona

Twenty kms west of the river on PR 201 at Highway 30, mostly Mennonite **Altona** (pop 4,088) sits outside the flood zone. The town, which bills itself as Canada's sunflower capital, is best known for its seven-storey replica of Van Gogh's *Sunflowers*. Modest **Buffalo Creek Nature Park** has a campground and a catch-and-release fishing pond. There's also a downtown farmers' market, operating Saturday mornings from July through September.

You can sample Mennonite food at the mid-June **Sunflower Festival**. Year round, try the farmers' sausage pizza at **Ang's Pizza & More** (daily, 58 Second Ave. NE, 204.324.8955) or go for egg salad sandwiches at **Jasmine Tea Room** (Mon-Sat, 41 Second Ave. NE, 204.324.1847), located inside a craft shop. Obviously, Altona's not a party town.

Altona is surrounded by a dozen small Mennonite communities that make the region seem more like Germany than Manitoba.

The most-quaint hamlet is **Reinland**, on PR 243 near Highway 32, where families display their names on signs before their homes. And if you don't mind a straight, flat walk across farmland, a 10-km trail connects Altona to the small town of **Gretna** (pop. 563) and a US-hugging portion of the Trans Canada Trail.

Southwest of Winnipeg

Although the farmland immediately southwest of Winnipeg is flat and boring – it was once the vast and glorious Boyne Marsh – daytrippers who continue west along highways 2, 3, or 23 will be rewarded for their patience. The gently rolling terrain offers good biking and cross-country skiing in the Roseisle area, decent day-hiking in the Pembina Valley, and Mennonite-flavoured culture in Winkler and Morden.

This area is home to the southeast reaches of the Manitoba Escarpment, a ridge that separates the flat Red River Valley from higher and western Manitoba. The other dominant feature of this chunk of the province is the Pembina Valley, a glacial spillway that once carried the southern portion of the Assiniboine River. Although the valley itself isn't wide, the term "Pembina Valley" is used to describe a 100-km-wide population corridor above the US border.

Carman

Southwest of Winnipeg on Highway 3, **Carman** (pop. 3,027) sits on the Boyne River, a tributary of the Morris, which in turn spills into the Red. A five-kilometre footpath circumnavigates the quiet town, where ice cream sales at **Syl's Drive Inn** (May-October, 132 Fourth Ave. SE, 204.745.2432) signify it is summer.

The real attraction in Carman is higher up. In 1975, mysterious orange lights appeared in the night sky around Carman and kept reappearing for months. The unidentified object, eventually dubbed Charlie Redstar, briefly made the town the "UFO Capital of the World." Unlike Roswell, NM, Carman doesn't try to cash in on its former fame as a UFO hotspot. Official town literature makes no mention of alien spacecraft or extraterrestrials, which is an oversight – Paul Bunyan isn't real, either, but he still makes a great ambassador for Bemidji, Minn.

Ten kms west of Carman on PR 245, **Stephenfield Provincial Park** consists of a campground (May-Thanksgiving, sites $15.75-$21, yurts $56.50) on the shore of a reservoir, with an eight-kilometre hiking trail circling the entire small park. You'll need a Manitoba park pass for your vehicle.

The Manitoba Escarpment

Farther west on PR 245, you hit a picturesque section of the Manitoba Escarpment with excellent cross-country skiing, mountain biking, and road cycling. It's also a gorgeous, compact place to simply drive or walk around, especially in the summer and early fall.

**MUST SEE:
Manitoba
Escarpment**
*Fantastic moun-
tain-biking,
great cross-
country skiing,
and picturesque
back roads
southwest of
Winnipeg*

An old railbed
now serves as
bike path between
Miami and
Altamont, along
the Manitoba
escarpment.
Note the absence
of dolphins and
palm trees.

Just west of the small town of **Roseisle**, keep your eyes peeled for a sign marking the **Birch Ski Area** (40120 Road 32 North, birchmountainsports.com), home to 25 kms of cross-country ski trails groomed weekly during the winter. There are enough hills to make it loads of fun. Trail access fees are $5. The same area is home to 40 kms of mountain-bike trails in the summer. For insurance purposes, cyclists must purchase a $25 Birch Trail Pass from the Manitoba Cycling Association (mbcycling.ca) to access the single track, some of which crosses private land. To reach the parking lot from PR 245, head south at Road 40 West for three kilometres and make a right at Road 32 North.

A nearby ski alternative is the 20-km **Pumpkin Creek** cross-country ski trail system, nestled into idyllic Snow Valley. From PR 245, turn south on Road 40 West, but quickly make the first right turn onto a gravel road. Head west 2.5 kms, past the mothballed Snow Valley ski lift, until you see the trailhead on the right side of the road. The user fee is $5, which you can place into a drop box at the Pumpkin Creek trailhead.

During the warmer months, this same gravel road through picturesque **Snow Valley** makes for a gorgeous little detour, especially during the fall. Continuing southwest for a few more kms, you'll eventually reach tiny **St. Lupicin** (gravel Road 31 North at 45 West), a good place to stage a 12.5-km bike loop around the valley. Take a topographical map or a copy of *Backroads Mapbook* if you're prone to getting lost.

About seven kilometres northwest on PR 244, the village of **Notre Dame de Lourdes** (pop. 589) has a museum celebrating the Chanoinesses, an order of French nuns that moved into the area in

Bartley Kives

1895. Unlike most rural museums, **Musée des Pionniers et des Chanoinesses** (weekdays, 55 Rogers St., 204.248.2687) is open year-round. So is **Andy & Wendy's Drive Inn** (daily, 164 Notre Dame Ave., 204.248.2343), where you can grab a burger.

South of Notre Dame, it's impossible to miss a much grander attraction — the **wind farm** that stretches southwest toward the village of **St. Leon**. The presence of 73 giant turbines above on the rolling prairie is dramatic. You can see them along PR 244 between PR 245 and Highway 23 as well Highway 23 toward St. Leon. You can arrange to go inside one of the turbines through the **St. Leon Interpretive Centre** (35 Baie du Lac, 204.242.4374, cistleon.com), open Saturdays all year and daily during the summer. The centre offers information about the wind farm and the **grey tiger sala-mander**, an amphibian that migrates from pond to pond in the area at the height of the summer. There's an aquarium and terrarium at the centre if you don't want to go searching for salamanders along St. Leon-area roads or the 2.7-kilometre Round Lake trail.

Farther south along the escarpment, the town of **Miami** (Highway 23 and PR 338) is the starting point for a **20-kilometre bike ride** up the 190-metre escarpment along an abandoned rail line to the village of Altamont. The unmarked path runs along the north side of Highway 23 for about 600 metres before it crosses South Tobacco Creek on an old railway bridge. It then snakes up the escarpment in a long, gentle loop past the Miami Golf & Country Club, over Provincial Road 240 and up to the edge of the Deerwood Wildlife Management Area before it rolls up the top of the gentle grade. At the top of the escarpment, the final nine kilometres to Altamont are relatively flat and straight.

Winkler and Morden

With a combined population of 19,000, **Winkler** and its slightly smaller neighbour **Morden** are destined to grow into a single city at some point. Superficially, Winkler is the economic engine and Morden has more cultural attractions – although this is not exclusively the case.

The first thing you notice about Winkler is the depth of the Mennonite influence, as even the Dairy Queen sign says "Welkommen." Mennonite immigrants from Germany are fuelling the economy, but Paraguayans and Mexicans have also streamed in, to the point where Winkler's Sunny Day Products makes the best corn and flour tortillas in Manitoba. Look for them at local groceries. You can also find passable Tex-Mex food, along with some Mennonite dishes, at **Del Rios** (Mon-Sat, 644 Main St., 204.325.5273). You can also try Menno dishes at **Co-Op Café** (Mon-Sat, 370 Main St., 204.325.1655).

Winkler's greatest contribution to the culinary world, however, is the skinless farmer's sausage produced by Winkler Meats. This perennially popular pork product is available at groceries across Manitoba in the form of patties, finger-sized wieners, and big, phallic sausages that are perfect for the barbecue. There are imitators, but they're not as smoky-good.

Halfway between Winkler and Morden on Highway 3, the **Pembina Thresherman's Museum** (daily May-September, 204.325.7497, threshermensmuseum.com) is a collection of vintage agricultural equipment. Admission is $7.50 for adults.

More modern artifacts can found in Morden proper at the **Pembina Hills Art Gallery** (Tues-Sat, 352 Stephen St., 204.822.6026), a non-profit artists' co-op renovated in 2015. And way more ancient exhibits are the star attraction at the **Canadian Fossil Discovery Centre** (daily except holidays, 111-B Gilmour St., 204.822.3406, discoverfossils.com), a small natural history museum in the basement of the Morden Recreation Complex. The centre still sports the largest marine reptile collection in Canada, with the prized possession being Bruce, a 15-metre-long mosasaur discovered in bentonite clay outside the city. Admission is $8 for adults and $5 for students. The museum also offers paleontological tours to dig sites in the Pembina Hills, ranging in length from a half a day to five days, for $60 to $525 per adult.

Instead of Mennonite food, try the **Restaurante dos Banderas** (Wed-Sun, 212 First St., 204.822.6045), which offers Mexican food and dishes from Belize.

Heading outdoors, **Morden Park** plays host to the **Back Forty Folk Festival** (back40folkfest.com) the first Sunday in June, while the entire downtown closes to cars during the last weekend in August for the **Morden Corn and Apple Festival** (cornandapple.com), a town fair offering free sweet corn and apple cider.

In the summer, you can stroll the prairie gardens of Agriculture Canada's **Morden Arboretum Research Station** (daily May to September, 101 Route 100) or visit **Colert Beach** in **Minnewasta Recreation Area** (May-September, off PR 434, $8 per vehicle). In the winter, drive eight kms west of Morden and head north on Road 34 West to reach the **Shannondale Cross Country Ski Trails**, an excellent 22-km system. Pay for your trail use under the honour system – there's a drop-box for donations.

MUST SEE:
Pembina Valley Provincial Park
Uncrowded day-hiking up and down the Pembina River Valley, a remnant of a glacial spillway.

Pembina Valley Provincial Park

One of the newer parks in Manitoba, **Pembina Valley Provincial Park** protects a narrow slice of river valley about 50 kilometres southwest of Morden, close to the US border. Despite its small size, the park boasts an excellent network of short day-hiking trails that descend the 100-metre-deep river valley. The most satisfying route is the 6.5-km **Pembina Rim trail**, which dips down to the river and back. The best time to visit is late September, when the leaves are turning.

To reach the trailhead, take PR 432 then 201 southwest from Morden or take PR 201 east from Highway 31. Keep your eye out for a picnic table sign – larger signage at the park entrance won't be visible until you're almost at the parking lot. There is no staff on site, so purchase a Manitoba park pass before you go.

Manitou and La Rivière

Thirty-five kilometres west of Morden on Highway 3, diminutive Manitou (pop. 808) hosts the **Pembina Valley Honey, Garlic, and Maple Syrup Festival**, a harvest-time event usually held during the second week of September. It's also home to the 385-seat **Manitou Opera House** (325 Main St., manitouoperahouse.com), which hosts occasional concerts. A statue of Nellie McClung, the former Manitou resident who led the fight for women's voting rights in Canada, stands outside the venue.

Another 11 kilometres west, you hit the actual Pembina River Valley and the town of **La Rivière**. In the winter, ski hill and resort **Holiday Mountain** (holidaymountain.com or 242-2172) has eleven runs down the valley, ski and snowboard instruction, and

Charles Shilliday

accommodations in chalets and conventional rooms. Lift tickets are $40 for adults. The resort also operates zip lines capable of propelling riders up to 88 km/h; the first ride is $30. Just east of La Rivière, **Oak Valley Outdoor Theatre** (888.264.2038, passionplay. ca) produces Passion plays in early July; tickets are $20.

South of La Rivière, near the town Snowflake, **Star Mound School Museum** (daily, May to October) makes a fascinating statement about colonial history. The pioneer schoolhouse, built in 1886, serves as an interpretive museum. It, however, was erected on sacred ground, right next to an indigenous burial mound shaped like a beaver. To reach the site from La Rivière, drive south on PR 242 to PR 201 and turn right; drive 3.2 kilometres west to Road 56 West, and turn right: then drive 1.6 clicks north; you will see the school and mound on Road 4 North, to the left.

Post-glacial torrents carved out spillways, such as the Pembina Valley, pictured here at La Rivière.

Northwest of Winnipeg

The dullest possible drive in Manitoba is the 75-km stretch between Winnipeg and Portage la Prairie along the featureless Trans-Canada Highway. But don't let that discourage you from tooling around the northwestern quadrant of Winnipeg's hinterland, home to the meandering Assiniboine River and world-class birding at Delta and Oak Hammock marshes.

If you're heading to Portage, consider taking the scenic route. Not only does two-lane Highway 26 have a lot more character than the Trans-Canada, it's less exposed from prevailing winds and is safer to drive when the snow blows horizontally during the winter.

Portage la Prairie

Most motorists heading west from Winnipeg bypass **Portage la Prairie** (pop. 12,996), Manitoba's fifth-largest city. That isn't true to history: Quebec explorer la Vérendrye paddled up the Assiniboine River in 1738 and established Fort La Reine northeast of the city, using it as a base of operations for 15 years.

La Vérendrye's fur trade-era post survives in the form of **Fort La Reine Museum** (2652 Saskatchewan Ave. East, 204.8573259,

Lynne Skromeda

fortlareinemuseum.ca), albeit no longer at the original site. It's a pioneer village at the junction of Highway 1A and Highway 26, open daily from mid-May to early September. Admission is $10 for adults, $8 for students/seniors and $5 for children.

If history doesn't turn your crank, visit **Island Park**, an oval of land almost entirely surrounded by Crescent Lake, an oxbow left behind by an earlier course of the Assiniboine River. The park has an aquatic centre, **Splash Island Water Park**

The Bittersweet Cross-Country ski trails are carved into the Assiniboine River Valley, southwest of Portage la Prairie.

($7 for adults, $5 youths/seniors and $2.50 for infants), a windmill, a U-pick strawberry field, an arboretum, and a large enclosure of fallow deer, an ornamental species from Europe. There are also occasional performances at the **William Glesby Centre** (11 Second St. N.E., 204.239.5591, glesbycentre.com).

For a bite in Portage, **Horfrost** (Wed-Sun, 190 River Rd., 204.857.7203) boasts a playful fusion menu; there are bison mango spring rolls and chocolate-dipped bacon cubes. More straight-ahead fare can be found at rib shack **Bill's Sticky Fingers** (daily, 210 Saskatchewan Ave. East, 204.857.9999) and **Grindstone Bakery** (weekdays, 61 Saskatchewan Ave. East, 204.239.0610).

Around Portage la Prairie

Southeast of Portage, **Hoop & Holler Bend** (PR 331, four kms east of PR 240) is worth a short detour for Manitobans curious to see the infamous spot where provincial flood-fighters deliberately breached a dike during the height of the 2011 Assiniboine River flood. Fears of an uncontrolled Assiniboine River dike breach downstream from Portage la Prairie led authorities to deliberately flood Hoop & Holler Bend. There's nothing to see now but the restored curve of road, however. Southwest of Portage, **Portage Spillway Provincial Park** (Yellowquill Trail, west of Highway 1), offers a view the Portage Reservoir, where part of the Assiniboine's flow is carried north to Lake Manitoba along the Portage Diversion during flood seasons.

Ten kilometres south of Portage along PR 240, **Portage Sandhills Wildlife Management Area** offers cross-country ski and walking trails over grass and tree-covered dunes. Unlike in most

Manitoba wildlife management areas, here, motorized vehicles aren't allowed.

About 30 minutes southwest of Portage, there are 20 kms of regularly maintained skinny-ski routes at the fantastic **Bittersweet Cross Country Ski Trails**, which descend the north side of the Assiniboine River Valley. From Portage, head west on the Trans-Canada Highway to Bagot and then south on PR 242. The trailhead sits on the west side of the road, north the Assiniboine River. If you've crossed the river, you've gone too far.

Delta Marsh

The biggest attraction in the vicinity of Portage la Prairie is one of North America's largest wetlands — **Delta Marsh**, which covers 220 square kms of shallow freshwater habitat at the south of end of Lake Manitoba. Almost 300 bird species – roughly three out of every four ever spotted in Manitoba – have been recorded at the 50-km-wide marsh, making Delta one of Canada's top birding destinations. The marsh also attracts canoeists, hunters, and thanks to the windy, open water on Lake Manitoba, windsurfers.

There are three built-up areas offering easy access to the marsh, each sporting a campground, boat launches, at least one beach, and places to observe (and shoot) birds. **Lynch's Point** sits at the southwest corner of Lake Manitoba at the edge of the **Lynch Point Game Bird Refuge**. It's 45 kms northwest of Portage la Prairie – take the Trans-Canada west to Highway 16, drive northwest to PR 242, then head north to the end of the road.

Charles Shilliday

Delta Beach, in the centre of the marsh, was ravaged by high water levels on Lake Manitoba in 2011, when record volumes of Assiniboine River floodwater were sent into the lake through the Portage Diversion. Delta Beach used to be home to a cottage area, the University of Manitoba's Delta Marsh Field Station and the private Delta Waterfowl Research Centre. Most of the structures were smashed to bits by high waves during a 2011 storm. Birders and disaster tourists can visit the beach from Portage la Prairie by taking PR 240 north for 24 kilometres.

Delta Marsh, one of the province's top birding destinations.

On the northeast corner of the marsh, you'll find the town of **St. Ambroise** and **St. Ambroise Beach Provincial Park**, whose campground was destroyed in the 2011 flood. The beach at the park reopened for day use in 2013. From Winnipeg, take either the Trans-Canada or Highway 26 west to PR 430 and then drive north to Lake Manitoba.

St. François Xavier and Headingley

The closest "country" destination available to Winnipeggers is **St. François Xavier,** a village on the Assiniboine River fifteen kms west of the Manitoba capital. The main attraction is one of the more poignant village statues in the province: The White Horse at the junction of Highway 26 and the Trans-Canada Highway commemorates the *Romeo and Juliet*-like story of a Cree brave and Assiniboine bride who were slaughtered by jealous rivals.

Southeast of St. FX, **Beaudry Provincial Heritage Park** sports 16 kms of cross-country ski trails branching off a trailhead just north of PR 241. The trails are usually busy, due to the proximity to Winnipeg.

Due west of Winnipeg, the suburb of **Headingley** – once part of the city, but oddly allowed to secede – is home to a fantastic greasy spoon, **Nick's Inn** (daily, 5392 Portage Ave., 204.889.4548). This is the place to load up on chili-drenched, Winnipeg-style burgers and fries if you're heading west on the Trans-Canada.

If that doesn't sound sufficiently healthy, **Adrenaline Adventures** (600 Caron Rd., 204.800.2060, adrenalinemb.com) offers snow tubing ($10/hour) and a snowboard terrain park ($12/day) in the winter. In the summer, there's cable wakeboarding ($30/two hours), a high-ropes course with a zipline ($20/hour) and paintball ($22, gear included).

Stonewall and Vicinity

Northwest of Winnipeg, the quiet bedroom community of **Stonewall** (pop. 4,536, Highway 67 and PR 236) is named after a limestone quarry that is now **Quarry Park**. It has a campground, artificial lake, and an interpretive centre (daily, July and August) that explains the geo-cultural history of the area. **Quarry Days,**

Stonewall Quarry Park in winter.

the town's annual fair, is held in the park during the third weekend in August. **McLeod House Tea Room** (weekdays, 292 Main St., 204.467.2303) offers nostalgic, dainty lunches.

Due east of Stonewall on Highway 67, strawberry-growing **Boonstra Farms** (76135 Road 8 East, 204.467.8480, boonstrafarms.com) operates **Murray's Corn Maze,** a labyrinth open in September and October. The $12 admission covers the maze, a petting zoo and hayrides.

Off Highway 7, the village of **Stony Mountain** is best known for the federal penitentiary that looms over the road. During the Great

Charles Shilliday

Flood of 1826, the high ground near the town provided refuge for Red River Valley settlers on the west bank of the river. Today, the slope of the same hill is known as **Stony Mountain Ski Area** (Wed-Sun, 204.344.5977, skistony.com) which caters to snowboarders and downhill skiers. Lift tickets are $23.80 for adults. To reach the hill from Winnipeg, take Highway 7 north for 10 kms, turn right into town, and follow the signs to the hill.

If you're a fan of old trains, the **Prairie Dog Central Railway** (April-October, 204.832.5259, pdcrailway.com) carries passengers in vintage rail cars on a 2.5-hour return trip from Inkster Junction Station on the outskirts of Winnipeg to the town of Grosse Isle. Trains depart at 11 a.m. Inkster Junction Station is located in the Rural Municipality of Rosser on Prairie Dog Trail, between Inkster Boulevard and Sturgeon Road.

Grosse Isle marks the south end of the **Prime Meridian Trail**, a 10-km walking trail that runs up to the village of Argyle along an abandoned rail line. The trail, once part of a 116-km distance-hiking trail, may not be maintained.

Charles Shilliday

Oak Hammock Marsh

Whether you call yourself a birder or have any interest in flying feathered creatures, make the 20-kilometre trip from Winnipeg to **Oak Hammock Marsh Wildlife Management Area** (204.467.3300, oakhammockmarsh.ca), which protects 36 square kilometres of wetlands for 296 avian species. The best birding takes place at dawn and dusk during the spring and fall migrations. A 30-km network of dike trails covers the whole marsh, but it's best to start at the excellent Oak Hammock Marsh Interpretive Centre (daily except Christmas, New Year's Day and Remembrance Day) at the north end of PR 220, accessible from Highway 67.

You can get an up-close view of Oak Hammock Marsh in a war canoe.

MUST SEE:
Oak Hammock Marsh
World-class bird watching minutes north of Winnipeg.

The walking trails are free, but it's worth spending $7 to enter **Oak Hammock Marsh Interpretive Centre**, which has info on many of the animals and plants in the area, as well as displays about wetlands conservation. The centre is open 10 a.m. to dusk from May to October, and 10-4:30 p.m. from November to April. There are also summer canoe rentals and winter snowshoe trails.

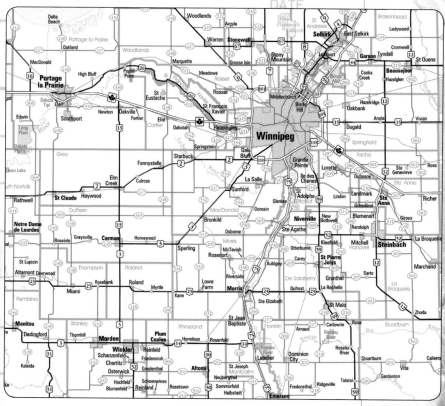

Map ©2006 Sherlock
Publishing Ltd.

Red River Valley Daytrips

Beginning and ending at Winnipeg

Red River Valley North

When to go: Mid-May to Labour Day

1. Drive north on Main Street and go for breakfast just outside Winnipeg's city limits at West St. Paul's **Red Eye Diner** (daily, 3132 Main St., 204.334.6424). Try the pickerel & eggs or the saskatoon pancakes.

2. Continue north 700 metres to the Perimeter (Highway 101). Head 2.5 kms west to Highway 8. Drive 19 kms north to Highway 67. Drive 6.5 kms west to PR 220. Drive four kms north to **Oak Hammock Marsh Interpretive Centre** (daily, 204.467.3300, oakhammockmarsh.ca). Walk off that breakfast with a walk around the dikes, keeping your eyes open for waterfowl. Head inside the interpretive centre to learn a bit about the wetlands that used to cover much of the Red River Valley.

Opposite: An aerial view of Lockport and the lower portion of the Red River Floodway.

3. Backtrack to Highway 67. Drive 15 kms east to **Lower Fort Garry National Historic Site** (5925 Highway 9, 204.785.6050, parkscanada.gc.ca/garry), the last stone Fur trade-era fort still standing on the prairies.

4. Drive three kms south to Highway 44 and **Lockport**. Flip a coin and decide whether to get a hotdog at **Skinners** (daily, 608 River Rd., 204.757.2951) on the west side of the Red River or **Half Moon** (daily, 6860 Henderson Hwy., 204.757.2517) on the east side.

5. Stop in at the **Kenosewun Visitor Centre and Museum** (north side of Highway 44, east of the Red) to learn about early indigenous history. Up until late August, check out the pelicans on the downstream side of **St. Andrews Lock & Dam**.

6. Take the scenic route back to Winnipeg on **River Road**, which ends at Main Street, also known as Highway 9.

Pembina Hills and Valleys

When to go: May to Thanksgiving.

1. Go for breakfast in Winnipeg at the **Original Pancake House** (daily, 1049 Pembina Highway, 204.452.1040). Try the baby apple pancake, or the giant version if you can easily burn off carbs.

2. Continue south to McGillivray Road. Past city limits, it becomes Highway 3. Follow Highway 3 south past the Perimeter (Highway 100) 64 kms to **Carman**. Head west on PR 245 for 27.5 kms to Road 40 West. Now it's time for a short scenic drive through Snow Valley: Drive 450 metres south and take the first gravel road on the right. Follow it 11 kms west through the valley to the hamlet of **St. Lupicin**. Drive five kms west on Road 31 North to PR 244.

3. You're now entering Manitoba's largest **wind farm**. Drive eight kms south to Highway 23. Drive three kms west to Road 50 West. Drive 2.5 kms south to St. Leon, where you can learn about the turbines and the grey tiger salamander at **St. Leon Interpretive Centre** (daily in summer, Saturdays all year, 35 Baie du Lac, 204.242.4374, cistleon.com).

4. From St. Leon, take Road 25 North three kms east back to PR 244. Drive 13 kms south to Highway 3. Drive 17 kms east to Highway 31. You're now about to enter the Pembina Valley proper. Drive south 21 kms to PR 201. Head east five kms and then south 450 metres to the access to **Pembina Valley Provincial Park**. Walk the 6.5-km **Pembina Rim trail**, which takes you down the river valley and back up again.

5. Return to PR 201. Follow it 14.5 kms north, east and north to PR 432. Drive north 17 kms to Morden. If you're hungry, try the central American food at **Restaurante dos Banderas** (Wed-Sun, 212 First St., 204.822.6045). If not, head straight to the **Canadian Fossil Discovery Centre** (daily except holidays, 111-B Gilmour St., 204.822.3406, discoverfossils.com) and check out Bruce, the mosasaur.

6. Still hungry? Head east on Highway 3 and 14 to **Winkler** and try the kjielke at **Co-Op Café** (Mon-Sat, 370 Main St., 204.325.1655) or continue back to Winnipeg on Highway 3, optionally stopping in Carman for ice cream at **Syl's Drive Inn** (May-October, 132 Fourth Ave. SE, 204.745.2432).

Red River Valley South

When to go: June and early July.

1. Go for old-school breakfast in Old St. Vital at **Red Top Drive Inn** (daily, 219 St. Mary's Rd., 204.233.7943). Harden your arteries and then continue south on St. Mary's Road, which becomes PR 200 south of Winnipeg's city limits.

2. From the Perimeter (Highway 100), take PR 200 south kms to PR 305 and **Ste. Agathe**. Cross the Red River and learn about the near-destruction of the town at the **Red River Valley Floods Interpretive Centre** (PR 305 at Highway 75, 1-9 p.m., 204.882.2696).

3. Back on PR 305, drive east 14 kms to Highway 59. Drive south 28 kms to St. Malo. Go for a swim or pedal the reservoir at **St. Malo Provincial Park**.

4. Now it's time to see some orchids. Continue 33 kms south on Highway 59 to Tolstoi. Head east on PR 209 a couple of kms to the south block of the **Manitoba Tall-Grass Prairie Preserve** and hike the Prairie Shore Trail. Continue east and then north on PR 209 to PR 201. Drive east 1.5 kms to Road 37 East and turn north into the preserve's north block and walk the Agassiz Interpretive Trail. If you're lucky, the western fringed prairie orchids will be blooming.

5. Return to PR 201 and drive nine kms east to PR 302. Drive 17 kms north to Highway 12. Take Highway 12 33 kms north to Steinbach. Try Mennonite food at **MJ's Kafe** (Tues-Sat, 408 Main St., 204.326.2224) or Menno farmer's sausage on your pizza at **Niakwa Pizza** (daily, 197C Main St., 204.320.9955).

6. Head west from Steinbach on Highway 52 for 13 kms to PR 216. If you want honey, head south to **Kleefeld** and look for "honey for sale" signs along the road. If you want cheese, head north to **New Bothwell** and **Bothwell Cheese** (Mon-Sat, 61 Main St., 204.388.466). Then go west to Highway 59 and back north to Winnipeg.

THE CANADIAN SHIELD

7

Rivers, lakes, and wild spaces are the main attractions in Manitoba's sparsely populated southeast, a Group of Seven-worthy landscape protected by three big provincial parks – Whiteshell, Nopiming, and Atikaki – as well as a patchwork of provincial forests.

A post-glacial playground of exposed granite and coniferous trees, the Canadian Shield is the largest of Canada's physical regions, covering almost half the country, including most of eastern and northern Manitoba. This chapter deals with the southeast portion of Manitoba's Shield, as well as the sandy deciduous forests that mark the transition and between the Shield and the open prairie.

Cree and other Algonkian peoples hunted and fished here during pre-colonial times, living off sturgeon, deer, grouse, and other critters. The area opened up to Europeans after la Vérendrye paddled down the Winnipeg River in 1733, leading the way for French-Canadian fur traders, trappers, and, in all likelihood, pea-soup merchants.

After the completion of the Canadian Pacific Railway in 1877, timber from Shield forests fuelled Winnipeg's construction industry as immigrants from all over Europe began flooding into western Canada. Logging, gold mining, and finally hydroelectric power dominated the economy until Whiteshell Provincial Park was established in 1961, followed by Nopiming in '76 and Atikaki in '85.

Today, tourism and recreation are the main industries in the southeastern Shield, although logging continues in the forests and on Crown land.

Summertime Shield attractions include paddling, fishing, hiking, and mellowing out at numerous cottage areas, lakes, and campgrounds. Winter is all about snowmobiling and cross-country skiing.

Wildlife in the area includes deer, wolves, moose, river otters, black bears, bald eagles, great blue herons, and, up in Nopiming, a small population of threatened woodland caribou.

The Shield also boasts many year-round cabins and lodges, so this is the best place to go for a quick winter getaway from Winnipeg if you can't afford a flight to the Dominican Republic. Just don't expect to suntan in December.

Opposite: Rock cairns serve as navigational guides on the Manitoba Trail, in Whiteshell Provincial Park.

Bartley Kives

The spare fall canopy in Whiteshell Provincial Park.

Whiteshell Provincial Park

At 2,726 square kms, the **Whiteshell** is southern Manitoba's largest provincial park. It takes its name from small, white seashells used in ceremonies by the Anishinaabe, who hunted and gathered in these forests for centuries. The park's logo – the rock outline of a turtle – is inspired by petroforms assembled by Algonkian-speaking peoples who lived here even earlier. Some archeological sites within the park date back to 6000 BC and remain sacred to many First Nations.

Created out of a former forest preserve, Whiteshell is bounded by the Winnipeg River to the north, the Ontario border to the east, and transitional prairie to the south and west.

Every visitor entering Manitoba at the Ontario border passes through the Whiteshell's southeast corner, zooming past meteor-created West Hawk Lake – Manitoba's deepest at 111 metres – and heavily developed Falcon Lake. But Manitobans know the park as an all-season playground, swarming in during the summer but maintaining a year-round presence.

The park can be divided into four regions. The densely populated southeast is dominated by cottage developments at Falcon, West Hawk, and Caddy lakes. The northwest also has cottage areas, campgrounds, and lodges, all snaking along a string of lakes between Highway 44 and the Winnipeg River. The northeast is undeveloped except for lodges, canoe routes, and a Manitoba Hydro generating station at Point du Bois. No industry, motorized

MUST SEE:
Whiteshell
Provincial
Park
Manitoba's most-popular provincial park, with dozens of resorts and hundreds of lakes, including meteor-created West Hawk, the deepest in the province.

vehicles, or permanent dwellings of any kind are permitted in the eastern Wilderness Section, home to a sizable wolf population and the 66-km Mantario Trail, the longest dedicated hiking trail in the province.

The park entrance fee is the standard $5 per vehicle, often but not always collected at gates at Rennie, West Hawk Lake, and Seven Sisters from May to September. Gate staff will waive the fee if you're driving straight through the park along Highway 44.

Falcon Lake

About 75 minutes from Winnipeg by car on Highway 1, **Falcon Lake**'s proximity to the Prairie metropolis makes it one of the most popular lakes in Manitoba, for better and for worse. Three-quarters of the cigar-shaped lake is lined by cottage developments, which means rarely a summer day goes by without the roar of personal watercraft and powerboats reverberating across the water.

Despite the racket, Falcon Lake remains one of the province's prettier resort areas. The **Falcon Lake townsite**, located at the west end of the lake, is home to **Falcon Beach**, two **campgrounds** (mid-May to Thanksgiving, $17.85 to $27.30), **Falcon Lake Bakery Bistro** (daily, 21a Park Blvd., 204.349.8993), a marina, tennis court, a run-down hotel, an 18-hole golf course (home to a four-km ski loop during the winter), and, best of all, one of the largest and most challenging miniature golf courses in the province. There's also a horse stable and a 2.2-km (return) self-guiding trail just northeast of town.

The road along the south side of lake ends at the year-round, excellent **Falcon Trails Resort** (100 Ridge Rd., 204.349.8273, falcontrails.mb.ca), which encompasses a lodge, cabins, the eleven-run Falcon Ridge ski-and-snowboard hill, and a modest but well-maintained trail system groomed for hiking and mountain biking in the summer and cross-country skiing in the winter. The longest ski route, the 7.5-km **High Lake Trail**, takes you past the resort's

A vintage aerial view of meteorite-created West Hawk Lake, Manitoba's deepest at 111 metres.

two solar-powered eco-cabins, on to the High Lake ice, and then back to the resort. Just watch out for snowmobiles. Rooms range from $110 to $350, depending on the cabin and the season.

On the north side of Falcon Lake, the 13-km **South Whiteshell Trail** hooks up with West Hawk Lake, swooping beneath the Trans-Canada Highway. You can bike in the summer or cross-country ski in the winter, when the trail connects to three ski loops south of West Hawk Lake. There's also a four-km winter ski trail that crosses the east end of Falcon Lake, connecting the West Hawk ski loops with the Falcon Ridge and the High Lake trails.

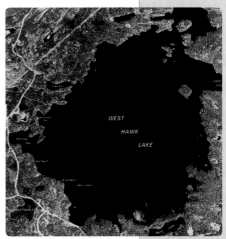

Manitoba Department of Natural Resources

133

West Hawk Lake

Only one click away from the Ontario border at the east end of Highway 44, **West Hawk Lake** is smaller than Falcon but almost as busy, thanks to cottages that ring its southern and western shores. The unusually deep lake, formed when a meteorite smashed into the Shield about 150,000 years ago, attracts scuba divers to a **permanent dive site** near the West Hawk townsite, and to a marina at the south end of the lake.

Sights below the surface include a submerged windmill, the wreck of a sailboat, and freshwater fish. The water gets frigid below 10 or 15 metres, so divers must suit up. For more information about this site – and Manitoba diving in general – contact the Manitoba Underwater Council (manunderwater.com).

If diving into the deep, cold blackness doesn't sound like fun, you can learn about the lake's origins at **West Hawk Museum** (daily, mid-May to Thanksgiving) at the **West Hawk Campground** (mid-May to Thanksgiving, $15.75 to $23.10). The town, meanwhile, offers the usual assortment of services, including burger joint **Nite Hawk Café** (daily in summer, Thurs-Sun winter, Highway 44, 204.349.2580).

If you're looking to stretch your legs, the longest day hike in the Whiteshell begins just east of the townsite. The 12.6-km **Hunt Lake Trail** is a pulse-stimulating there-and-back scramble over granite ridges on the east side of West Hawk Lake. There's a warm-up shelter at the turnaround point in case the wind is howling.

West Hawk Lake to Rennie

The six-km (return) hike from Hwy 44 to Bear Lake may also be undertaken in the winter.

One of the nicer short drives in Manitoba is a winding stretch of Highway 44 from West Hawk Lake to the Whiteshell's eastern gate at Rennie.

Heading west, the first paved road on your right is PR 312, one of the access points to **Caddy Lake**, a staging ground for canoe trips along the **Whiteshell River**. Paddling north from Caddy, you can circumnavigate the Whiteshell's Wilderness Section or head all the way up to the Winnipeg River. One of the highlights of the Caddy Lake paddle is accessible to daytrippers, as Caddy is connected to northern neighbour South Cross Lake not by a portage but by a tunnel blasted below the Canadian Pacific Railway line. The **Caddy Lake tunnel** is only four paddling kms northwest of the lake's boat launches. Caddy Lake also has a resort and a campground (May-September, $13.65).

Continuing east on PR 312, you'll find a parking lot that serves as the southern staging ground for the Mantario Trail. This is the place

Charles Shilliday

to clip your toenails and jettison extra weight in preparation for the 66-km slog to Big Whiteshell Lake. If that sounds too daunting, you can always whip around the easy 2.8-km **White Pine Trail**, which starts at the same parking lot. The 312 continues east into Ontario, where it dead-ends at the small community of **Ingolf**, home to network of mountain-biking trails accessible from the CPR tracks.

Back on Highway 44, there are four diversions between Caddy Lake and Rennie. The **McGillivray Falls** self-guiding trail offers walks of 2.4 or 4.6 kms along a set of rapids. The Lily Pond, a picnic spot, attracts climbers to a set of steep cliffs. The moderate **Bear Lake Trail** offers a slightly more strenuous six-kilometre scramble, while the 25-km **Centennial Trail** can take you all the way from Caddy Lake to the Bear Lake trailhead along a portion of the Trans Canada Trail. For a more manageable but still outstanding day hike, shorten the route to 12 clicks by starting at the McGillivray Falls trailhead and heading west; stash a car or bike at the Bear Lake trailhead so you can shuttle back.

The main attraction in **Rennie** is **Alfred Hole Goose Sanctuary**, a pond harbouring thousands of Canada honkers. The best times to visit Alf Hole are the spring, when impossibly cute goslings are yellow and fuzzy, or right before the fall migration, when adult geese congregate in disturbing numbers. **Alfred Hole Interpretive Centre** (daily, June to Thanksgiving), will give you the lowdown on the geese and other wildlife you'll find in the Whiteshell. A 2.5-km walking trail follows the pond, while in the winter, a seven-km ski loop extends east to Jean Lake and then back to the interpretive centre.

MUST SEE:
Mantario Trail
Manitoba's longest dedicated backpacking trail, a 66-kilometre trek over granite ridges and alongside lakes in Whiteshell Provincial Park's wilderness zone.

Bartley Kives

The Mantario Trail

Straddling lakes and climbing ridges in the eastern fringe of Whiteshell Provincial Park, the **Mantario Trail** is the prettiest, most pristine, and most strenuous hiking route in Manitoba. Disturbingly fit trail runners complete the 66-km slog from Caddy Lake to Big Whiteshell Lake in 24 hours, but they're insane. Backpackers typically take three to five days, depending on their fitness level and on how much time they want to chill out and enjoy the scenery and solitude.

Mantario Lake campsite along the Mantario Trail, within the Whiteshell's wilderness zone.

Compared to high-elevation Rocky Mountain hikes or the tidal challenges of the Pacific Coast Trail, Mantario is a literal walk in the park. But every year, dozens of people who've never hiked a day in their life head out on this trail and are defeated within 36 hours; they carelessly discard cooking utensils, clothing, and food along the way, and sometimes bush-crash into cottage areas at isolated Florence and Nora lakes in a desperate – and usually futile – attempt to get a lift back to civilization.

Jason Sorby

Hard to reach but worth it: Granite cliffs and bogs along the 66-kilometre Mantario Trail, the province's longest and best backpacking route.

If you've never strapped on a backpack, this is no place to start. Hikers with wilderness-camping experience should have no problem. Navigation is fairly easy, as most of the trail is well marked and well used. But you need a compass and map for a handful of tricky areas. Pick up a $12 laminated trail guide at Manitoba Conservation's Map Sales office in Winnipeg (1007 Century Ave., 204.945.6666, canadamapsales.com).

Most hikers find it easier to hike the route from south to north, as the stretch around the north trailhead at Big Whiteshell is flat and easy. Leave a vehicle at each trailhead. There is no fee for using the trail. The best time to go is between Labour Day and Thanksgiving, when days are cool, bugs are non-existent, the autumn foliage is beautiful, and low-lying areas are dry. Consider packing a pair of gaiters and hiking poles to remain dry and upright while negotiating at least three beaver-dam crossings along the way.

There are nine dedicated campsites along the route, plus one dead-end site on the west side of Caribou Lake, the latter perfect for a there-and-back overnight. Each site has a firepit, tenting space, a bear box, and outdoor biffies. Keep the Wilderness Section wild and you will be rewarded: The first time I hiked the Mantario, I was serenaded by a pack of wolves at Olive Lake.

The only service along the trail can be found at **Mantario Lake**, where the **Nature Manitoba** (204.943.9029, naturemanitoba.ca) runs wilderness-education programs and guided canoe trips out of the rustic **Mantario Wilderness Education Centre** on an island in the lake. Week-long canoe trips take place in July and August at a cost of $415. Subject to availability, you may also rent a room in **Mantario Cabin** for $35 per night, provided you undertake an orientation session.

North Whiteshell

Leaving Highway 44 at Rennie, PR 307 snakes north past five lakefront cottage communities until it parallels the Winnipeg River and heads west to the park's northwestern gate at Seven Sisters Falls. You can spend a fantastic day checking out trails and scenery along this route, or spend the night at one of six campgrounds or 11 lodges/rental cabins. Just don't drive through if you're in a hurry, especially during the summer, as the 307 is notoriously busy and slow.

Heading north from Rennie, the first community is **Brereton Lake**, which has a campground, two beaches, and the **Amisk hiking trail**, a 4.8-km loop that leads to **Inverness Falls**, home to the year-round **Inverness Falls Resort** (204.369.5336, invernessfalls. mb.ca; minimum stays of two nights, $210 to $490) and an eight-km cross-country ski-trail system.

A side road at **Red Rock Lake** takes you to the 4.6-km (return) **Cabin Lake Trail**, while five paths across the highway from Jessica Lake are groomed for cross-country skiing in the winter and walking in the summer. The loops range from almost two to eight kms.

White Lake offers a beach, campground (mid-May to Labour Day, $13.65), and a fishing spot at **Rainbow Falls**. Less than a km farther on, PR 309 heads east to **Big Whiteshell Lake**, home to more cottages and cabins, a marina, a beach campground (May-Thanksgiving, $13.65 to $18.90), and the north end of the Mantario Trail.

Continuing north on 307, **Betula Lake** has yet another campground (May-Thanksgiving, $15.75) and the only dedicated **mountain-bike trail** in the Whiteshell, a 4.2-km loop that shares space with the short **Forester's Footsteps hiking trail**.

The next trailhead along the highway is the start of the most-travelled trail in the Whiteshell, the 8.2-km walk to **Pine Point Rapids**, two sets of falls on the Whiteshell River. This is a very popular picnic spot, so consider a midweek visit or go early in the morning to avoid crowds. In winter, you can ski a 6.5-km stretch of this trail.

Next up along the highway are the **Bannock Rock petroforms,** the most-accessible archeological site in the Whiteshell and a sacred place for Anishinaabe and other First Nations. The petroforms are 2,500-year-old artworks created by indigenous ancestors, who placed rocks on the ground to form the outlines of turtles, snakes, and people. The petroforms likely served both navigational and spiritual purposes. They've very sacred today, so moving the rocks or tampering with any offerings left at the site is strictly forbidden — never mind insensitive and absolutely moronic.

PR 307 meets the Winnipeg River at Nutimik Lake just below **Sturgeon Falls**, an excellent playboating spot for whitewater paddlers, accessible via short path and suspension bridge. In the 18th and 19th centuries, sturgeon were so plentiful that anglers had only to place sharpened sticks in the rapids and wait for a large fish to impale itself. Nutimik Lake also offers a modest **natural history museum** (daily from May long weekend to Labour Day), with

MUST SEE:
Bannock Point
Petroforms
Centuries-old rock arrangements depicting turtles, people, snakes, and abstract forms tie modern Manitobans to the teaching of our indigenous predecessors.

exhibits about sturgeon, wild rice, and the petroforms. There's also the five-km (return) **Picket Creek cross-country ski trail**.

There are more cottage communities along the highway in the Whiteshell's northwestern arm, at Nutimik Lake, Barrier Bay, Dorothy Lake, Otter Falls, and Eleanor Lake, all of which are wide sections of the Winnipeg River. Campgrounds can be found at **Nutimik Lake** (May-Thanksgiving, campsites $13.65-$18.90, yurts $56.50), **Barrier Lake** (May-Labour Day, $13.65 to $17.85) and **Otter Falls** (May-Thanksgiving, $13.65 to $17.85). There are also two cross-country ski loops (three and seven kms) at Otter Falls.

There are four lodges northern Whiteshell, including excellent riverfront cabins with decks and lofts – and hotel rooms – at year-round **Pinewood Lodge** (204.348.7549, mypinewood.com) at **Dorothy Lake.** The lodge also has a pool and fitness centre and offers room service. Guests rooms go for $89 to $189 per night and cabins rent for two nights from $325 in the low season; from Summer Solstice to Labour Day, cabins rent by the week, starting at $1,225. There's also a three-km snowshoe trail south of Pinewood Lodge.

Bryan Scott

Seven Sisters Falls along the Winnipeg River, just west of the northern entrance to Whiteshell Provincial Park.

At any time of year, your best bet for a meal in the north Whiteshell is just outside the park in the hydro town of **Seven Sisters Falls**. Old-world restaurant **Jennifer's** (Tues-Sun, 63052 PR 307, 204.348.7135), offers central European dishes such as schnitzel, shots of Czech liqueur, and decor from rural Slovakia.

Just west of Seven Sisters Falls, the Whitemouth River tumbles into the Winnipeg River at **Whitemouth Falls**, which can be viewed from **Whitemouth River Wayside Park**.

North Whiteshell Gateway Towns

The billion-year-old Canadian Shield bedrock is among the most stable land on the planet. In this part of the continent, earthquakes occur as often as tsunamis. Knowing this, Atomic Energy of Canada Limited built a nuclear laboratory on the north side of the Winnipeg River in 1960 and built the nearby town of **Pinawa** (pop. 1,444, 15 kms east of Highway 11 on PR 211) to house scientists and technicians. At its peak in 1991, the lab employed 1,100 people.

The feds pulled the atomic plug in 2003, but Pinawa survived, reinventing itself as a retirement community and commuter residence for Winnipeg professionals. To visitors, the main attractions are a 10-metre-wide sundial built as a millennium project, a beach, and an extensive series of trails, including the **Ironwood Interpretive Trail** along the Winnipeg River, the excellent **Whiteshell Cross-country Ski Trails** east of the town (six loops totalling 37 kms, and the **Pinawa Channel Heritage Walk**. This last walk follows the north side of the Pinawa Channel from the Winnipeg River to a suspension bridge.

Across the bridge, a section of the Trans Canada Trail continues north toward **Pinawa Dam Provincial Park** (by road, 10 kms north of Pinawa on PR 520), which preserves what's left of Manitoba's first hydroelectric project, a generating station that operated from 1906 to 1951. Today, water tumbles wistfully through the concrete ruins, which were partly destroyed during army training exercises. The park also has canoe launches and an interpretive trail.

Northwest of Pinawa, **Lac du Bonnet** (pop. 1,328) lines the shore of the Winnipeg River at the confluence of Highway 11 and Provincial Roads 317, 313, and 502. The logging town and cottage community has a beach, a marina, and the free **Lac Du Bonnet & District Museum** (Saturdays May & June, daily July & August). Most visitors merely travel through on their way to the northern Whiteshell or Nopiming Provincial Park; heading into the bush from Winnipeg, this is the last place on any size to load up on provisions.

The ruins of Manitoba's first hydro dam are being reclaimed by nature at Pinawa Dam Provincial Park.

To the east of Lac du Bonnet on PR 313**, Pointe du Bois** is Manitoba's newest ghost town. Built in 1911 around a hydroelectric generating station, it wound up entirely within Whiteshell Provincial Park. Manitoba Hydro decided to shut it down in 2013 and ordered all remaining residents out by 2015. By the time you read these words, Pointe du Bois will be returning to a natural state.

Nopiming Provincial Park

Nopiming Provincial Park is the Whiteshell's younger, wilder sibling. Most roads are gravel instead of paved, there are fewer cottages and lodges, and even canoeists and hikers are not allowed to camp in the summer months inside a caribou-calving zone in the centre of the park.

Nopiming came into being like most Manitoba parks. First, lumberjacks logged the heck out of it. Then, it was protected as a provincial forest so it could be logged some more. Logging even continued after Nopiming was granted provincial-park status in 1976, when it was connected by road with the gold-mining town of Bissett.

To reach the park from Lac du Bonnet, head east on PR 313 and turn north at the junction with PR 315. From there, it's a

Bartley Kives

Sunset along the Manigotagan River, rendered easier to see thanks to a vegetation-clearing forest fire.

Taking a breather along a hike in Nopiming Provincial Park, where solitude is easier to find than in the more popular Whiteshell.

30-km drive to the park. Shortly before the entrance, you'll pass a turnoff to Bernic Lake, where mining company Tanco exploits the world's richest deposit of rare, volatile cesium, which is used in electronic components. Pure cesium is fun: it ignites spontaneously in air and reacts explosively with water. Needless to say, you won't be getting a tour of the mine.

It's easy to miss the entrance to Nopiming: there's no gate, and visitors are expected to obtain a park pass in Lac du Bonnet. Most visitors keep going east on PR 315 to the **Bird Lake** area in Nopiming's southeastern corner, home to most of the park's cottage developments, as well as campgrounds at both the Bird Lake townsite (May-Thanksgiving, $11.55) and **Tulabi Falls** (May-Thanksgiving, $11.55 to $15.75).

Bird Lake is also the staging ground for canoe trips up the **Bird River** into Elbow Lake, McGregor Lake, Snowshoe Lake, and eventually Crown land in Ontario. This short route sees a lot of paddlers during summer weekends, so go during the week or shoulder seasons if you want a quiet campsite.

The main artery in Nopiming is PR 314, which heads north from the park entrance. After 30 kilometres of winding nothing-ness, you'll pass the abandoned Irgon Mine and then come to access points to three canoe routes. The **Rabbit River route** is an overnight trip upriver to Cole Lake and back. Head downriver at the same point to embark on a five-day, 100-km paddle down the **Black River**, out of the park, and to the edge of Lake Winnipeg. Water levels are only high enough in the spring, usually. A short distance to the north lies the start of the **Seagrim Lake trail**, anoth-er short, popular paddling route.

A couple of kms up the highway, pull into the **Black Lake** campground (May-September, $16.80), the start of a nine-km (return) lakeshore path marked with rock cairns. The campground also houses an outdoor exhibit about Nopiming's small herd of woodland cari-bou, the southernmost cari-bou herd in Manitoba. The critters are so skittish while calving that the area around Flintstone Lake and Lost Claim Lake is closed to over-night visitors all summer.

You can get a glimpse of Flintstone Lake, albeit from a long distance, from the top of the **Walking on Ancient Mountains trail**, a short

Bartley Kives

self-guiding trail that climbs up a granite ridge. The trail is piddly in length – only 1.8 kms, return – but offers a nice panoramic view of the area, including Tooth Lake stretching out to the west.

Continuing north on PR 314, you'll cross the **Manigotagan River,** the most accessible A-list whitewater river in eastern Manitoba. Put in at Long Lake, and you can spend six days paddling 120 kms down the scenic Manigotagan to Lake Winnipeg, passing dozens of rapids, waterfalls and probably river otters along the way. To shorten the trip to four days, put in at Caribou Landing on Quesnel Lake, south of the Bissett (*see PR 304*). The lower 55 kms of the river is protected from logging, mining, and hydro development by **Manigotagan Provincial Park**, which follows the river down to the town

of Manigotagan. If you're interested in paddling the river, there's good advice in Hap Wilson's *Wilderness Rivers of Manitoba* and the *Manigotagan River Interpretive Map.* The river is usually navigable from May through September. Car shuttles from Manigotagan can be arranged by calling Charles Simard at **C&M Shuttle Service** (204.363.7355); he'll drive you to the put-in of your choice and store your vehicle

Bartley Kives

on his property, which is a short walk from the takeout at the government yards above Wood Falls.

There are two cottage areas in Nopiming's northern section: **Beresford Lake**, which also sports a campground (May-Thanksgiving, $16.80), canoe launch, and the remains of an old trapper's cabin; and **Long Lake**, home to the only lodge in this part of the park. Before the Beresford Lake turnoff, the short **Fire of '83 trail** takes you through an area of recovering forest. The most interesting features in this part of the park are the remains of gold and silver mines that operated in the area between 1927 and 1951. You can see the capped remains of four mine sites near Beresford Lake and Long Lake, the latter accessible via a short but slightly gnarly four-wheel-drive track that starts at the end of PR 314. You know you've come to the right place when you see a big pile of old core samples.

In the extreme north of the park, at the beginning of PR 304, you'll drive through a large clearing that looks like a giant mudflat. It's actually the remains of a mining town called **Wadhope**, which was dismantled after the nearby Kitchener mine was closed during the Depression. A small plaque stands at the site, which you could call a ghost town, if there were any town left here at all. The clearing has an eerie quality, especially since vegetation has yet

MUST SEE: Manigotagan River
Spend a few days or a week paddling Manitoba's most accessible A-list whitewater river, which flows from Nopiming Provincial Park to Lake Winnipeg.

to reclaim the site, even after 60 years. Who would have guessed mine tailings could be bad for the environment?

Provincial Road 304

PR 304 extends in an arc from Nopiming's north entrance to the Lake Winnipeg town of Manigotagan, then down to the twin communities of Pine Falls and Powerview on the Winnipeg River. The east-west drive between Nopiming and Powerview is dusty and lonely, and seems longer than its 88 kms. People mostly come up here to hunt, fish, or paddle – or to charter a floatplane to do more of the same.

Just northwest of Nopiming, you'll find a turnoff to **Wallace Lake** and **Wallace Lake Provincial Recreation Park**, which has a campground and boat launch. This fishing spot marks the start of the most infamous set of portages in Manitoba – the Siderock and Obukowin portages, six boggy kilometres of misery that allow paddlers access into roadless Atikaki Provincial Wilderness Park without having to pony up big bucks for a floatplane ride. Canoeists can also head west from Wallace Lake to begin a 90-km, three-to-four-day paddle down the narrow but mostly pristine **Wanipigow River**, which enters Lake Winnipeg at Hollow Water First Nation. **Wallace Lake Lodge** (204.755.3473, wallacelakelodge.com) has cabin rentals and also outfits canoeing, hunting and fishing trips.

Continuing west on the 304, the town of **Bissett** (pop. 125) is most famous for the San Antonio gold mine, where 1.2 million ounces of gold and 190,000 ounces of silver have been extracted in fits and starts since 1932. Manitoba's modest gold rush started here in 1911, when an Anishinaabe trapper named Duncan Twohearts gathered up some yellow rocks on Rice Lake and showed them to a trader in Manigotagan. Bissett is now used as a gateway to Atikaki Provincial Wilderness Park.

There are three campgrounds between Bissett and Manigotagan. **Quesnel Lake Caribou Lodge** (877.305.5526, qlakelodge.com) sits at Caribou Landing on Quesnel Lake in the western arm of Nopiming Provincial Park; it offers cabin rentals, boat rentals and outfitted paddling or fishing trips. **Wanipigow Lake** is popular for fishing. **English Brook** is usually empty.

MUST SEE:
Kasakeemee-
misekak
Islands

A spectacular archipelago on the east side of Lake Winnipeg, with impressive numbers of bald eagles, blue herons, double-crested cormorants, and white pelicans.

West of English Brook, a new all-season road departs north to **Bloodvein First Nation**. Thirty kilometres up, the road crosses the **Rice River**; Canoeists and kayakers park here, paddle about five kilometres down to Lake Winnipeg, and explore a gorgeous archipelago called the **Kasakeemeemisekak Islands**, where large numbers of white pelicans, double-crested cormorants, blue herons and bald eagles gather during the summer. The islands make for a fantastic daytrip, as long as you're prepared to deal with open water on Lake Winnipeg and the navigational challenges of finding your way in this maze. Bring a GPS, just in case. You may also reach the Kasakeemeemisekak Islands and spend several days exploring the Lake Winnipeg narrows region from **Hollow Water First Nation,** an Anishinaabe community located eight kms north of the 304.

South of the Hollow Water turnoff, PR 304 becomes a paved road, and the settlement of Manigotagan appears. The main attraction is the impressive falls at the Manigotagan River, overlooked by a campground to the south.

The 71-km drive between Manigotagan and the Winnipeg River is fast and mostly featureless. The lower portion of the **Black River** is accessible from a launch on the west side of the highway; you can paddle a few hours to Little Black River First Nation, shooting a few sets of Class II rapids, and arrange a ride back to your vehicle. There's also a two-km hiking loop just north of Powerview.

Atikaki Provincial Wilderness Park

Bartley Kives

In 1985, Manitoba protected 4,000 square kms of Canadian Shield forests and wetlands on the east side of Lake Winnipeg with the creation of Atikaki Provincial Wilderness Park, home of five of the province's most celebrated rivers and a woodland caribou population of about 350.

Since there are no roads in the park, the only way to enter is by floatplane, canoeing up from Garner Lake in Nopiming Provincial Park, or taking the arduous Obukowin Lake portage. The expense and effort required to reach Atikaki has helped keep the park pristine, as the only visitors are hunters and fishers flying to one of five wilderness lodges, and paddlers heading down the Gammon, Bloodvein, Sasaginnigak, Leyond, and Pigeon rivers.

The most popular attraction is the **Bloodvein River**, a fur-trade waterway that flows 340 kilometres from Red Lake, Ont., to Lake Winnipeg. One of 17 Canadian waterways designated as a heritage river, the Bloodvein possesses spectacular beauty, historical significance, and dozens of rapids, most of them runnable Class I, II and III. But almost all of the Bloodvein's whitewater can be bypassed via portages, making this river accessible to any paddler with some prior wilderness experience.

Canoe-in paddlers approach the Bloodvein from the **Gammon River**, accessible from PR 304 via the Obukowin portage. This trip is a total of 256 kms and takes 18 to 20 days. The classic fly-in route begins at the Ontario border at **Artery Lake**, home to

MUST SEE: Bloodvein River Adrenaline junkies and wilderness lovers are wowed by dozens of runnable rapids, awe-inspiring Shield scenery and sacred pictographs along this gorgeous pool-and-drop river flowing through Atikaki Provincial Wilderness Park.

143

Brenda Schritt

Running 'Shangri-La,' a Class III rapid on the Bloodvein River. Note the canoe has been emptied of gear, just in case.

spectacular pictographs in eastern arm, and continues 225 kms to Lake Winnipeg. The latter trip takes 10 to 14 days. A third option is to fly into Kautunigan Lake and paddle 120 kms to Lake Winnipeg over the course of six or seven days. You don't need to fly out from your take out, as an all-season road connects the lakefront Bloodvein First Nation to PR 304.

Atikaki's other attractions include the less-visited **Leyond** and **Pigeon** rivers, the latter regarded as one of Canada's most exciting whitewater rivers. This northernmost Atikaki waterway has almost twice the Bloodvein's flow, which makes it too hairy for anyone but paddlers comfortable with running long stretches of Class III rapids.

The Bloodvein, Pigeon and other Atikaki rivers can be navigable from May to October, but high spring flows create volume hazards and low fall flows expose rock gardens. Hap Wilson's *Wilderness Rivers of Manitoba* (see *Selected Sources*) offers the best intel about paddling the Bloodvein, Gammon, Leyond and Pigeon.

Fully outfitted or guided Bloodvein, Pigeon, and Manigotagan river trips can be arranged through **Northern Soul Wilderness Adventures** (866.425.9430, northernsoul.ca). Guided Bloodvein trips start from $2,250 a person; outfitting services include car shuttles, canoe and equipment rentals and meals.

For floatplane charters, **Blue Water Aviation** (204.367.2762, bluewateraviation.ca) carries hunters, fishers, and paddlers and their canoes from a floatplane base at Silver Falls on the Winnipeg River and from a sub-base on Rice Lake near Bissett. Gimli-based

Interlake Aviation (888.642.4799, interlakeaviation.com) also offers floatplane charters out of Pine Dock, on the west side of the Lake Winnipeg Narrows.

If you'd rather stay in a fishing lodge within Atikaki, you have two options. **Aikens Lake Lodge** (800.565.2595, aikenslake.com) is situated in the middle of the Gammon River system in the southern portion of the park. **Sasa-ginni-gak Lodge** (888.536.5353, saslodge.com) sits farther north on Sasaginnigak Lake, which drains through the Sasaginnigak River into the Bloodvein and can also be used to access the Leyond River. Both lodges cater to fly-in fishing tourists but will accommodate paddlers if arrangements are made ahead of time.

The Shield-Prairie Transition

Between the rocky Canadian Shield and the open Prairie farmland, you'll find mixed forests with sandy soils created by the retreat of glacial Lake Agassiz. Most of this area – a rough triangle extending south from Pine Falls to the US border and across to Lake of the Woods – is covered by provincial forests, the largest being Agassiz, Whiteshell, Sandilands, and Northwest Angle.

Logging is the main activity here, followed by fishing, hunting, snowmobiling, and ATVing. Since most of these practices are restricted if not completely banned in provincial parks, the forests of the southeast can be playgrounds for rednecks on ATVs.

Don't get offended: I use the term in the most affectionate way possible, because there's no longer a big cultural gap between urban ecotourist types and rural outdoorsmen. Hunters are committed conservationists, catch-and-release sport fishing is both sustainable and growing in popularity, and modern snowmobiles are quieter and produce fewer pollutants than their archaic counterparts. But I have nothing good to say about ATV users, who do more to disfigure the landscape than any other group of backcountry users.

In any case, take care while hiking, mountain biking, or skiing in the southeast, as you may be sharing a trail with motorized vehicles. And, if you head into the bush during hunting season, wear bright colours such as blaze orange to avoid being mistaken for something with fur, claws, or antlers. You'd look stupid up on somebody's mantle.

Pine Falls to the Trans-Canada Highway

Highway 11 is the main north-south artery in southeastern Manitoba. Beginning at the edge of the Eastern Beaches region (see the Beaches and Interlake chapter), it follows the Winnipeg River southeast until Seven Sisters Falls, when it parallels the Whitemouth River to the Trans-Canada Highway.

About 4,000 people live in a cluster of communities, each with its own character, at the top of the highway near the confluence with PR 304. Driving southeast, you'll pass through the mostly Aninishinaabe **Sagkeeng First Nation**; hydroelectric centre **Powerview-Pine Falls**, where you can walk across the boiling froth of the Winnipeg River at PR 304; and the partly Francophone **St-Georges**, home to the **Musee de St-Georges** (June-September, 19 Baie Caron).

Go back 100 years and most of the Winnipeg River was a raging ribbon of whitewater. Today, six dams between the Ontario border and Lake Winnipeg have mellowed it out and swollen its width to create Lac du Bonnet and other pseudo-lakes within the Whiteshell.

The drive from St-Georges to the town of Lac du Bonnet is more pastoral than wild, as Highway 11 heads south through a narrow band of cleared farmland east of the Brightstone Sand Hills Provincial Forest. The road grows tamer as you head south, as the road follows a ribbon of open prairie between Agassiz and Whiteshell Provincial Forest, past the towns of Whitemouth and Elma to Hadashville at the Trans-Canada Highway.

For a very short detour, take PR 406 between Whitemouth and Elma to stick close to a string of rapids along the **Whitemouth River**. Whitewater paddlers practice at Nakka Falls, Oak Falls, and Cook Falls. Campgrounds at the latter two falls are open from May to October; you may also continue north to the Winnipeg River as part of a two-day trip.

In winter, the town of Whitemouth grooms six kms of cross-country ski trails, while the **Whitemouth River ski-trail system** south of Hadashville offers loops of 2.5, 5.5, and seven kms. To find the trailhead, drive south on Highway 11, cross Highway 1, and follow the access road as it curves to the right. Hadashville also has a forest centre with interpretive displays.

Sandilands Provincial Forest

Driving east on the Trans-Canada from the Red River Valley, the flatness gives way to a wide, green ridge created by sediments left behind when the final glaciers retreated from southern Manitoba. This is **Sandilands Provincial Forest**, the highest area in southeastern Manitoba, home to forests intercut with logging roads and fireguards.

The maze of dirt tracks is a playground for ATV yahoos as well as hunters in pursuit of moose and deer. To stay out of their way, mountain bikers and cross-country skiers focus their attention on **Sandilands Cross-Country Ski Trails**, 40 kms of trails near the confluence of PR 210 and PR 404. The volunteer-maintained system is accessible from a trailhead across PR 210 from **Marchand Wayside Park**, just east of the 404.

Popular with motorcyclists, PR 210 is a gently winding road that curves southeast through the southern Sandilands, where a slew of small communities are cut into breaks in the forest. If you choose to carve out a backcountry campsite in the Sandilands, stick to the north of the forest and avoid areas near the towns of

Woodridge, Carrick, Badger, and St. Labre. But do pay a visit to the town of **McMunn** at the northeast corner of the forest. Right on the Trans-Canada Highway, the diner at the unassuming-looking **McMunn Motor Inn** (Highway 1 at PR 308) serves enormous cinnamon buns and slathers them in butter – the perfect, high-carb pick-me-up after a day of skiing, either in the Sandilands or the Whiteshell. In the summer, you can peruse hand-made crafts at **Birch River Arts and Crafts**, an artists' co-op on the south side of the highway.

Bartley Kives

Early-spring conditions on the trails in Sandilands Provincial Forest.

Northwest Angle Provincial Forest

Manitoba's extreme southeast corner is mostly comprised of wetlands passable only in the winter on snowmobile. Most of the area belongs to Northwest Angle Provincial Forest, which takes its name from a chunk of Minnesota that wound up affixed to Manitoba when the final borders between Canada and the US were set.

The only road cutting through the forest is PR 308, which is entirely gravel and extends from the delightfully named community of East Braintree to tiny **Moose Lake Provincial Park**, which has a campground (Victoria Day-Labour Day, $11.55 to $15.75). The road to Angle Inlet, Minn., is just northeast of the park.

The two main attractions in this area are **Whitemouth Lake**, a popular fishing spot accessible from a gravel road that connects Woodridge to PR 308, and **Buffalo Bay**, a tiny corner of Lake of the Woods that belongs to Manitoba.

The southernmost reaches of Sandilands and Northwest Angle provincial forests are traversed by Manitoba Highway 12, which passes by the towns of Piney, South Junction, and Sprague on the way to Warroad, Minn., the southernmost port on Lake Of The Woods.

Just before the US border, at the turnoff to cottage area Buffalo Point, the modest **Buffalo Point Cultural Centre** offers Aboriginal crafts and cultural displays. **Buffalo Point Resort** (buffalopoint.ca) has a marina, seasonal campground (sites $19 to $27) and year-round cabin rentals ($100 to $285).

Northwest Angle, Minnesota

If you look at a map of North America, you'll notice the Canada-US border follows a nice, even path along the 49th Parallel until you get to Lake Of The Woods, where a little thumb of Minnesota known as the **Northwest Angle** sticks up into the Great White North.

When the UK and US were settling their North American borders at the end of the American Revolution, they agreed to separate Ontario from Minnesota along the historic voyageur canoe route between Lake Superior and Lake Of The Woods. All the lakes and rivers along the way — including Rainy Lake and Rainy River — were divided down the middle. For some reason, Lake Of The Woods was supposed to be divided at its northwestern point, which was later determined to be a small bay called Angle Inlet.

This became a problem when the rest of the Canada-US border was set at the 49th Parallel, creating a 43-km gap. So in 1841, border negotiators decided to draw a line south from Angle Inlet, connect the dots on paper and call it a day.

MUST SEE: Angle Inlet, Minn.

There's part of the USA you can only visit by driving through Manitoba – unless you brave the waters of Lake Of The Woods by boat.

This decision meant a chunk of Minnesota wound up an orphan, attached by land only to Manitoba and separated from the rest of the US by the choppy waters of Big Traverse Bay. Today, the bulk of this mapmaking oddity belongs to Minnesota's Red Lake Ojibwe Nation, while the shoreline is protected by Northwest Angle State Forest. The sole town, **Angle Inlet**, sits on the north side of the peninsula. Residents of this small fishing community periodically threaten to secede from Minnesota whenever Ontario makes it tougher for US residents to fish in Canadian waters. The protests are never serious; even orphaned Americans take their nationality seriously.

The chief attraction in the Angle is history, and bloody history at that. On **Magnusons Island** in Angle Inlet, explorer La Vérendrye established **Fort St. Charles** soon after he reached Lake of the Woods in 1732. Four years later, the star-crossed adventurer sent his son Jean Baptiste, local priest Jean Pierre Aulneau and 19 other men east to pick up supplies from what's now Thunder Bay. Along the way, the canoe party was ambushed by a Sioux war party, which beheaded all 21 men and left their corpses on **Massacre Island**, which sits inside Canadian waters in Little Traverse Bay.

From Angle Inlet, you can take a motorboat ride to Magnusons Island and tour **Fort St. Charles**, which was rediscovered in 1890 by St. Boniface Jesuits and rebuilt in the 20th century by Minnesota Catholics. Kayakers may also retrace the route of the doomed canoe party from Magnusons to Massacre islands, a 15-km trek across choppy, open water.

Some Americans, however, claim a smaller island inside US waters, **Ile du Massacre**, is the real site of the massacre. Yet again, borders are an issue in Lake of The Woods.

To reach the Northwest Angle from Winnipeg, take the Trans-Canada Highway east to the town of East Braintree, PR 308 south to PR 525 and head east to an unmanned US border post, where you'll show your passport to a US customs guard stationed elsewhere. From here, it's a short drive northwest to Angle Inlet. Allow two hours for the entire jaunt.

Heading north from the US border, Angle Inlet can be reached by taking Highway 12 northwest to Sprague and then PR 308 northeast to PR 525.

Respecting Rock Art

Indigenous rock art is one of the greatest cultural treasures in Manitoba and northwestern Ontario. It must be treated with tremendous respect, as it is sacred to First Nations – not to mention fragile, ancient and utterly irreplaceable. There are three basic types.

Bartley Kives

Pictographs are paintings on rock surfaces, most commonly cliff faces just above water level. Well-known examples include the red ochre paintings on Artery Lake on the Bloodvein River, Long Lake on the Manigotagan River, Tramping Lake on the Grass River and on Stephen Lake in northwestern Ontario.

Petroforms are groups of rocks arranged into the forms of animals or other figures on the ground. The most famous example is the Bannock Point petroforms in Whiteshell Provincial Park.

Whatever you do, do not touch: Pictographs are sacred and extremely fragile.

Petroglyphs are forms carved into rock surfaces. They are less fragile than pictographs and petroforms but are far less common.

Viewing rock art requires care and etiquette. For starters, never touch a pictograph with any object – especially your hands, which contain oils which may dissolve the red-ochre dye. Never move any part of a petroform, whose placements were deliberate many centuries ago. Obviously, do not decorate, paint, remove or damage any form of rock art.

Less obviously, do not camp in close proximity to rock art of any sort; such an act would be comparable to pitching a tent inside a church, synagogue, mosque, temple or gurdwara.

When viewing rock art around other people, keep your voice down to the same level you would use in another place of worship; other visitors may be meditating or praying at the site.

In a wilderness setting, consider leaving an offering of loose tobacco near the art. Even better, contemplate the context in which the art was created; the persistence of these works allow modern generations of First Nations to commune with their forebears.

The question of whether to take photographs is contentious. There is little harm in doing so for your own purposes. The sharing of those images through social media, however, may be considered offensive to indigenous Canadians. The commercial sale of sacred images is most definitively offensive.

Happily, the vast majority of people who take the time to approach rock art are already predisposed to viewing the sites with respect.

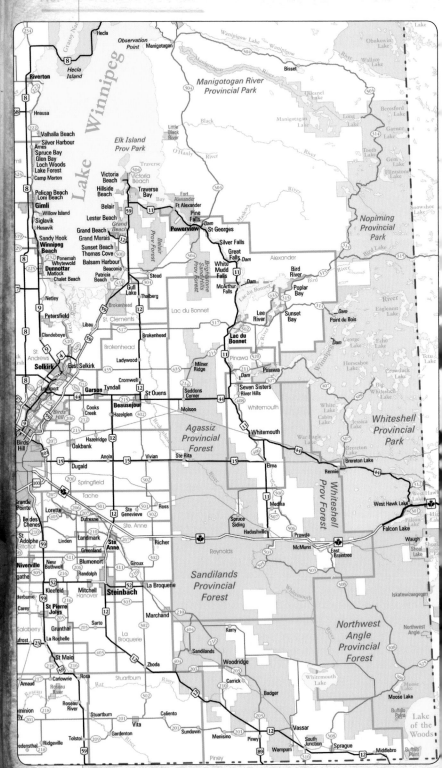

Canadian Shield Daytrips

Beginning and ending at Winnipeg

North Whiteshell Walks

When to go: Late April to late October.

1. Go for breakfast at **Marion Street Eatery** (daily, 393 Marion St., 204.233.2843). Continue east on Marion Street, north on Lagimodiere Boulevard and then east on Dugald Road, which becomes Highway 15 past city limits.

2. From the Perimeter (Highway 101), head east on Highway 15 for 88 kms to Highway 11. Drive seven kms north to Highway 44. Drive east 44 kms to **Alfred Hole Goose Sanctuary** at the edge of Whiteshell Provincial Park. Stretch your legs on the 2.5-km walking trail around the pond behind the interpretive centre.

3. Continue two kms east on Highway 44 to PR 307. Drive 36 kms north to the **Pine Point Rapids** trailhead. Walk the 8.2-km loop, stopping at three sets of rapids along the way.

4. Another 1.3 kms north on PR 307, pull into the parking lot for the short walk to **Bannock Point Petroforms**, home the centuries-old indigenous rock art.

5. Continue six kms north on PR 307 to the entrance to **Nutimik Lake**. Turn right and drive through the campground to the Whiteshell River. Walk the **Whiteshell River Suspension Bridge** and continue up to the Winnipeg River to view **Sturgeon Falls**. Return to your vehicle.

6. Back at PR 307, visit the **Nutimik Lake Natural History Museum**, if it's open. Then drive 34 kms north and west out of the park, to Highway 11. Head south five kms to Highway 44. Then 31 kms west to Beausejour. Go for a Cheez Whiz-topped bison burger and fries at **Vickie's Snack Bar** (719 Park Ave., 204.2681922).

7. Head back to Winnipeg along Highway 44 and Highway 59.

Ski Falcon and West Hawk

When to go: Late December to mid-March, weather permitting.

1. Load up on carbs with an old-school breakfast at **Southdale Village Family Restaurant** (daily, 35 Lakewood Blvd., 204.254.7039). Continue east on Fermor Avenue, which becomes the Trans-Canada Highway, or Highway 1.

2. From the Perimeter, take Highway 1 east 128 kms to the **Falcon Lake** entrance in Whiteshell Provincial Park. Take South Shore Road and Ridge Road south and east 13 kms to **Falcon Trails Resort**.

3. Ski the 7.5-km High Lake Trail. Return to the resort lodge for hot chocolate.

4. Cross Falcon Lake on the 4-km **Falcon Lake Trail** and ski the nine-km **McHugh Lake Loop**.

5. Back at your vehicle, return to Highway 1. Drive 30 kms west to **McMunn Motor Inn**. Stop in for a giant cinnamon bun.

6. Continue back to Winnipeg on Highway 1.

Bryan Scott

C rusty Manitobans can often be heard griping about the weather, the government or the Blue Bombers. But nothing really stirs emotions like the province's most dominant feature, Lake Winnipeg. The world's 11th-largest freshwater lake is the destination of choice for vacationing Winnipeggers, a meal ticket for thousands of fishers – and an environmental disaster waiting to happen.

Despite its massive size – roughly 24,000 square kms, which is bigger than all of Israel or El Salvador – Lake Winnipeg is very shallow, with an average depth of only 12 metres. That gives it a very small volume – 284 cubic kms – relative to its immense drainage basin, a 950,000-square-kilometres chunk of North America that includes much of Manitoba, Saskatchewan, and Alberta, sizable pieces of Ontario, North Dakota, and Minnesota, and a couple of corners of Montana and South Dakota.

As a result, Lake Winnipeg is the lucky recipient of pollution created by farms, factories, mines, logging operations, cities, towns, and cottage communities from Edmonton to Fargo to Atikokan, Ont., all places where few of the residents think about where their wastewater winds up. Undertreated sewage, fertilizers, industrial effluent, and sediments all threaten the lake, whose ecology has already been messed up by the destruction of lakeshore habitat and the introduction of foreign fish, invertebrates, and micro-organisms since Europeans showed up en masse in the 1800s.

In recent years, high phosphorus loads from a variety of sources have led to summertime algae blooms in the lake's larger northern basin, while freshwater snails, mussels, and other rungs on the food chain are disappearing due to increasing turbidity. If the situation worsens, as freshwater scientists predict, the lake could lose its lucrative commercial

Opposite page: The mayfly, colloquially known as the fish fly in Manitoba, lives only several days but can still be found by the millions during the summer along the shore of Lake Winnipeg.

Enjoy yourself! Warning signs along Lake Winnipeg.

Bartley Kives

Gulls at Winnipeg Beach, one of the largest of dozens of cottage communities ringing the southern basin of Lake Winnipeg.

walleye fishery and become unattractive to vacationers. Almost every Manitoban shoulders some responsibility for the future of the lake, and most want the provincial government to do whatever's necessary to prevent or at least mitigate the looming disaster.

In the meantime, it's still perfectly safe to visit Lake Winnipeg, whose densely populated southern basin is the main focus of this chapter. I've only dished out the bad news to instill a sense of urgency in travellers: Enjoy this big, shallow baking pan right now, while you still have the opportunity.

Lake Winnipeg's southern basin is lined by dozens of sandy beaches, several excellent provincial parks, and the fishing community/resort of Gimli, once the capital of a self-proclaimed New Iceland. Meanwhile, the low-lying marshes, forests, and meadows to the west – dubbed the Interlake, due to its location between Lake Winnipeg and Lake Manitoba – sport attractions like the garter-snake pits of Narcisse, and the limestone cliffs at Steep Rock.

In the lakeshore communities, the bulk of the population is seasonal. Among the year-round population, dominant ethnic groups include Icelandic, Cree, Anishinaabe, and Métis, along with the usual Manitoban mix of British, German, and Ukrainian.

The best time to visit both the beaches and the Interlake is the summer, but ice fishing, snowmobiling, and cross-country skiing draw year-round visitors. I've personally snowshoed straight across the frozen southern basin of Lake Winnipeg in the middle of March, so a little cold weather is no reason to avoid cottage country.

Eastern Beaches

Two provincial parks, a dozen beaches, and two dozen cottage communities line the east side of southern Lake Winnipeg, a fifty-km shoreline characterized by unusually fine sand, impressive glacial erratics (large boulders left behind by retreating glaciers), and a mix of deciduous and coniferous trees. A transition zone between prairie and the Canadian Shield, this ecologically diverse area feels a lot wilder than the west side of the lake – and not just because of the hard-partying twentysomethings who flock to Grand Beach.

To reach most of the beaches, you have to saunter through quiet cottage areas. But there are no barriers to three of the best, each with its own distinct character: Grand is the biggest and busiest, Patricia is the best choice for families, and Beaconia is the most secluded and least developed.

For the purposes of orientation, I've listed the beaches from north to south.

Victoria Beach

If any place in Manitoba couldn't care less about tourism, it's **Victoria Beach**, a community that bars motorized traffic from its streets during the summer and gears all but a handful of services to resident cottagers. Except on special occasions, cottagers are required to leave their vehicles at a parking lot at the entrance to the community and walk in. This once-exclusive cottage area works extremely hard at being relaxed. Victoria Beach feels more like a New England island resort than a Manitoba beach town, especially when you factor in the presence of a sailing club and numerous social events throughout the summer.

Still, Victoria Beach is hardly xenophobic – visitors are more than welcome to stroll its quiet streets and swim at its **sandy beach**. If you make the trek, stop in at **Einfeld's Bakery** (112 Birch Ave., 204.756.2533), an 80-year-old establishment famous for its dream cookies.

Victoria Beach is located at the end of Highway 59, about 110 kms northeast of Winnipeg. The parking lot charges a nominal fee.

Elk Island Provincial Park

One of the weirder (and wetter) day hikes in Manitoba is the trek to **Elk Island Provincial Park**, a 900-hectare protected wilderness located off the north shore of the Victoria Beach peninsula. To reach the island, you have to wade across a narrow strait that's a metre deep or more, carefully following a submerged sandbar. Venture too far to the left or right and you'll end up swimming – or worse.

There's nothing on the other side of the strait but forest, sand, and rock; hence the attraction. You can circumnavigate Elk Island (about eight kms) or merely hang out and the south end and enjoy the solitude. Overnight camping, however, is not permitted.

To reach the island, drive north on Highway 59 but go straight past the turnoff to Victoria Beach at PR 504. At the end of the road, turn left on Olafson Road and drive until you can't go any farther. Park, walk as far north as you can, and begin wading cautiously across the strait, being mindful of currents and waves. You might want to take a PFD and, in cooler weather, a drybag full of warm clothes.

Grand Beach Provincial Park

On hot July and August weekends, the remarkably fine silica sands of **Grand Beach Provincial Park** can attract tens of thousands of Winnipeggers, creating a scene that looks a lot more like southern California or Florida than the Canadian Prairies. Originally served by rail, this seasonal sunspot causes traffic headaches on Highway 59.

MUST SEE:
Grand Beach Provincial Park
Manitoba's most-popular beach, packed with tens of thousands of sun-worshippers on hot summer days.

The three-kilometre-long beach is the best open-air meat market in Manitoba, as the young, the genetically gifted, and the surgically augmented crowd along the **West Beach**, home to a boardwalk with beachwear vendors, some so-so food concessions, a tennis court, and a cramped cottage area. On busier days, families usually stick to the middle of the beach or the **East Beach**, which sports a **campground** (Victoria Day-Labour Day, $17.85-$22.05), an amphitheatre, and access to most of the trails in the park.

Aside from the beach and lake, natural attractions include active sand dunes that reach a height of 12 metres, a large lagoon and marsh full of fish and waterfowl, a small protected nesting ground for the endangered piping plover, and eight trails totalling 32 kms.

Three of these trails are short walks suitable for the young kids or people pressed for time. The one-km **Spirit Rock trail** rounds a bluff near the West Beach; the equally brief **Wild Wings trail** circles part of a marsh along the causeway that connects the East and West Beaches; while the two-km **Ancient Beach trail** offers a glimpse of the mixed forest that characterizes the mostly undeveloped east side of the park.

A separate East Beach trailhead is the staging ground for five longer trails that make for dull hiking but fun mountain biking and excellent cross-country skiing. The longest route is the 13-km **Beaver Pond trail**, which is officially closed during the summer but is passable to anyone willing to make two stream crossings.

Grand Beach is about eighty kilometres northeast of Winnipeg. Take Highway 59 north and then Highway 12 west to reach both the East Beach and West Beach gates. A Manitoba Park Pass is required for vehicle entry from the start of the Victoria Day long weekend to Labour Day.

Around Grand Beach

Immediately outside the West Beach gate, the town of **Grand Marais** – literally, "big marsh" – is a quaint but faded beach town offering cheap cabin rentals and greasy comfort food. The most popular destinations for munchies are **Lanky's** (daily in summer, 85 Grand Beach Rd., 204.754.2106), a shack that specializes in hot dogs, and pizza joint **Potenza's** (daily, 42 Parkview Ave., 204.754.8825), which has a small lounge, a screened-in porch and is open year round. For coffee – and wireless Internet access – visit **Spirit Rock Café** (Highway 12 at Donald Street, 204.754.2265, rooms $65-$100), while the no-nonsense **Sand Bar Motor Inn** across the street is your best bet for a burger outside the summer season.

The marsh that gives Grand Marais its name extends southeast from the town and is best explored by canoe. From mid-June to mid-August, you're all but guaranteed to see great blue herons, red-winged blackbirds, double-breasted cormorants, and white pelicans, the latter two nesting on narrow **Stevens Island,** which is usually covered with Hitchcockian quantities of gulls. Unfortunately, idiots on personal watercraft routinely buzz the nesting grounds, while the marsh itself is slowly being destroyed by the one-two punch of introduced, vegetation-chewing carp and high water levels.

You can also bike or walk into the interior of the marsh along a section of the **Trans Canada Trail** that follows a railbed used during Grand Beach's early-twentieth-century heyday. Starting at an entrance hidden behind the Sand Bar Motor Inn, the path leads across the marsh, then through seven cottage communities, until it veers toward Highway 59 at Beaconia, eight kilometers to the south.

Immediately outside the Grand Beach's east gate, you'll find **Turtle Tide Waterslides** (mid-June to August, East Gate Road, 204.782.4692, $16 admission) and a more unusual attraction: a Manitoba Hydro substation capped by an enormous osprey nest. This is an easy place to spot North America's most spectacular fishing bird: two to four of the big raptors usually perch in the nest all summer.

Two kms up Highway 59, northeast of the park, an off-road driving route called the **North Star Trail** curls around the glacial moraines of Belair Provincial Forest to PR 304, offering eastward views across the Catfish Creek Valley to the Brightstone Sand Hills near Pine Falls. An old fire observation tower is officially off-limits to climbing.

Beaconia and Patricia Beach

If you love beaches but can't stomach crowds, head to idyllic **Beaconia Beach**, which has two kilometres of pristine sand and absolutely nothing else. There are no services here, and in some places, no bathing suits – the southern section the beach is clothing-optional, albeit by custom and not official sanction.

Charles Shilliday

Patricia Beach.

Generally speaking, the north end of the beach is for people in bathing suits, straight nudists frequent the middle section, and the bottom of the sandbar is a gay nude beach. You can wear clothing wherever you like, but don't go naked on the north section, as some of the locals aren't cool with exposed flesh.

To reach Beaconia Beach, drive north on Highway 59, turn left at PR 500, and enter the hamlet of Beaconia. When the main road veers to the right, go straight and follow a gravel causeway to the sandbar that comprises the beach. Since this is a wilderness area, pack out all your trash.

A similarly mellow vibe can be found at **Patricia Beach Provincial Park**, where the beach is about 1.5 kms long but usually busier and a little more family-friendly. You'll find actual washrooms and a snack bar here, but little of the hustle and bustle of

MUST SEE:
Beaconia and Patricia Beach
Idyllic, white-sand beaches where you won't have to worry about crowds.

Grand Beach. The secluded eastern corner (that is, the right-hand side of the sandspit) is another unofficial nude beach. To reach the park, take Highway 59 north, turn left at PR 319, and follow the winding road to the beach.

Just one warning: high water levels in recent years have reduced the width of both Patricia and Beaconia beaches; when a heavy north wind blows, much of the sand can be submerged.

Brokenhead Ojibway Nation

Perched on the northeast corner of Netley Marsh, the Anishinaabe community of **Brokenhead Ojibway Nation** serves as the gateway to the Eastern Beaches. Passing through, you cannot help but notice **South Beach Casino & Resort** (Highway 59, 204.766.2100, rooms $99-$259), a year-round gaming facility with a Miami Beach motif.

North of the reserve, **Brokenhead Wetland Ecological Preserve** protects 23 rare or uncommon plant species growing within a spring fed alkaline fen and a surrounding white cedar forest. No fewer than 28 of Manitoba's 36 orchid species can be found here. A boardwalk with interpretive signage (west of Highway 59, two kms north of Stead Road) was completed in 2014.

South of the reserve, the **Mars Hill Wildlife Management Area** encloses a tangle of sandy trails used by horseback riders and ATVs during the summer and cross-country skiers and dogsledders in winter. This is also a popular forage spot for mushroom, herb, and berry pickers. Take a map and compass, because most trails aren't marked, or follow a section of the Trans Canada Trail through the area. The hills are accessible from PR 317, east of the community of Libau.

Netley-Libau Marsh

In stark contrast to the dense cottage developments on the east and west sides of Lake Winnipeg, the very bottom of the inland ocean remains wild. A 240-square-km wetland called **Netley-Libau Marsh**, one of the largest waterfowl nesting areas in North America, is uninhabited aside from a handful of communities on its fringes.

Although larger than Delta Marsh, Netley-Libau sees relatively few visitors. Boaters pass through the three mouths of the Red River on their way to Lake Winnipeg, while anglers, the occasional canoeist, and a handful of intrepid birders negotiate the labyrinth of canals and shallow lakes in the rest of the marsh. Needless to say, it's incredibly easy to get lost here – take a GPS unit as well as a topographical map or nautical chart if you decide to go exploring. Also be aware of the tide-like effect of winds: gusts from the north engorge the shallow marsh with water from Lake Winnipeg, while south winds empty it out, turning navigable channels into impassable muck.

The only road-accessible destination inside the marsh is **Breezy Point**, a cottage area, campground, and small marina at the end of PR 320, a northern extension of Selkirk and Winnipeg's

Main Street. An observation tower at the end of the road offers views of the massive marsh. South of Breezy Point, dozens of cottages were destroyed by fast-moving ice during the Red River flood of 2009.

Southwest of the marsh, off Highway 9, a string of marinas at **Petersfield** offers water access to the marsh via Netley Creek, the most northern tributary of the Red before the river splits into three branches.

Western Beaches and New Iceland

While the Eastern Beaches are all about nature, the west side of Lake Winnipeg's southern basin offers culture. In 1875, immigrants from Iceland established a colony near the present-day town of Gimli, where the Scandinavian influence remains.

Fishing and farming dominated this shoreline before crowds from boomtown-era Winnipeg discovered the beaches about 100 years ago, brought *en masse* by a branch of the Canadian Pacific Railway. In recent years, retirees and a handful of artists have started to move in and transform the character of Dunnotar, Winnipeg Beach, and Gimli from purely rural communities into extensions of the Manitoba capital. But due to the seasonal nature of the cottage business, the area has largely resisted colonization by fast-food franchises and other tendrils of corporate culture. The main arteries are Highway 9 and PR 222 along the shore of Lake Winnipeg, and the faster but less scenic Highway 8, which continues north to the marine playground of Hecla/ Grindstone Provincial Park.

Winnipeg Beach and Dunnotar

Sixty kms north of Winnipeg, the lakefront hamlets of Matlock, Whytewold, and Ponemah, collectively known as the **Village of Dunnotar**, own the closest set of beaches to the Manitoba capital. These communities only sport a handful of small beaches and the year-round **Julia's Ukrainian Restaurant** (Mon-Sat, 30 Gimli Rd. in Matlock, 204.389.5303), but they're cute enough to warrant the brief detour off Highway 9 – PR 232 follows the shore through the entire village.

Immediately to the north, **Winnipeg Beach** is no rival to Grand Beach when it comes to sand, but the lakefront services are vastly superior and are open for more of the year. The main attraction is the beach itself, part of it protected by tiny **Winnipeg Beach Provincial Park**, but the town offers superior country food from May to October along or near the lakefront boardwalk at the nouveau-Italian **Casa Bianca** (Tues-Sat, 22 Murray Ave., 204.389.5007) or diners **The Boardwalk** (daily, 30 Main St., 204.389-5945) and **Bonnie Lynn's Café** (Fri-Wed, 14 Main St., 204.389.5639). In the off season, you're eating Chinese-Canadian at **New Sing Fei** (Tues-Sun, 22 Main St., 204.389.5888).

MUST SEE:
Winnipeg Beach
An increasingly artsy beachfront community within 45 minutes of Winnipeg.

Also on the boardwalk, leaf through dog-eared titles at **Tale Of The Raven Used Books** (daily in summer, 48 Main St.) or stop into one of the most creative art retailers in small-town Manitoba, the **Fishfly Gallery** (18 Main St., 204.389.5661), which sells works by 40-odd Manitoba artists, including several from the Interlake.

There are at least three dozen potters, jewellers, painters, sculptors, luthiers, and other artists working full-time along a strip of Lake Winnipeg shoreline from Matlock to Gimli – and a few dozen more elsewhere in the Interlake. Many sell their work out of their studios, but only by appointment.

For two weekends a year – mid-June and early September – you can drop in unannounced at more than 50 studios in the area as part of the **Interlake WAVE Artists' Studio Tour**. This in itself makes for a worthwhile daytrip. Visit watchthewave.ca for specific dates and to download a brochure.

Along the same Matlock-to-Gimli strip, dozens of Lake Winnipeg outfits sell fresh and frozen pickerel, pickerel cheeks, and fantastic smoked goldeye from garages or storefronts advertised along the road. Don't be squeamish about the cheeks – they're boneless nuggets of meat, perfect for pan-frying. Keep heading north to Gimli if you'd rather have a restaurant cook 'em for you.

Nine kms north of Winnipeg Beach, **Willow Creek Heritage Park** marks the landing site of the Interlake's original Icelandic and Ukrainian settlers. The creek itself is navigable to paddlers. You can head upstream during the spring and early summer, when water levels are high, or downstream all summer through the community of **Siglavik** to Lake Winnipeg.

Gimli

The capital of all things Icelandic in Manitoba, **Gimli** combines the hardscrabble hardiness of a maritime fishing village with the Neverland vibe of a summer resort. It's also the largest community in the Interlake, with about 5,000 people living in and around the lakefront town – and more retirees coming from Winnipeg every year.

Gimli Harbour – quaint, but don't expect to meet Captain Highliner.

From 1875 to 1887, Gimli was the unofficial capital of New Iceland, a semi-autonomous political entity. You can learn about the twelve-year republic at the **New Iceland Heritage Museum** (204.642.1001, nihm.ca) whose exhibits are divided between the Waterfront Centre (daily, 94 First Ave.), the Lake Winnipeg Visitor Centre (just west of Gimli Harbour, May to September), and Gimli Public School (62 2nd, May to September). The Waterfront Centre houses multimedia displays and the visitor centre has a freshwater

Charles Shilliday

Bryan Scott

fish aquarium, while the school maintains a heritage classroom. Museum admission is $6 for adults and $5 for students/seniors.

Over the August long weekend, downtown Gimli hosts **Islendingadagurinn** (icelandicfestival.com), a cultural festival that celebrates the 140-year Norse presence in the Interlake. It's basically your typical town fair, with Viking hats, a dubious demonstration of Viking village warfare tactics and best of all, a Fris-Nok competition. While the latter may sound Icelandic, it actually involves using a Frisbee to knock down beer bottles. There are also free performances by musicians who usually include some Icelandic-Canadian talent.

Islendingadagurinn is so popular, the **Gimli Film Festival** (gimlifilm.com) has been moved to the last weekend in July. It features screenings and four indoor venues as well as outdoor nighttime movies on a 10-metre screen right on the lake, facing the beachfront.

Gimli Beach, a decent stretch of sand, is the biggest summer draw. At the east end of Centre Street, you'll also find **Gimli Harbour**, a working wharf where you can rent kayaks and windsurfers.

You absolutely must take a walk along First Avenue and make a meal out of pan-fried pickerel – among half a dozen downtown restaurants, **The Beach Boy** (daily, 70 First Ave., 204.642.7560) and **Kris' Fish & Chips** (daily, 78 First Ave., 204.642.8848) compete for fried-walleye supremacy. Again, go for the cheeks if they have 'em. To purchase fresh pickerel (in season), smoked goldeye or smoked whitefish to eat at home, try **Sveinson's** on Highway 9 just south of town.

If you can't stand fish, the year-round **Brennivins Pizza Hüs** (daily, 70 Main St., 204.642.5555) will put perogies or kubasa on

MUST SEE:
Gimli
Once the capital of a New Iceland, now an Interlake fishing town with a laid-back summer resort vibe.

your pizza. Also try the vinarterta, the prune-filled Icelandic layer cake, at **Reykjavík Bakery** (J-41 Centre St., 204.642.7598).

For shoppers, the compulsory Gimli stop is **H. P. Tergesen & Sons** (82 First Ave., 204.642.5958), a retail store established in 1899 that now specializes in beachwear and street clothes, among many other items.

If you want to stay the night, the most modern property is **Lakeview Resort & Conference Centre** (10 Centre St., 204.642.8565, lakeviewhotels.com, rooms $79 to $185), which dominates the lakefront and books up months in advance for summer long weekends.

Gimli to Hecla

Eight km north of Gimli on PR 222, **Camp Morton Provincial Recreation Park**, a former Roman Catholic summer camp, has seven kms of footpaths along the shore of Lake Winnipeg. The highlight is the formal gardens in the northern section of the small park. Camp Morton also a campground (May-September, sites $16.80, yurts $56.50) or cabins for rent ($72.60 to $79.15). In winter, the **Gimli Cross-Country Club** maintains 13 kms of ski trails along both sides of the road.

There's another province-run campground at tiny **Hnausa Provincial Park**, located 21 kms farther north on PR 222 (May-September, $18.90-$23.30).

Another 11 kms up, the fishing village of **Riverton** (pop. 594) is worth a detour for a summer swim at underused **Sandy Bar Beach**.

Ten kms north of Riverton along Highway 8, artisanal bakery **Integrity Foods** (Road 141 North, 204.378.2887, integrityfoods. ca) is located on a farm with alpacas, rabbits, goats, chicken, and peacocks, a walking trail and a public garden. There's a retail store for the baked goods and a wood-fired oven selling made-to-order pizzas, baked with spelt and kamut crusts, on Friday and Saturday evenings (5-9 p.m.) from late June to late September. Sales are cash only. Integrity also offers artisanal baking classes. The farm is 500 metres east of Highway 8.

Hecla/Grindstone Provincial Park

MUST SEE: Hecla/ Grindstone Provincial Park
An undervisited marine park near the Lake Winnipeg Narrows, now with a restored year-round resort.

Eleven km north of Riverton, Highway 8 veers east toward Lake Winnipeg and **Hecla/Grindstone Provincial Park**, a 1,084-square-km block of open water, islands, and peninsulas that comprises Manitoba's only real marine park. This is one of the best places in Manitoba for sea-kayak touring and sailing, and also offers a glimpse into the past at the fishing village of Hecla, one of the original New Iceland settlements.

The park can be divided into three components: Grindstone Peninsula, road-accessible Hecla Island, and a wilderness area encompassing Black Island, Deer Island, and hundreds of smaller islets.

The mainland peninsula has a pair of cottage communities and public beaches at **Blacks Point** and **Little Grindstone**. Most visitors

Grassy Narrows Marsh in Hecla/Grindstone Provincial Park.

head to Hecla Island, crossing over the Grassy Narrows Causeway to **Grassy Narrows Marsh**, a waterfowl nesting area ringed by 25 kms of hiking and bike trails along a system of dikes just outside the park gate. The two longest trails are the 10.5-km **Fox Loop** and the 7.5-km **Turtle Loop**, located on either side of Highway 8.

A few clicks down the road, a wildlife-viewing tower offers a chance to spot moose from a distance. It's 14 more kms to **Hecla Village**, which resembles a Newfoundland fishing outport. The 25-km **Black Wolf Trail**, one of the longest day-hiking routes in the province, connects the Grassy Narrows area with Hecla Village.

At the end of Highway 8, the resort of **Gull Harbour** has a **campground** (May-September, sites $17.85-$23.10, cabins $38.10-$69.16) and a marina that serves as the launching point for sailing and sea-kayaking excursions. There are also two trails: the 10-km (return) **West Quarry Trail** and the shorter walk to the **Gull Harbour lighthouse**, which serves as Hecla's trademark. The renovated **Hecla Island Resort** at Gull Harbour (204.279.2041, lakeviewhotels.com, rooms $95 to $155) is surrounded by the trails, a golf course and also has a spa and restaurant. The resort is a bargain, considering the setting.

If you'd rather rough it and have experience paddling on open water, you can spend three to five days circumnavigating the park's **wilderness area by sea kayak**, whose highlights include impressive numbers of pelicans and cormorants, a heron rookery at Cairine Island, limestone cliffs at the northern tip of Hecla Island, an amazing, secluded beach at the east end of Deer Island, and, best of all, the **Kasakeemeemisekak Islands**, a stunning archipelago on the east side of Lake Winnipeg. There are also several beaches along large Black Island, the largest used for spiritual ceremonies by nearby Hollow Water First Nation. Obtain permission

Charles Shilliday

The lighthouse at Gull Harbour, in Hecla/Grindstone Provincial Park.

Bartley Kives

The general store at the historic Hecla village on Hecla Island.

from the band (204.363.7278) before camping at this particular beach — it's the only one with a lawn.

The most awe-inspiring part of this wilderness trip is the way the landscape changes from the limestone-dominated Manitoba Lowlands at Gull Harbour to Prairie-Shield transition landscape on Black Island to rugged Canadian Shield granite in the Kasakeemeemisekak Islands, all in the span of 25 kms. There are dozens of natural harbours in this area for sail-boats, but the waves are often too freaky for canoeists. Alternate water access is available on the east side of the lake at Manigotagan, Hollow Water First Nation, or the Rice River. See *the Canadian Shield* chapter for more info.

Lake Winnipeg Narrows

Branching off Highway 8 just before the turnoff to Hecla/Grindstone, gravel PR 234 snakes along the west side of Lake Winnipeg's southern basin until it reaches a point where the lake's shallow southern basin meets the larger, wilder north. This is the **Lake Winnipeg Narrows**, a two-km gap prone to crazy currents, especially when winds force water from one basin to another through the narrow bottleneck.

PR 234 winds for forty km before you reach **Beaver Creek Provincial Park**, the most northerly campground (Victoria Day-Labour Day, $16.80) on Lake Winnipeg, which faces the top of Grindstone Peninsula across Washow Bay. Next up is the float-plane terminal of Pine Dock at Biscuit Harbour, where canoeists heading to Atikaki Provincial Wilderness Park catch a one-way ride.

After 93 kms, PR 234 ends in a ferry terminal that used to offer the only access to Bloodvein First Nation, across the narrows,

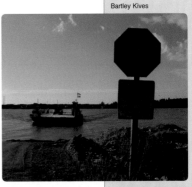

before a road was completed in 2014. A few kms further, you can take a cable ferry to cross over to the quaint fishing community of **Matheson Island** (pop. 117).

Central Interlake

Drive north through the middle of the Interlake, and you'll see why they call this area the Manitoba Lowlands. The forests and swamps are as flat as the Red River Valley, with only the occasional limestone crevice offering some relief. The chief attraction is the world's largest agglomeration of snakes at Narcisse. The main arteries are north-south Highways 7 and 17, and the east-west Highway 68.

The cable ferry to Matheson Island.

Teulon to Arborg

Heading north from Winnipeg's hinterland on Highway 7, **Teulon** (pop. 1,124) offers the requisite **pioneer museum** (Tues-Sun, July to September, $5 adults/$2 students), while **Komarno** is worth an ironic visit if you want to see a town named, in Ukrainian, after Manitoba's most celebrated organism, the mosquito. A giant skeeter swings with the wind but, unfortunately, does not suck blood from other over-sized statues, which means Oak Lake's giant ox and Onanole's elk are safe, for the time being.

Thirty-eight uneventful kms later, **Meleb** sports the only culinary monument in Manitoba, a statue of three edible wild mushrooms prized by Polish and Ukrainian *babas*: the boletus, the morel, and the honey mushroom. Highway 7 ends at **Arborg** (pop. 1,152), one of the few Interlake towns where Icelandic is still spoken as a first language. If an Arborgian tells you his name is Thor, he isn't messing with you.

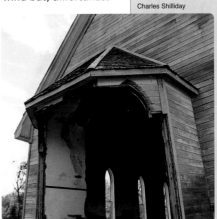

Derelict structures, such as this church, are common sights in the central Interlake.

Narcisse Snake Dens

On warm, sunny days in late April and early May, more than 70,000 red-sided garter snakes wriggle out of underground pits in a corner of the **Narcisse Wildlife Management Area**. The four dens rank as the largest concentration of reptiles in the world, and are easily among of the planet's weirdest wildlife-watching destinations: Few ecotourism hotspots allow visitors actually to handle the creatures they observe.

Normally antisocial, the snakes have somehow learned to huddle together all winter in porous limestone caves in the middle

Bryan Scott

of the Interlake. They emerge in the spring in massive mating balls, where – in a scene reminiscent of closing time at any human bar – dozens of males coil around a single female. Manitoba Conservation staff are on hand during the spring to show you how to pick up the non-poisonous serpents without harming them.

The snakes are absent from the dens during the summer, but return in September to gather at the mouths of the pits until frosty weather drives them back underground. Most Manitobans make a visit to this spot at some point in their lives, and tourists are usually amazed – just make sure the reptiles are present before you make the drive. Call Manitoba Conservation and Water Stewardship at 204.945.6784 just to make sure.

To reach the snake dens from Winnipeg, take Highway 7 north to Teulon and take a left on Highway 17, following it north to **Inwood**, home to a statue of two giant garters. Continue north on Highway 17 for 23 kms until you pass the town of Narcisse. The entrance to the snake dens is another six kms up the road, clearly marked alongside the highway. There is no entrance fee.

Interlake Pioneer Trail

In the 2000s, volunteer trail-builders attempted to convert a former railway line that ran up the centre of the Interlake into a hiking-and-cycling route called the Prime Meridian Trail. They didn't entirely succeed.

Most of what's now the Interlake Pioneer Trail, a 116-km route connecting Grosse Isle northwest of Winnipeg to Fisher Branch, is primarily used by ATVs and snowmobiles. It also crosses a diverse landscape that transitions from grain fields around **Argyle** to the marshes of Inwood Wildlife Management Area, and eventually into boreal forest.

While the southernmost 10 kms are supposed to be free from motorized vehicle traffic, anyone on foot or on a bike should expect to encounter ATVs north of Argyle. A staging area for ATVs is located north of Argyle; take PR 322 to Road 86 North, turn right and head 400 metres.

North-Central Interlake

Driving north on Highway 17 past Highway 68, the scrubby, swampy ranch land gives way to boreal forest and the occasional glacial ridge. Nine kilometres north of **Fisher Branch**, a gravel road on the right marked "Interlake Forest Centre" leads to a pair of short trails: the one-km **Spruce Grove loop**, home to orchids in late spring, and a wider three-kilometre (return) walk along a rough road that leads east to an old quarry. Both trails are buggy in mid-summer, so consider a June or September visit, if you're in the area.

Continuing north, Highway 17 becomes PR 224 at **Peguis First Nation** (see *Selkirk* in *Red River Valley & Around*, for the history) and follows the Fisher River to Lake Winnipeg at Fisher Bay. Most of the bay's shoreline, as well as Moose Island, are protected as Fisher Bay Park Reserve, with the expectation Fisher River Cree Nation, and the province will eventually develop some form of camping or ecotourism infrastructure.

Between Peguis and Fisher River, a side road heads north to Kinonjeoshtegon First Nation, passing between narrow Lake St. Andrew – home to bat hibernacula – and Lake St. George, site of the rarely visited **Lake St. George Provincial Park** and its camp-ground (Victoria Day to Labour Day, $16.80). Kinonjeoshtegon Nation hopes to make these lakes part of an even larger provincial wilderness park stretching west to the Mantagao River and north to existing Lake Winnipeg park reserves at Sturgeon and Kinwow bays.

Lake Manitoba

At 4,624 square km, Lake Manitoba is the third-largest lake in the province and is second only to Lake Winnipeg in importance as a commercial fishery. The east shore of the lake is a cross-section of Interlake culture – there are cottage areas, Métis fishing towns, Icelandic farming communities, Cree nations, and a pair of modest provincial parks.

Many lakefront communities were devastated by the Assiniboine River flood of 2011, which saw record volumes of river water diverted into the shallow lake, which became engorged and engulfed much of its shoreline. Most towns and cottage areas have yet to recover. Nonetheless, you can explore Lake Manitoba's 250-kilometre east shoreline from Highway 6, which loosely parallels the lake as it heads northwest from Winnipeg.

Twin Lakes, St. Laurent, and Lundar

Heading northwest from Winnipeg through the towns of Grosse Isle, Warren, and Woodlands (see *Central Plains and Valleys*), Manitoba Highway 6 hits Lake Manitoba right above **Lake Francis**, an eastern extension of the Delta Marsh system. To take the scenic route here, exit Highway 6 at the town of Woodlands and drive north on PR 518 through the West Shoal Lake Provincial Wildlife Management Area, then due west on PR 415.

Otherwise, keep going northwest on Highway 6 until you reach Twin Lakes Road, the turnoff to the cottage community of **Twin Lakes Beach**, which occupies a sandspit between Lake Francis and Lake Manitoba. This is one of the closest natural beaches to Winnipeg – only Matlock takes less time to reach, if getting the heck out of Winnipeg is a matter of urgency. Unfortunately, many properties along this lakebottom ridge were destroyed during the 2011 flood and the beachfront is far less pleasant as a result.

Just north of the Twin Lakes turnoff, the fishing town of **St. Laurent** is one of the few places on the Prairies where you can still hear *Michif*, a Métis language. While few Winnipeggers visit, the town's unique culture is on display at the National Museum of the American Indian, part of the Smithsonian Institute in Washington, DC, where Métis hunting and fishing implements – including the Bombardier, a motorized ice-fishing sled – are featured. The town celebrates its culture during Métis Days, held during the August long weekend.

Thirteen kilometres northwest of St. Laurent, **Marshy Point Provincial Game Refuge** preserves a chunk of Lake Manitoba shoreline between the Métis settlement of Oak Point and **Lundar Beach Provincial Recreation Park**, the latter accessible via PR 419 from the Icelandic-settler-founded town of **Lundar**. The refuge sees about 10,000 geese per year.

The provincial park, meanwhile, has a beach, a campground (Victoria Day to Labour Day, $18.90-$23.10), and a three-kilometre hiking trail. Lundar itself has an oversized statue of a Canada goose, a pioneer museum in a former railway station, and from July to September, a farmer's market (Tuesdays and Fridays, 4-6 p.m.).

Lake Manitoba Narrows

While Lake Winnipeg's blustery narrows are only traversable by ferry boat, you can drive right across the narrow strait dividing Lake Manitoba's northern and southern basin. Highway 68 crosses the **Lake Manitoba Narrows** 60 kms west of Highway 6, after exiting about 10 kms north of the community of Eriksdale.

The Narrows is a fishing hotspot. Aside from fishing, the sole attraction is **Manitou Island**, a small chunk of land just north of the Narrows Bridge purported to have provided the province with its name. To some, pounding waves on the north side of the island evoked the sound of Kitchi Manitou, the great spirit of pantheistic indigenous cosmology, thereby giving the lake – and the entire province, by extension – its moniker.

About 40 kms north of Eriksdale, **Ashern** is a haven to motorists, as the Petro-Canada outlet is the last 24-hour gas station on Highway 6 before the road gets lonely on its way north. The small community also sports a – yep, you guessed it – pioneer museum in the former CNR station, and holds a rodeo every September long weekend.

Twelve kms to the north, PR 237 heads west from the town of Moosehorn to **Watchorn Provincial Park**, a campground (Victoria Day to Labour Day, $18.90-$23.10) at Watchorn Bay, on Lake Manitoba.

Bryan Scott

Steep Rock

Limestone is the official rock of the Interlake, and there's no better place to see it than the town of **Steep Rock**, a small Lake Manitoba hamlet blessed with stunning cliffs that wind along the shore for kilometres. Thousands of years of wave action and winter ice have carved the cliffs into ledges, seats, and other eroded shapes that make this shoreline an interesting place to stop on the long drive north to Thompson or elsewhere in Manitoba. As a daytrip destination, it's a little out of the way – Steep Rock is 210 kilometres from Winnipeg's northwest edge.

To reach the cliffs from Highway 6, drive five kms north past Grahamdale and turn left at PR 239. Follow the road into town and then down to a government dock, where you can leave your car for walks along the shoreline.

To see the cliffs from the water, bring a canoe or kayak – or rent one from **Steep Rock Kayak & Canoe** (June weekends, daily

MUST SEE:
Steep Rock
Eroded lime-stone cliffs at a Lake Manitoba pit stop for motorists heading to the province's north.

July and August, thesteeprock.com), which also doubles as beachfront concession, selling burgers, smokies and ice cream. It's cash only.

Given the distance from Winnipeg, you may want to stay overnight. The non-profit **Steep Rock Beach Campground** (204.449.2221, steeprockbeach.ca) has 208 campsites ($23.14 to $36.78) and one cabin for rent ($87.80). Reserve in advance, especially in July and August. There's a three-night minimum stay during long weekends.

Fairford

Continuing north up Highway 6 for 23 kms past the turnoff to Steep Rock, you'll reach a bridge over the **Fairford River.** The bridge is actually a dam: The Fairford River Water Control Structure, which controls the sole outflow for Lake Manitoba.

At the height of the 2011 flood, the capacity of the Fairford outflow was smaller than the volume of water flowing into Lake Manitoba from its two main natural sources and the Portage Diversion. The resulting lake-level rise created calls for a new means of draining water from Lake Manitoba to Lake Winnipeg. Downstream of the dam, meanwhile, high Fairford River flows flooded out Lake St. Martin, prompting the province to cut an emergency channel.

You can contemplate the futility of all this hydrological engineering from the bridge – or just stare at the white pelicans that usually gather here from June to August. On the north side of the river, **Roviera Campground** (204.659.5248) usually has space when Steep Rock Beach Campground is full.

Take heed of the time of day and your fuel gauge if you plan to continue north toward The Pas or Thompson from here. **St. Martin Junction**, 14 kilometres north of Fairford, has the last gas station for 178 kms. The next section of Highway 6 is the loneliest stretch of asphalt in the entire province.

Snowmobilers, beware: In winter, pressure ridges can run for kilometres on Manitoba's big lakes.

Bartley Kives

Beaches & Interlake Daytrips

Beginning and ending at Winnipeg

Reach the Beach

When to go: Mid-June to late August.

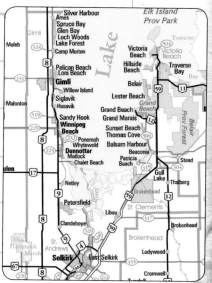

1. As early as you can stand it on what promises to be a warm day, head north on Lagimodiere Boulevard, which becomes Highway 59 outside city limits. From the Perimeter (Highway 101), drive 11 kms north to the western entrance of **Birds Hill Provincial Park**.

2. Go for quick spin on your mountain bike on the off-road course adjacent the **Nimowin Trail** (South Drive) or the paved Pine Ridge Trail (North Drive).

3. Return to Highway 59 and drive north 52 kms to PR 319. Turn left and drive six kms to **Patricia Beach Provincial Park**. Chill out at placid Patricia Beach until you get antsy.

Map ©2006 Sherlock Publishing Ltd.

4. Heading back toward Highway 59, turn left three kms before the beach and take gravel Point Road for five kms, through Beaconia Wetland Ecological Preserve, to PR 500. Turn left, toward the water.

5. If you want to check out another quiet beach continue straight to unserviced **Beaconia Beach**. Otherwise, head north on PR 500 for 10.5 kms to Highway 12. Make a right on the highway and quick left on Road 38 East into **Grand Beach Provincial Park**. Head to the **West Beach** if you're into people watching. Head to the East Beach if you want yet another placid beach. Or head toward the East Beach and go for a spin on your mountain bike along the ski-trail network.

6. Back on Highway 12, head south four kms until it merges with Highway 59 and another 10 kms south until the two split again. Take Highway 12 south 19.5 kms to PR 307. Turn left at PR 307 and grab an excellent grass-fed burger at **Robyn's Drive Inn** (summer, 204.265.3456).

7. Take PR 307 back to Highway 59 and then back to Winnipeg.

Lakes and Snakes

When to go: Late April to mid-September.

1. Head north on McPhillips Street, which becomes Highway 8 outside of city limits. From the Perimeter (Highway 101), head north 10 kms on Highway 8 to PR 230. Follow PR 230 10.5 kms north to Highway 9. Turn left and follow Highway 9 22 kms

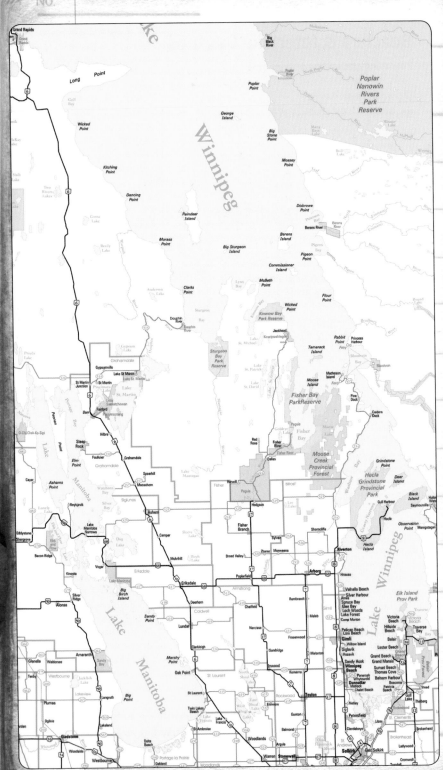

Map ©2006 Sherlock Publishing Ltd.

north to **Petersfield**. Cross Netley Creek and turn right on Edith Avenue for the start of the slow, scenic route up the west side of Lake Winnipeg's southern basin.

2. Take Edith Avenue 800 metres east to Tom Prince Drive. Turn right and follow it south and east three kms to Gimli Trail. Turn left and follow Gimli Trail 12 kms north until it merges with Cochrane Road. Turn right and follow it north three kms to **Matlock**, the first of three communities in the Village of Dunnotar.

3. Deke left on Matlock Avenue for 300 metres and turn right on Gimli Road, also known as PR 232. Stop for perogies and kubasa 900 metres north at **Julia's Ukrainian Restaurant** (Mon-Sat, 30 Gimli Rd., 204.389.5303) or keep up Gimli Road.

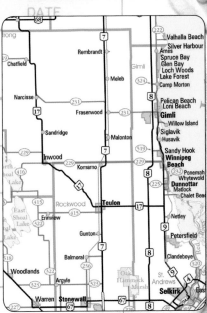

Map ©2006 Sherlock Publishing Ltd.

4. Follow the PR 232 signs seven kms north to **Winnipeg Beach**. Turn right on Hamilton Avenue, park along the Main Street boardwalk and check out the beach or local art at **Fishfly Gallery** (18 Main St., 204.389.5661). Then follow Stitt Street northwest to Highway 9.

5. Drive north on Highway 9 for 14.5 kms to Gimli. Turn right at Centre Street and park as close as you can to the waterfront. Check out local retail institution **H. P. Tergesen & Sons** (82 First Ave., 204.642.5958), Gimli's harbor and beach and flip a coin over a choice of fried pickerel filets or cheeks at **The Beach Boy** (daily, 70 First Ave., 204.642.7560) or **Kris' Fish & Chips** (daily, 78 First Ave., 204.642.8848). Head home if it isn't snake season, or continue snaking up the lake along PR 222 to Riverton.

6. If it's late April or mid-September, leave Gimli to see a few thousand snakes. From downtown Gimli, drive north until you hit North Fifth Avenue. This becomes PR 231 west of the town. From Highway 8, follow PR 231 15 kms west until it merges with Highway 7. Follow the combined highways three kms north and turn left at PR 231. Follow it 22 kms west to Highway 17, turn right and drive five more kms to the **Narcisse Wildlife Management Area**. Check out the red-sided garter snake dens, which will be active as the snakes leave their hibernation spots in the spring and return in September.

7. Head back to Winnipeg on Highway 17 and then Highway 7, which becomes Route 90 inside city limits.

*

Canadians have a distorted view of south-western Manitoba, thanks to the unfortunate placement of the Trans-Canada Highway. For the most part, Highway 1 crosses some of the most yawn-inducing terrain in the province, which makes for great long-distance trucking but lousy sightseeing.

The gently rolling prairie south of the Trans-Canada is way more interesting, thanks to the winding Souris River Valley, the western reaches of the Pembina Valley, forested Spruce Woods and Turtle Mountain provincial parks, and a couple of biggish bodies of water, including birdwatching spots Oak Lake, Pelican Lake, and Whitewater Lake.

North of the Trans-Canada, the Yellowhead Highway marks the transition between Prairie farmland and the more rugged parkland on the approach to Riding Mountain National Park.

And smack in the middle of the region is the second-largest community in Manitoba – Brandon, an underappreciated city where even the residents don't seem to recognize what they have.

Getting out to this region from Winnipeg usually demands an overnight, but you can hit certain destinations as a daytrip if you're really motivated.

Opposite: No, it's not a desert. The dunes at the Spirit Sands in Spruce Woods Provincial Park were left behind by glacial Lake Agassiz.

The Yellowhead

A ribbon of road extending northwest from Portage la Prairie, the Yellowhead Highway – also known as Highway 16 – marks the transition between southwestern Manitoba's prairie and the wilder Parkland. The Yellowhead leads through the pretty towns of Neepawa and Minnedosa, where the Whitemud and Little Saskatchewan rivers flow down from the Manitoba Escarpment, before continuing across a relatively empty stretch of farmland on its way to the Assiniboine River and the Saskatchewan border.

Gladstone and Big Grass Marsh

Heading west on the Yellowhead, the first community of any size is **Gladstone** (pop. 879), infamous for the **Happy Rock**, a supremely silly statue that looms over Highway 16 near the junction of

Highway 34. Pull in anyway and pick up a cinnamon bun at **Gladstone Bakery** (5 Morris St., 204.385.2225) as a provision for a visit to nearby **Big Grass Marsh**, the first conservation project ever undertaken by Ducks Unlimited in North America.

The marsh originally encompassed about 400 square kms before misguided drainage between 1909 and 1916 dried up the wetlands and created a dusty, peat-fire-prone wasteland by the Great Depression. In 1938, a fledgling Ducks Unlimited tried to restore part of the marsh to its original soggy state. Today, what's now **Big Grass Marsh Provincial Game Bird Refuge** protects 50 square kms for the likes of Franklin's gulls, snow geese, and sandhill cranes. To reach the refuge from downtown Gladstone, drive north of Morris Street until the end and zigzag north until you reach the east-west PR 265, which bisects the marsh. Head east and you'll wind up on the south side of Jackfish Lake, the largest body of water in the wetland.

Continuing west on the Yellowhead from Gladstone, the community of **Arden** (PR 352, six kms north of Highway 16) offers a chance to stretch your legs along a five-km walking trail at the Whitemud River, where you'll also find a swinging bridge and an oversized statue of a crocus. The surrounding area is covered with crocuses, which bloom spectacularly right after the spring snowmelt.

Neepawa

MUST SEE: Neepawa and Minnedosa Quaint Yellowhead Highway towns on the approach to Riding Mountain Provincial Park.

One of the most idyllic-looking towns in Manitoba, **Neepawa** (pop. 3,629) is best known as the home of the late novelist Margaret Laurence, whose fictional hamlet of Manawaka was based on this picturesque community. The very definition of quaint, the town bills itself as the lily capital of the world. Needless to say, there are few biker bars here.

If you want to buy lilies, no less than 1,500 varieties are on sale at **The Lily Nook** (204.476.3225), four kms south of Neepawa on Highway 5. Other Neepawa attractions include **Rotary Park** (Park Lake Drive, at the south end of First Avenue), a quirky lakeside picnic area with a bird sanctuary; and **Margaret Laurence House** (daily, June-August, 312 First Ave., 204.476.3612, $5 adults/$2 students), the author's former home.

Inspired by Laurence's prose, **Manawaka Gallery** (Tues-Fri, 293 Mountain Ave., 204.476.3232) displays local art, while **Beautiful Plains Museum** (weekends May and June; daily July and August, 91 Hamilton St. West, 204.476.3896) offers the usual assortment of pioneer artifacts in an old CNR station.

At lunchtime, grab a bite **Brews Brothers Bistro** (weekdays, 376 Mountain Ave., 204.476.4279), which despite its name is actually a soup-and-sandwich joint. To avoid franchise fare at night, **Brahma's Grill & Steakhouse** (daily, 564 Main St. East, 204.476.3600) is a Yellowhead roadhouse option.

Neepawa also marks the start of one of Manitoba's most road-free portions of the **Trans Canada Trail**. A 49-kilometre stretch of TCT's Rossburn Subdivision follows an abandoned railbed between Howden, a hamlet five kms north of Neepawa on Highway 5, and the town of Erickson, just south of Riding Mountain National Park. Trail conditions vary from fair to awful, but the attraction here is solace – head out and you'll probably have the route to yourself.

Charles Shilliday

Green and yellow canola stands out against a bright blue Manitoba sky.

Minnedosa and Beyond

Another attractive Yellowhead town, **Minnedosa** (pop. 2,587) sits on the Little Saskatchewan River at the junction of Highway 16 and Highway 10. Media mogul Izzy Asper, founder of Winnipeg's Canadian Museum for Human Rights, was born in this quiet valley town and began his career here sweeping up the family-run movie theatre.

Today, the main attraction is **Lake Minnedosa** (PR 262, northeast of Main Street), an artificial lake and beach created by a dam on the Little Saskatchewan. Classic rock festival **Rockin' The Fields of Minnedosa** (rockinthefields.ca) is held at the lakefront during the August long weekend.

Below the dam, a short network of walking trails criss-crosses a low-lying area with a marsh boardwalk, a swinging bridge, and a **bison compound**. After your walk, pop into **Sun Sun** (13 Main St. North, 204.867.1913) for small-town Chinese-Canadian fare.

West of Minnedosa, the next 100 kilometres of the Yellowhead can be fairly dull, except in July, when bright-yellow canola and deep-green wheat fields stand out against the blue sky. Diversions along the way include the **Mounted Police Museum** (July and August, 204.759.3326), a replica of a 19th-century North-West Mounted Police barracks at the town of **Shoal Lake** (Highways 16 and 21); hiking or cross-country skiing along picturesque **Birdtail Creek Valley** at Birtle (10 kms south of the Yellowhead at Highways 42 and 83).

Long, narrow Lake Minnedosa, created by the damming of the Little Saskatchewan River, complements the idyllic setting of one of western Manitoba's most picturesque towns.

Farther west, treat the kids with a round of minigolf and a chlorinated dip in the heated

Charles Shilliday

pool at **Binscarth Park & Pool** (daily, late June through August, 204.532.2353), immediately off the highway two kilometres south of the town of Binscarth (Highway 16, just north of the Highway 41 junction). Swimming fees are $5.50 adults/$4.50 students and minigolf is $2. Campsites are $15-$45.

Spruce Woods Provincial Park

MUST SEE:
Spruce Woods Provincial Park
An island of greenery on the southwestern prairie, home to a network of trails and the famous Spirit Sands, a collection of active sand dunes.

A remnant from a time when forests covered southwestern Manitoba, **Spruce Woods Provincial Park** is a 250-square-kilometre island of greenery in the middle of Prairie farmland. This popular park is famous for the Spirit Sands, a small patch of active sand dunes. But it also encompasses a particularly scenic stretch of the Assiniboine River Valley, and one of the best long biking and cross-country skiing routes in the province, the Epinette Creek/ Newfoundland Trail system.

Located east of Highway 5 between the Trans-Canada and Highway 2, Spruce Woods is a patch of forest and grassland with sandy soil that used to mark the bottom – and later, edge – of glacial Lake Agassiz. All the sand prevented the area from being developed in the late 1800s, when the rest of southwestern Manitoba was getting plowed to shreds. Spruce Woods formally became a park in 1964.

Today, the vast majority of visitors head straight to the southwest corner of the park and the nine-km **Spirit Sands trail system**, which offers easy access to the still-active dunes, an unusual colour-shifting sinkhole called the **Devil's Punchbowl** and the Assiniboine River Valley. The trailhead is located on the west side of Highway 5, just north of the river. Given the fragility of the

Bryan Scott

landscape, bikes, ATVs, and off-trail hiking are not allowed. That doesn't stop idiots from occasionally scarring the dune faces.

On the south side of the river, the only developed portion of the park houses the **Kiche Manitou campground** (May-October, sites $21.20-$25.20, yurts $56.50) and a swimming hole/beach at an oxbow called **Kiche Manitou Lake**. The site also has a replica **Pine Fort**, a **visitor centre** (mid-May to early September, 204.827.8850) with a restaurant, bookshop, museum and minigolf course. Canoe rentals are on the river to the northeast. There

Bryan Scott

are also two short walking trails: the 1.4-km **Isputinaw Trail** is just east of the campground; meanwhile, the 1.2-km **Springridge Trail,** four kilometres to the northeast at Steels Ferry Overlook, offers views of the Assiniboine River Valley.

Kiche Manitou Campground also marks the start of a 10-km section of the Trans Canada Trail that heads to an **equestrian campground** (bookings 204.82.2654) and a network of dirt tracks used by horseback riders and hikers in the southeast corner of the park. The highlight of this area is an unusual, bald-faced ridge called the **Hogsback**, about five kilometres east.

Only a small portion of Spruce Woods Provincial Park is open sand. Colonized dunes – that is, sand covered in spare forest – make up most of the park's rolling terrain.

North of the Assiniboine, a 1.5-km interpretive trail called **Marshs Lake** explains the formation of oxbow lakes, the crescent-shaped sloughs created when meandering prairie rivers forge a more direct course. It's located about one kilometre north of the Spirit Sands trailhead.

Another six kms north, just outside the park boundary, you'll find the entrance to the **Epinette Creek/Newfoundland trail system**, one of the few Manitoba provincial park loops to offer hike-in, bike-in, and ski-in camping. This is a fantastic trail. There are five campsites and four warm-up shelters along the 42-km route, which traverses sandy hills, grasslands, forests, and two ravines. The first 10 kilometres of the trail are okay for hiking, but the entire route is more fun for mountain bikes – you can whip through here in four to six gruelling hours. Just be prepared to push your bike up the occasional patch of deep sand. **Jackfish Cabin**, at the far end of the loop, may be reserved as an overnight winter shelter for cross-country skiers who traverse the loop in two days (bookings 204.834.8800 after Oct. 1).

During the winter, the near side of the Epinette trail system makes for good day-skiing and there are 25 more kms of cross-country loops nearby. The **Seton Cross Country Ski Trails** depart from a trailhead on the west side of Highway 5, one km south of the Epinette turnoff, while the **Yellow Quill Trails** are on the east side, another two clicks down the road. The northeast and southern sections of the park are devoted to snowmobiles.

In addition to hiking, biking, skiing, sledding, and horseback riding, you can also see Spruce Woods from the water. The Assiniboine River is navigable for canoes and kayaks from the spring snowmelt until the end of the summer. Paddlers usually put in east of the park at PR 340 or at Stockton Ferry and spend two to four days on the river, taking out at Highway 34 east of the park. There's one established canoe campsite inside the park itself, near the Hogsback. Bring your own drinking water, as it's inadvisable to drink Assiniboine water, even when it's filtered, thanks to dissolved pesticides from agricultural runoff.

Visitors to Spruce Woods are subject to the usual fees: $5 per vehicle for one day, $12 for a three-day pass, or $40 for a seasonal pass covering all Manitoba provincial parks.

Around Spruce Woods

Immediately to the west of the provincial park, **Spruce Woods Provincial Forest** has more interesting hills that few people ever get to see: The Canadian Forces out of Shilo use this area as a training ground and artillery range. If you think you hear shells going off while you're in the park itself, you're not imagining things.

The largest town outside the park is **Carberry** (pop. 1,669), Manitoba's self-proclaimed potato capital, located ten kms north of the boundary on Highway 5 near the Trans-Canada Highway. **Carberry Plains Museum** (daily, July and August afternoons, 520 Fourth Ave., 204.834.6609) has exhibits honouring pioneer wildlife painter Norman Criddle (see Criddle/Vane Homestead) and former resident Tommy Douglas, the architect of medicare, Canada's publicly funded healthcare system. The even tinier **Seton Centre** (Mon-Sat, June to August, 116 Main St., 204.834.2509, thesetoncentre.ca) is dedicated to the life of British-born wildlife illustrator, naturalist, and indigenous rights activist Ernest Thompson Seton, who spent his early 20s in the Carberry area. The Spirit Sands inspired his life's work.

Farther north at Highway 1 near the Highway 5 junction, **Robins Nest Café** (daily except winter Sundays, 204.834.28780) is the spot for a post-trail burger.

Horse team at the Threshermen's Reunion at Austin, a big community along the Trans-Canada Highway.

There's a statue of a camel at the Spruce Woods gateway town of **Glenboro** (Highway 2 at Highway 5) in honour of the Spirit Sands. Southwest of the park, the last remaining river ferry in Manitoba carries vehicles across the Assiniboine northeast of the hamlet of **Stockton** (Road 88 West, three kms north of Highway 2).

Northeast of the park at **Austin** (Highway 1 at Highway 34), the **Manitoba Agricultural Museum** (weekdays

Charles Shilliday

October-May, daily otherwise, 204.637-2354, ag-museum. mb.ca, admission $10 adults, $8 students/seniors, $5 kids) is a 32-hectare shrine to farm implements, vintage tractors, and the like. The museum grounds also sport a campground that hosts the **Austin Threshermans Reunion & Stampede**, a fair usually held the last week of July.

Bartley Kives

Early spring along the Rae Trail in the Assiniboine Corridor Wildlife Management Area.

East of the park, the northeast unit of the **Assiniboine Corridor Wildlife Management Area** is the home of the 14-kilometre (return) **Rae Trail**, a nice but poorly signed day hike along the north bend of the Assiniboine River. The trailhead is a small clearing on the west side of Highway 34, about 2.5 kilometres past the Assiniboine River. The trail leaves from the northwest corner of the lot. Given the terrible signage, bring a GPS unit or a topographical map. Also watch out for ATVs.

Southeast of the park, **Holland** (Highways 2 and 34) is home to the **Tiger Hills Art Gallery** (Tues-Fri, 103 Broadway Street, 204.526.2063). Southeast of the town, you'll find the **Abbey of Our Lady of the Prairies**, a community of Trappist monks that moved here from St. Norbert in 1978 to get away from Winnipeg's urban sprawl. Their current residence is a modernist concrete structure with a small gift shop up front. Hours vary, but these are monks after all — if they wanted a constant stream of visitors, they'd have stayed in Winnipeg. The monks make a fantastic raw-milk cheese that tastes like a more complex cousin of Oka; look for it at high-end cheese shops in Winnipeg. The sign marking the road to the monastery is on Highway 34, 350 metres west of the junction with PR 245.

Bryan Scott

Storm clouds gather near the town of Holland, southeast of Spruce Woods.

Pembina Valley West

Carved out of southern Manitoba by a torrent of glacial meltwater, the Pembina River Valley snakes across southern Manitoba along a course roughly parallel to the US border. The eastern portion of this valley, described in the *Red River Valley & Around* chapter, is the most affluent rural region in the province. The western Pembina Valley has a different character – it's seen a lot less growth in recent years, but remains a picturesque stretch of the Prairies, especially in the middle of the summer.

West of Highway 34, the valley widens out into three trough-like lakes: Swan, Rock, and Pelican, the latter a busy cottage area.

Farther west, the Pembina is merely a stream that tumbles down from the Boissevain area.

Away from the river, the farmland is dotted with thousands of tiny lakes and sloughs, colloquially known as Prairie potholes, which attract impressive numbers of birds. As a result, a pair of binoculars is compulsory for any spring, summer or fall trip through this region.

Heading east or west, you have three routes to choose from: Highway 23 skirts the north side of the valley, Provincial Road 253 heads straight through it, and Highway 3 curves below the river, hugging the US border.

Pilot Mound and Around

Tucked into a bend in Highway 3, **Pilot Mound** (pop. 676) takes its name from a 36-metre-high glacial formation with a fascinating history. In late prehistoric times, indigenous people – Sioux ancestors, in all likelihood – used the hill for ceremonies and built a mound on its summit. The western slope of the hill became a graveyard in the 1850s, after hundreds of Dakota were killed in a battle with Métis bison hunters on a plain just north of the mound.

In the decades to come, white settlers used the mound as a navigational aid and built a town on the site in 1881. Sir John A. Macdonald, Canada's first prime minister, held a political rally here in 1885. But when the Canadian Pacific Railway bypassed the town, the hill was abandoned for a new site two kms to the south. The original mound sits north of the current village on Road 64 West, but treat it with respect – Dakota from North Dakota occasionally hold ceremonies on the summit. More mounds built by indigenous ancestors line the north shore of **Rock Lake**, a prime birding area about 15 kms west of Pilot Mound on PR 253.

Eight kilometres southwest of Pilot Mound, the village of **Crystal City** (pop. 414) is worth a stop for the **Crystal City Community Printing Museum** (Mon-Fri by appointment only, 212 Broadway South, 204.873.2095), a quirky monument to 100-year-old typesetting and publishing gear. Some of the vintage equipment is fully operational, as the museum staff still handles print jobs.

Six kms west of Crystal City on Highway 3A, the even tinier hamlet of **Clearwater** is on the map thanks to the three-day **Harvest Moon Festival** (harvestmoonfestival.ca), a folk and roots music festival usually held the third weekend in September. Originally created to promote organic farming in the region, this cross-cultural event carved out a niche as the last Manitoba folk festival of the season and has grown to attract more than 2,000 fans. Tickets usually sell out in advance.

Continuing west, the village of **Cartwright** (pop. 304, Highway 3 at Highway 5) offers another glimpse at pre-European history. Three kms to the north, a set of cliffs known as the Clay Banks were used 2,500 years ago as buffalo jumps by indigenous peoples.

Pelican Lake and Around

The largest navigable body of water in southwestern Manitoba, **Pelican Lake** sits above the spot where the Pembina River spills into the long, post-glacial trench that once held the lower portion of the Assiniboine River. The lake is nine times longer than it is wide, with cottage communities and rental cabins ringing the shoreline.

Pelican Lake peaked a century ago as a resort area, but a yacht club remains at the largest community, **Ninette** (Highways 23 and 18, at the northwest corner of the lake). Aside from boating and fishing, birding is the chief activity, especially during the fall migration season.

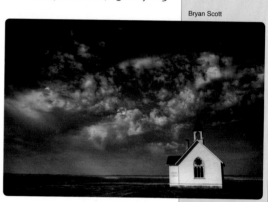
Bryan Scott

About fifteen kilometres west of Ninette, north of the town of Margaret (Highway 23 and PR 346), there's more attractive valley scenery in the **Souris Riverbend Provincial Wildlife Management Area**, a protected patch of riverbottom forests and grasslands. This is the place where the Souris River abruptly turns northeast to flow into the Assiniboine. Equestrians and hikers use about ten kilometres of trails, some of which cross private land. From Margaret, drive about eleven kilometres north on PR 346, cross the Souris River, and look out for a trailhead on the east side of the road.

Little church on the prairie: A common southwestern sight.

South of Pelican Lake, **Killarney** (pop. 2,197, Highways 3 and 18) is a quiet town that's lucky enough to have its own beach and marina at small, often algae-covered **Killarney Lake**. Playing off the town's Irish name, or perhaps the shamrock-green algae blooms, **Blarney Stone Pub & Grill** (daily, 531 Broadway, 204.523.7782) will sell you a pint of Guinness with your burger and baked potato.

Brandon

Manitoba's second-largest city, **Brandon** (pop. 46,061), is a lot like Winnipeg in that the locals tend to be unusually and unfairly hard on their hometown. Built up on the Assiniboine River Valley where Highway 10 and the Trans-Canada meet, the small city with the big inferiority complex is particularly gorgeous in September, when the leaves on more than 20,000 elms begin to turn. Brandon also makes an excellent base of operations for a weekend exploration of southwestern Manitoba.

Brandon's similarities to Winnipeg are numerous, starting with the city's beginnings as a railway boomtown in the 1880s, a long period of stagnation in the 20th century, and a relatively

Bryan Scott

Rosser Avenue, in downtown Brandon.

MUST SEE: Brandon
Manitoba's second-largest city serves as a great base to explore nearby attractions such as a Second World War airforce training museum, a reptile menagerie, and the Brandon Hills.

recent period of renewed growth. Brandon also has its own urban-doughnut problem, as the handsome, 100-year-old buildings of its turn-of-the-last-century downtown seem deserted at night, when Brandonites flock to the franchise restaurants on the suburban fringe of 18th Street, the city's main north-south artery, and Victoria Avenue, the primary east-west route.

Brandon's most attractive feature is the river valley, which runs east-west through the northern part of town. The **Assiniboine Riverbank Trail System**, a seventeen-kilometre network of mostly paved footpaths, lines both sides of the river and connects to both downtown and small **Eleanor Kidd Gardens** (18th Street at the river). A good place to begin a walk is the **Riverbank Discovery Centre** (daily, 545 Conservation Drive, 204.729.2141, riverbank. mb.ca), where you can pick up a trail map and tourism info for the whole region. While on the north side of the river, try the meatloaf burger or scratch-made soups at **Lady Of The Lake** (Mon-Sat, 135 17th Street North, 204.726.8785).

It's also worth a stroll through the city's inner core, a ten-block-wide rectangle bounded by 18th Street, Pacific Avenue, First Street, and Victoria Avenue. While the old residential streets are quaint, the most cosmopolitan stretch of downtown Brandon is **Rosser Avenue**, where you'll find some independent retailers and the Town Centre mall, home to the **Art Gallery of Southwestern Manitoba** (Tues-Sat, 2-710 Rosser Ave., 204.727.1036, agsm.ca), which specializes in contemporary Prairies art. Admission is free. A block away, **Brandon General Museum & Archives** (Mon-Sat June through August, Tues-Sat September through May, 19 Ninth St., 204.717.1514, bgma.ca) has a permanent Brandon-history exhibit and also houses the **B. J. Hales Collection**, comprised of 800 preserved birds, mammals, insects and plants. Admission is free.

Tours of **Daly House Museum** (daily in summer, Tues-Sat winter, 122 18th Street, 204.727.1722), the former residence of Brandon's first mayor, cost $6 for adults and $5 for seniors and students.

Downtown also boasts the **Double Decker Tavern** (daily, 943 Rosser Ave., 204.727.4343.), which has a good selection of brews on tap, and **Chilli Chutney** (daily, 935 Rosser Ave., 204.571.9310), a South Asian restaurant as strong as any in Winnipeg. One long block south on Princess Avenue, try **The Dock** (Mon-Sat, 1133 Princess Ave., 204.726.1234) for burgers and pub fare or **Komfort Kitchen** (daily, 835 Princess Ave., 204.727.6867) for carb-heavy breakfast and brunch fare. Further south in the inner core, **Pizza Express** (daily, 360 Tenth St., 204.727.2727) serves homey subs, while locals swear by the pizza at **Marino's** (Tues-Sun, 441 Tenth St., 204.578.5555). Need something lighter? Pan-Asian resataurant **Kim's** (daily, 241 McTavish Ave. East, 204.571.9266) offers dim sum, sushi and pho, a short drive southeast of downtown.

South of downtown, the **Keystone Centre** dominates five long blocks of 18th Street with exhibition grounds, curling rinks, and the 5,000-seat **Keystone Arena**, home of the Western Hockey League's **Brandon Wheat Kings** (wheatkings.com) the province's biggest spectator-sports draw outside of Winnipeg. Tickets to see the junior-aged Wheaties, who play from October to March, are $18 for adults.

In late March and into early April, the Keystone Centre hosts the week-long **Royal Manitoba Winter Fair** (brandonfairs.com), Manitoba's largest agricultural and equestrian show. On the other end of cultural spectrum, the **Brandon Folk Music and Art Festival** (brandonfolkfestival. ca) sets up on the centre's grounds over the third weekend in July. Weekend passes run from $56 to $80. The centre also sports a **Canad Inns** hotel franchise (canadinns. com); other brand-name chain hotels in Brandon are concentrated along the Trans-Canada Highway, far from the city's centre.

Up until recently, the most fascinating attraction in Brandon used to be ignored by local tourism authorities and was all-but-impossible to visit. The former **Brandon Mental Health Centre**, originally known as the Asylum for the Insane, looms over the northeast portion of city like a Gothic institution out of a *Batman* comic. This is the place where infamous psychiatrist Ewan Cameron, later reviled for experimenting on patients with LSD in Montreal, began to develop his controversial ideas about "recreating" entire personalities from scratch. Today, the four main buildings, constructed between 1912 and 1932, are in the midst of being transformed into a modern campus for **Assiniboine Community College**. You can visit at 1035 1st North, between the Low Road To Shilo and Ross Avenue.

The decommissioned Brandon Mental Health Centre, which looms over Brandon like a Gothic asylum out of a Batman comic.

Suzanne Braun

Around Brandon

The biggest bonus of visiting Brandon is the close proximity of great cycling in the Brandon Hills and a number of idiosyncratic attractions around the city. The following destinations are within 50 kms of Brandon, which translates into no more than a half-hour drive.

North of Brandon

Two minutes north of Brandon, World War II buffs will dig the **Commonwealth Air Training Plan Museum** (daily, 300 Commonwealth Way, 204.727.2444, airmuseum.ca), a monument to the wartime period when air force pilots and support crews from around the English-speaking world trained in the Brandon area before heading off to Europe to battle the Nazis. The museum boasts vintage aircraft and a pair of lovingly curated galleries, as well as a chapel displaying samples of terse telegrams informing parents and spouses of the loss of their loved ones. It's chilling stuff. The museum is housed inside Hangar 1 at Brandon Municipal Airport, accessible from Highway 10 just north of town. Admission is $7.50 for adults, $5 for university students and $4 for youths. In the early 1990s, the airport and some of the planes from the museum served as the backdrop in *For the Moment*, actor Russell Crowe's first North American feature.

Thirty minutes northwest of Brandon, **Rivers Provincial Park** sits on Lake Wahtopanah, a dam-created reservoir on the Little Saskatchewan River. The small park has a beach and campground (May-September, $21-$28.35). You can walk from the beach to the nearby town of **Rivers** (pop. 1,189) along three-km **Aspen Walking Trail**, which passes by a series of railway-excavated gravel pits.

In late April and early May, when water levels are sufficiently high, Rivers Provincial Park also marks the starting point for a 37-km **paddle down the Little Saskatchewan River**, which drops 100 metres and passes through many sets of Class I rapids before it meets the Assiniboine River northwest of Brandon.

Shilo and Wawanesa

East of Brandon on PR 457, also known as the Low Road to Shilo, **Westman Reptile Gardens** (daily May-September, Tues-Sun October-April, 204.763.4030, reptilegardens.ca) houses a large collection of snakes, iguanas, lizards, crocodiles, turtles, frogs

Winter on the Little Saskatchewan River northwest of Brandon.

Charles Shilliday

and other cold-blooded creatures inside a nondescript bunker of a building. Proprietor Dave Shelvey took care of unwanted reptiles for years before opening this menagerie, which is as impressive as it is hard to find: heading east on PR 457 from Brandon, drive south on Brown Road then east on Thompson Road. Keep your eyes peeled for a sign on the right. If you hit Waggle Springs Road, you've gone too far east. Admission is $6 for adults and $4 for kids.

One km to the east, PR 457 meets PR 340 and slides into the town of Shilo and Canadian Forces Base Shilo, once a home away from home for the German military, now a barracks-*cum*-blasting ground for the Canadian Forces. While most of the base is off-limits to civilians, armchair warriors can get up close to big guns at the **Royal Canadian Artillery Museum** (daily Victoria Day to Labour Day, weekdays off season, PR 340 at the base, 204.765.3000 extension 3570, rcamuseum.com), the largest collection of its kind in Canada. Admission by donation.

Ten kilometres south of Shilo, **Criddle/Vane Homestead Provincial Heritage Park** (east of PR 240) used to serve as a monument to one of Manitoba's most colourful pioneer clans. In 1882, British businessman Percy Criddle immigrated to Manitoba with his wife (Mrs. Criddle), his mistress (Ms. Vane), and a total of nine offspring. The family patriarch was a lousy farmer, but the women and children made the best of a miserable and awkward situation, somehow thriving on the land and excelling at sports and sciences. One of the sons, Norman Criddle, became a celebrated entomologist. The Criddle/Vane descendents maintained a presence at the hamlet of Aweme until 1960. In 2004, their land became a provincial park with a pair of interpretive trails; Arsonists burned their historic home to the ground in 2014.

Charles Shilliday

About 12 kms farther south, the village of **Wawanesa** (PR 340 at Highway 2) is familiar to most Manitobans in name only, thanks to Wawanesa Life Insurance, a multinational corporation founded here in 1896. With a population of 516, the town hasn't grown along with its financial offspring, but the 1903 Wawanesa Mutual building now houses **Sipiweske Museum** (afternoons and evenings in July and August, 102 Fourth Street), whose subjects include the Criddle/Vane Family and early feminist Nellie McClung, who lived in the area before moving to Winnipeg and winning women the right to vote in Manitoba. Admission is a loonie for adults and 50 cents for kids.

Sipiweske Museum in Wawanesa.

Brandon Hills

Due south of Brandon, some of the best mountain biking in Manitoba – and good cross-country skiing, too – can be found in **Brandon Hills Provincial Wildlife Management Area**, a glacial ridge that looms over the surrounding prairie. There are 45 kms of mostly unmarked trails, ranging in difficulty from easy loops on well-maintained single track to technical sections with plenty of challenging switchbacks and annoying deadfall.

The best place to hike in the hills, meanwhile, is near the southeast corner of the ridge, where the exposed hilltop offers long views of southwestern Manitoba. To reach the main ski-and-bike trailhead, drive south from Brandon on Highway 10 to the intersection of PR 349 but turn left on the gravel road opposite. Drive about three kilometres east, turn right, and drive about 1.5 kms up the ridge. Another left turn will lead to the Brandon Hills trailhead parking lot.

Charles Shilliday

Fog rises over Souris in morning.

Souris

MUST SEE:
Souris
A picturesque community on a bend in the Souris River, with Canada's longest suspension bridge swinging across the river valley – and an oddball rock-collectors' pit.

Southwest of Brandon, **Souris** (pop. 1,837) is one of the prettier towns in western Manitoba. The main attractions are the 182-metre **Swinging Bridge**, Canada's longest suspension bridge, originally built in 1904. It was destroyed or had to be dismantled during floods on the Souris River in 1912, 1976 and 2011. The current version was rebuilt in 2013 and straddles the river between Crescent Avenue and Boundary Street. A few hundred metres upstream, **Victoria Park** has free-roaming peacocks, six kilometres of walking trails, a campground, and access to hour-long cruises down the Souris River on a modified barge.

Between the park and the west side of the bridge, **Hillcrest Museum** (Victoria Day to Labour Day, 26 Crescent Avenue West, 204.483.2008) ups the usual pioneer-museum ante with an ento-mological oddity: a collection of 5,000 (quite dead) butterflies from all over the world. The museum is open Canada Day to Labour Day from 10 a.m. to 6 p.m. Admission is $3 for adults and $2 for kids. The nearby **Plum Heritage Church Museum** (Canada Day to Labour Day, 142 First Street South) offers just what you'd expect in a town with peacocks – a Victorian tearoom. More modern fare – wood-fired pizzas, focaccia sandwiches, espresso – can be found at **Woodfire Deli** (daily, 39 Crescent Ave., 204.483.2795).

The oddest attraction in town is the **Souris Agate Pits** (daily, Victoria Day to Thanksgiving; Highway 2 at PR 250), an open pit with precious stones scattered amidst the sand and grit. Rock collectors show up in the summer with buckets and start feeling their way through the gravel. You too can be a rockhound, after paying a pit permit – $20 per vehicle – at **The Rock Shop** (8 First St. South, 204.483.2561, sourisrockshop.ca), which also sells precious gems and fossils.

To reach Souris from Brandon, drive south on Highway 10 and then west on Highway 2.

Winter sunflowers, outside the town of Hartney.

Turtle Mountain Area

When the glaciers started retreating from southwestern Manitoba, the first patch of dry land to see the light of day was Turtle Mountain, a plateau that straddles the Canada-US border about 100 kms south of Brandon.

The first humans moved in about 12,000 years ago, making the area the oldest inhabited corner of the province. Hunter-gatherer cultures persisted until European colonists arrived in the 19th century, but Turtle Mountain remains a relatively wild place, home to Turtle Mountain Provincial Park, an excellent birding area at Whitewater Lake, and the interesting town of Boissevain.

Boissevain

American tourists heading up from North Dakota, and Brandonites heading south, have helped make **Boissevain** (pop. 1,572) a worthwhile stop on Highway 10, six kms north of Highway 3. The town actively promotes its **Outdoor Art Gallery**, a series of murals painted on the sides of 18 buildings, but the most unique attraction is the tiny **Moncur Gallery** (Tues-Sat, 436 South Railway St. in the public library, 204.534.2433, moncurgallery.org), an extremely impressive museum devoted to 12,000 years of Aboriginal presence in southwestern Manitoba.

If you have any interest in indigenous history, this will be the best $5 you'll ever spend. The small basement gallery features more than a thousand ancient and more recent artifacts found in fields and forests around Boissevain and Turtle Mountain, the first part of the province to emerge from glacial ice. Amazingly, a single collector – William Moncur – found most of the arrowheads, awls, and hammers. His donations form the basis of the collection. To fully appreciate this place, pick up the self-guided tourbook, which

MUST SEE:
Boissevain
A small town with four museums, including the excellent Moncur Gallery, which documents 12,000 years of indigenous presence in southwestern Manitoba.

explains the exhibits and helps illuminate Manitoba's early human history. The museum is open 9 a.m. to 5 p.m. If the librarians tell you it's closed, ask nicely and they may let you in anyway.

Boissevain also has three other museums: **Beckoning Hills** (afternoons May to September, 425 Mill Street South, admission by donation) is your standard pioneer museum. The much freakier **Irvin Goodon International Wildlife Museum** (daily, Victoria Day to Labour Day, 298 Mountain St., 204-534-6662, $7 adults/$3 kids) is a monument to taxidermy, featuring stuffed wolves, bison, bears, moose, eagles, and dozens of other critters. Basically, this place is a zoo where all the animals are dead. An attached gift shop specializes in fur clothing and rustic handicrafts. Neighbouring **Chokecherry Junction** (daily in summer, Mill and Mountain, admission $2) houses a model railway collection.

Charles Shilliday

One of the last remaining examples of the wooden grain elevator, once the symbol of the Canadian Prairies.

Outside the model railway museum, it's impossible to miss **Tommy the Turtle**, a seven-metre-high statue of a painted turtle at the corner of Mill and Mountain. Southeast of the town, a far more ancient monument sits above the Boissevain Reservoir – the **Boissevain Dancing Ground**, an ancient indigenous ceremonial site that served as the hub of a very large medicine wheel; rocks placed within sight of the hill line up with sunrise and sunset at the winter and summer solstices. This site, part of the vast Sourisford-Devils Lake mound complex that stretches across the prairies, is among the few sacred places where visitation by tourists has the blessing of Dakota elders. It sits above the reservoir at **Lorna Smith Nature Centre** (east side of Road 114 West, south of PR 443).

If you need sustenance, load up on caffeine at **Sawmill Tea & Coffee Co.** (296 South Railway St., 204.534.2232).

Turtle Mountain Provincial Park

MUST SEE: Turtle Mountain Provincial Park
The oldest inhabited corner of Manitoba now protects lakes and forests on a rolling plateau alongside the US border.

There's no shortage of irony in the fact that Manitoba's oldest inhabited spot is now a protected wild area. **Turtle Mountain Provincial Park**, established in 1961, encompasses 184 square kms of forests, marshes, and shallow lakes on rolling terrain along the US border, providing a playground for off-road cyclists, hikers, horseback riders, cross-country skiers, snowmobilers, and the occasional canoeist.

There are 175 kms of trails in the park, most of them concentrated in a built-up eastern section along Highway 10. **Adam Lake**, the most popular spot in the park, has a beach, campground (May-September, $16.80-$26.25), an interpretive centre (mid-May to Labour Day), a 1.6-km walking trail to a wildlife-viewing tower, and access to a 65-km trail system for day-hikers, trail runners, cyclists, horses, and cross-country skiers. While there are no backcountry campsites along these routes, the 15-km **James Lake Trail** leads to a backcountry cabin that must be reserved in advance at Manitoba Conservation Boissevain office (204.534.2028).

You can reach the wilder western side of the park from **Max Lake**, accessible from Highway 10 via McKinney Road, about 1.5 kms north of the park. This lake has a beach, campsites ($16.80), and a canoe launch for flatwater paddling trips down to seven other lakes connected by well-used portages. It also marks the start of the 43-km **Sharpe Lake Trail**, a former fireguard that circumnavigates the west side of the park, coming within metres of the US border. It's used both as a ski/bike route, and to provide motor-vehicle access to two short hiking trails: the one-kilometre **Disappearing Lakes** self-guiding trail, and a two-km hike to a back-country campsite at **Oskar Lake**.

Other long routes include the 30-km **Bella Lake Trail**, which requires cyclists to ford a chest-deep lake, and the 32-km **Gordon Lake Trail**, which straddles the north side of the park. After a big rainfall, the Sharpe, Bella, and Gordon trails all get obnoxiously muddy – cyclists better have calves of steel.

Visitors to Turtle Mountain are required to pay the usual fees: $5 per vehicle for day passes, $12 for a three-day pass, or $40 for a seasonal Manitoba Parks Pass.

International Peace Gardens

Tucked into the southeast corner of Turtle Mountain Provincial Park and extending south into the US, the **International Peace Gardens** (peacegarden.com) celebrate Canada's buddy-buddy relationship with its southern neighbour. Founded in 1932 as a Depression-era make-work project, the park is designed to allow both Canadians and Americans to visit without crossing an international border or passing through customs. The entrance sits precisely on the boundary, between the Canadian and American border stations on Highway 10, which means you *do* have to pass through customs when you leave the gardens. Bring identification for everyone in your vehicle to prevent a situation where you wind up stuck in transborder limbo.

The park is divided into a Canadian side, with a 2.4-km **Lake View Hiking Trail**; an American side, with a campground ($14-$22), sports camp, and **Game Warden Museum** (summer weekdays) and a central corridor housing three sets of gardens and a pair of poignant monuments that make the trip here worthwhile.

Just west of the park entrance, you'll find the **Formal Garden** and the year-round **Peace Gardens Interpretive Centre**, which has a café and an indoor plant conservatory containing a collection of succulents and cacti. Continuing west on foot, you'll pass through the **Sunken Garden** then walk up a gentle slope to the **Bell Tower**, which chimes every 15 minutes, and a **9/11 Monument** comprised of steel girders salvaged from the wreckage of the World Trade Center in New York.

MUST SEE: International Peace Gardens
A park dedicated to the long history of friendship between Canada and the United States, with gardens, the monolithic Peace Tower, and a monument to the victims of the September 11, 2001, terrorist acts.

Stan Milosevic

At the end of the corridor, the concrete columns of the **Peace Tower** eerily resemble the destroyed Twin Towers, although they were built in the early '80s. When you get up close, you'll notice there are actually four pillars here, each extending 37.5 metres off the ground. This concrete message of unity is illuminated at night, all year long.

The International Peace Gardens are open 24 hours a day, 365 days a year. Admission is $10 per vehicle or $5 per pedestrian, with Canadian and US funds at par. Self register from October to May.

William Lake Provincial Park

A small satellite of Turtle Mountain Provincial Park, **William Lake Provincial Park** sits about five kms east of its larger neighbour. This small crescent of a park has a beach, a campground (May-September, $21), and a decent day hike: the six-km **Turtle's Back loop**, which follows the shore of William Lake before climbing to one of the highest viewpoints in Turtle Mountain. To reach the park from Highway 10, take gravel PR 341 east for about seven kms and then head south.

Whitewater Lake

Water flowing north off Turtle Mountain winds up in Whitewater Lake, a closed-basin body of water that used to be prone to drying out completely. A wetlands restoration project on the east side of this shallow lake, at **Whitewater Lake Wildlife Management Area**, attracts impressive numbers of birds, including the usual Manitoba suspects – Canada geese, pelicans, cormorants, and smaller waterfowl – but also three egret species, white-faced ibises, American avocets, Wilson's phalaropes, tundra swans, sandhill cranes, and snow geese, the latter especially during the fall migration period.

During the middle of the summer, a system of dikes around the artificial marsh makes for an amazing walk at dusk and dawn, when clouds of swallows are so dense they look like airborne schools of fish. There's also a boardwalk and an observation tower.

To reach the viewing area and dike trails from Highway 10, head west on Highway 3 for 11 kms, turn north at Road 122 West and follow the "Wildlife Watching" signs eight kms north to the trailhead. One word of caution for the squeamish: hunting is allowed here and is very popular during the fall, so you may very encounter the carcasses of unretrieved dead waterfowl.

Along the way from Highway 3 to the marsh, you'll pass by oil wells and a captive bison herd that give the place a decidedly western feel. If you're lucky, you'll see cattle egrets perched on bison.

Metigoshe and Deloraine

Just west of Turtle Mountain Provincial Park, **Lake Metigoshe** straddles the Canada-US border, with one small bay belonging to Manitoba. There's a beach and cabin rentals at the town of

Metigoshe, plus a short interpretive trail, a boardwalk, and a viewing tower at nearby **Lake Metigoshe Natural Area**. The lake is at the southern end of PR 450, which heads south from Highway 3 a few kms west of the Whitewater Lake turnoff.

Fourteen kms west, **Deloraine** (pop. 1,026) is a former coal-mining town best known as the home of Peter Nygård, a Winnipeg clothing magnate. The main attraction here is Flags of the World, a collection of national emblems from 193 countries, located in the centre of town at Nygård Park. Give 'em a break — it's better than another stupid statue.

Oil country

Manitoba's extreme southwestern corner is unlike anywhere else in the province, thanks to distinctly Saskatchewan-like features such as oil derricks and dryish grasslands. Towns such as Melita and Virden are almost as close to Regina as they are to Winnipeg. But that's just geography – culturally, these places feel worlds away from the Manitoba capital.

This once-sleepy corner of the province has enjoyed (and in some cases, suffered from) an influx of people, motor-vehicle traffic and money following the rise of horizontal oil drilling and hydraulic fracturing.

Melita and Vicinity

The town of **Melita** (pop. 1,069) straddles a flood-prone stretch of the Souris River where Highway 3 meets Highway 83. The main thing to see in town is the **Antler River Historical Society Museum** (afternoons, June to August, 71 Ash St., 204.522.3103, admission by donation), a collection of pioneer and First Nations artifacts with a tearoom, open June to August.

For now, Parks Canada does not encourage visits to Linear Mounds National Historic Site, which is sacred to nearby Dakota.

There are a handful of natural attractions in the scrubland around the town, the driest region of Manitoba. Four km north of the American border, southeast of the oil-rich village of **Waskada**, **Lowe Farm Natural Heritage Area** protects a ten-hectare tract of unbroken grassland. From Waskada (PR 251 at 452), follow the signs six kms south and three kms east.

Bartley Kives

At the confluence of the Antler and Souris rivers, you'll find **Sourisford Park**, believed to be the oldest park in western Canada. It sits on Road 158 West, which can be reached by taking Road 10 North, east of Highway 83, or from PR 201 west of small community of Coulter.

South of the park, you can follow signs uphill on Road 8 North to the incorrectly named "Sourisford Burial Mounds," which are fenced off at the top of a hill. This is actually a sacred indigenous site protected by Parks Canada as **Linear Mounds National Historic Site**. The 200-metre-long burial mounds, which have been disturbed by archeologists and sacked by relic hunters, are part of a series of similar ancient earthworks erected by indigenous ancestors across Montana, Saskatchewan, Manitoba, and North Dakota. Parks Canada does not wish the mounds to be visited by the public, in deference to Dakota elders who wish to save them from further exploitation. Efforts to develop an interpretive centre off-site have also stalled, partly because continuing anger over removal of human remains – but also partly because of economic interests. Underground mineral-rights holders have little interest in drawing attention to the presence of ancient and culturally invaluable mounds all over southwestern Manitoba's booming oil patch.

And about 30 minutes northeast of Melita, **Lauder Sand Hills Provincial Wildlife Management Area** protects an area of sandy hills best visited in late June and early July, when prickly-pear and pincushion cacti are blooming. (Yes, there are small cacti all over southern Manitoba.) A maze of trails is accessible from PR 254 west of the town of **Hartney** (Highway 21 at the Souris River).

Trans-Canada West

The westernmost major waterfowl area in southwestern Manitoba is **Oak Lake**, a shallow marsh divided by a two-km-long dike. You can look for birds along the dike or launch canoes at either **Oak Lake Beach** or **Oak Lake Provincial Recreation Park**, both accessible from PR 254, which heads south from the Trans-Canada west of the town of Oak Lake.

An oil derrick amind a wheatfield, north of Virden.

To the west, **Virden** (pop. 3,114) is one of the worst speed traps along the entire 7,821-km length of *La Transcanadienne*. Slow down and assume the Mounties are watching you. When you come to a halt, check out the chateau-style former **CP Rail Station** (425 Sixth Ave. South), which now houses the **Virden Community Arts Council gallery** and gift shop, open weekdays. Another unusual structure is **The Aud Theatre** (228 Wellington St. West), a 450-seat opera house built in 1912 and still in use today. You likely won't be able to take a peek inside, however – it's usually only open for performances (virdencommunityarts.ca).

Bartley Kives

As the last sizable town on the Trans-Canada before Saskatchewan, Virden is a wise place to grab a bite if you're continuing west. Chow down on classic Manitoba fare – bison burgers, pan-fried pickerel and perogies – at **Farmhouse Bistro & Tavern** (daily, 558 Frame St. East, 204.748.6959) or a steak at **T's Dining & Lounge** (Mon-Sat, 235 Nelson St. West, 204.748.1141).

Continuing west, the village of **Elkhorn** (pop. 470) is home to the **Manitoba Antique Auto Museum** (daily May to September, 204.845.2161, $7.50 adults/$2 kids), a collection of 75 vintage cars built between 1902 and 1933. From Elkhorn, the Saskatchewan border is 18 kilometres to the west.

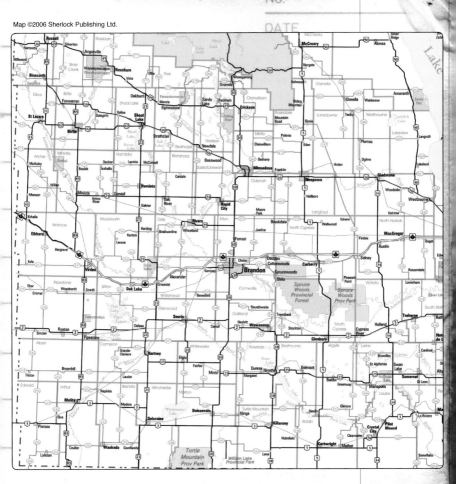

Map ©2006 Sherlock Publishing Ltd.

Southwestern Manitoba Daytrips

Spruce Woods Sojourn

Begin and end: Winnipeg.

When to go: May-September.

1. In Winnipeg, head west on Portage Avenue, which becomes Highway 1 west of the city limits. At the western edge of Headingley, stop at **Nick's Inn** (daily, 5392 Portage Ave., 204.889.4548) for a gloriously unhealthy breakfast.

2. From Headingley, cruise 147 kms west on Highway 1 to Highway 5. Turn left and drive 21 kms south into Spruce Woods Provincial Park and the Epinette Creek trailhead. Cycle or walk the 13-km (return) front section of the **Epinette Creek Trail**, up to the third shelter and back. To save time on foot, consider just the five-km return front section of the trail.

3. Back on Highway 5, drive eight kms south to the **Spirit Sands** trailhead. Hike to the dunes and back or walk the entire nine-km trail network, which also includes the colour-shifting Devil's Punchbowl.

Map ©2006 Sherlock Publishing Ltd.

4. Back at Highway 5, drive 11 kms south to Highway 2. Turn left and drive 15 kms east to Park Road, also known as Road 71 West. Head north 15 kms on Park Road back into the park to **The Hogsback**, a ridge affording a decent view.

5. Double back to Highway 2. If it's still daylight – which means you got up early or skipped one of the trails – drive east 16 kms to the town of Holland. Drive nine kms south on Highway 34; on your left, you'll see a "monastery" sign. Turn left and follow this road to the **Abbey of Our Lady of the Prairies**, where the monks will sell you fantastic Trappist cheese if the retail store is open.

6. About 350 metres east of the road to the abbey, Highway 34 meets PR 245. Follow PR 245 21 kms east to Notre Dame des Lourdes. Grab a burger at **Andy & Wendy's Drive Inn** (daily, 164 Notre Dame Ave., 204.248.2343), if it's still open.

7. Drive 13 kms north on PR 244 to Highway 2 and take it back to Winnipeg.

To the Turtle and Back

Begin and end: Brandon.
When to go: May-September.

1. Load up for breakfast at **Komfort Kitchen** (daily, 835 Princess Ave., 204.727.6867). Take Princess Avenue east to First Street and then north to PR 457, also known as the Low Road To Shilo.

2. Drive east on PR 457 for 17 kms to PR 340. Drive south 150 metres and exit on to Waggle Springs Road. Drive south on Waggle Springs 1.5 kms to Thompson Road, make a right and check out the snakes and lizards at **Westman Reptile Gardens** (daily, 204.763.4030, reptilegardens.ca).

3. Leaving the reptile gardens, head east on Thompson Road to PR 340. Drive south 32 kms to Highway 2, passing by **Shilo** and through **Wawanesa** along the way. Head east on Highway 2 for 4.5 kms and then south on Highway 18 for 18 kms to the Pelican Lake resort town of **Ninette**.

Map ©2006 Sherlock Publishing Ltd.

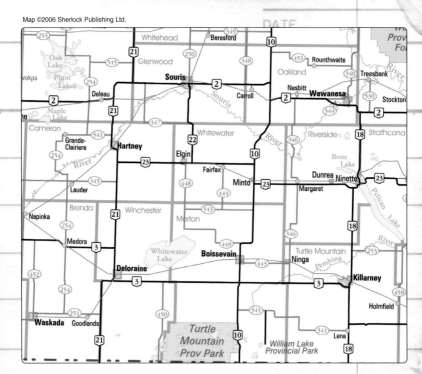

4. Drive west on Highway 23 for 29 kms, then south on Highway 10 for 22 kms to **Boissevain**. Visit the excellent **Moncur Gallery** (Tues-Sat, 436 South Railway St. 204.534.2433, moncurgallery. org), in the basement of the public library, to learn about the millennia-long indigenous presence in southwestern Manitoba.

5. Grab an Americano to go at **Sawmill Tea & Coffee Co.** (296 South Railway St., 204.534.2232) on your way out of town and drive 26 kms south on Highway 10 to **International Peace Gardens** (peacegarden.com) at the US border. You don't need a passport, but make sure you have I.D. in order to get back into Canada.

6. After checking out the gardens, drive six kms north to the **Adam Lake Recreation Area** at **Turtle Mountain Provincial Park** and take a dip.

7. Still have daylight? Good. Drive north 14 kms on Highway 10 to Highway 3. Drive 11 kms west to Road 122 West, also known as Strathallan Road, and follow the wildlife-watching signs eight kms north to **Whitewater Lake Wildlife Management Area**, a fantastic birdwatching spot.

8. Losing steam? Head back to Brandon by retracing your steps to Highway 3 and Highway 10 and driving north. Still have time for dinner? Leave Highway 10 at Highway 23, 27 kms north of Boissevain. Drive 16 kms west on Highway 23 to Highway 22 and 20 kms north to **Souris**. Check out the swinging bridge and grab a pizza at **Woodfire Deli** (daily, 39 Crescent Ave., 204.483.2795). Then head back to Brandon on Highways 2 and 10.

Bartley Kives

10

PARKLAND

A big, triangle-shaped chunk of western Manitoba, The Parkland takes its name from two of the largest natural areas in the province, Riding Mountain National Park and Duck Mountain Provincial Park.

Neither of these places are actual mountains, but plateaus that rise up to 400 metres off the Manitoba Lowlands. During the fur-trade era, travellers would ditch their canoes and switch to horses to make their way up the Manitoba Escarpment and across the forested high ground. During the pioneer era, most of the land in the region was cleared for agricultural use, which turned Riding Mountain and Duck Mountain into the ecological equivalent of islands on the prairie.

Within the parks, especially Riding Mountain, there are impressive numbers of moose, elk, black bears, beavers, coyotes, and other mammals, including small populations of wolves and cougars. Outside the parks, you're more likely to see white-tailed deer, relative newcomers to Manitoba that seem to thrive wherever humans go.

The largest community in the Parkland is Dauphin, a largely Ukrainian city in a valley between the prairie "mountains." The other dominant features are the west sides of lakes Manitoba and Winnipegosis, a dramatically deep stretch of the Assiniboine River Valley, and the tallest hills in Manitoba – Baldy Mountain in Duck Mountain Provincial Park, and Hart Mountain in the Porcupine Hills.

Opposite: A view from Reeve's Ravine, on the east face of Riding Mountain, which rises 343 metres from the flat Manitoba Lowlands.

Riding Mountain National Park

The only road-accessible national park in Manitoba, **Riding Mountain National Park** is one of the few places in the province you absolutely must visit. The 3,000-square-km park offers excellent wildlife-watching opportunities, a large cross-country ski-trail network, multi-day offroad bike trips, and hiking that actually involves some elevation gain. Add in deep, cold Clear Lake and the resort town of Wasagaming, and you have a park for all sorts of tourists, from merino-clad weekend warriors to young families to senior citizens in RVs.

MUST SEE:
Riding
Mountain
National Park
Manitoba's only road-accessible national park, with excellent wildlife-watching opportunities and hundreds of kilometres of hiking, cross-country skiing, and mountain-biking trails.

Riding Mountain lost much of its forest and grasslands to logging and fires when settlers arrived in numbers about a century ago. By the time the park was established in 1933, much of the wildlife had already been wiped out by a combination of hunting, trapping, and habitat destruction.

Most of the mammals have since recovered, as Riding Mountain now boasts 10,000 beavers, thousands of elk, moose and deer, hundreds of black bears and coyotes, about 70 wolves, a captive herd of 35 bison, a small number of lynx, and a handful of cougars. Motorists driving through the park on Highway 10 or 19 should drive slowly and cautiously to avoid wildlife collisions, as moose, deer, and bears are often spotted along roadsides. You may have more trouble spotting critters from the trail, as high brush during the summer will obscure your view. Wildlife watchers may want to travel by bike or horseback to get a better perspective, or visit during the leafless fall or winter.

There are more than 425 kms of hiking, biking, backpacking, and bridle paths within the park, with about 210 kms open for cross-country skiing, skate-skiing, or snowshoeing during the winter. Since many of the routes follow old logging roads, few are physically demanding or extremely technical. The biggest danger

Bartley Kives

you'll encounter in the Riding Mountain backcountry is the potential loss of your food to black bears – or run-ins with aggressive elk or moose during the spring rutting season. Needless to say, keep your distance from animals and lock your food up in bear boxes or vehicles.

Female moose grazing right along Highway 10 in early July. Drivers are urged to lay off the gas anywhere inside the park to avoid hurting themselves and wildlife.

As a national park, Riding Mountain charges a set of fees that are different from those in all provincial parks. Daily entrance fees are $7.80 for adults, $6.55 for seniors and $3.90 for youths – or $19.80 for a group of up to seven people. Annual passes are $39.20 for adults, $34.30 for seniors, $19.60 for youths or $98.10 for groups.

Car-camping sites range from $15.70 for unserviced campgrounds to $38.20 for campsites with full-service hookups at the extremely popular Wasagaming Campground. Backcountry camping is $15.70 per campsite, per night, while fishing permits are $9.80 per day or $24.30 for the season. You can reserve campsites at Wasagaming at 888.737.3783 and backcountry campsites at 204.848.7275 – or both at reservation.parkscanada.gc.ca.

Generally speaking, Riding Mountain can be divided into four main areas. The vast majority of visitors heads to heavily developed Wasagaming and Clear Lake, home to all hotels and restaurants in the park. Highway 10 slices through the middle of the park, connecting Wasagaming and Dauphin. The steeper trails of the Manitoba Escarpment, on the east side of the park, attract the largest numbers of mountain bikers and hikers. The western section of the park has most of the longer trails and truly wild places in Riding Mountain.

Bryan Scott

Wasagaming and Clear Lake

Like Banff, Jasper, and Grand Canyon Village, the seasonal resort of **Wasagaming** looks and feels like a national park town. Hundreds of cottages, a dozen hotels and souvenir shops, three golf courses, and the 500-site Wasagaming Campground are crammed into a townsite on the south side of Clear Lake, the largest body of water in Riding Mountain.

Wasagaming, which sits just inside the park on Highway 10, is the only place most Riding Mountain visitors see. They're drawn by the beach and marina at consistently chilly **Clear Lake**, but also by the town itself, as restrictions on neon signage and building materials have preserved the historic character of a community originally founded in 1908 as Clark's Beach. The name Wasagaming, Cree for "clear water," wasn't adopted until the park's 1933 opening.

Besides the lake, townsite attractions include the **Riding Mountain Visitor Centre** (daily July through August; Thursday-Monday Victoria Day to Canada Day and Labour Day to Thanksgiving, 133 Wasagaming Drive, 204.848.7275), where you'll find interpretive displays, a library, a gift shop and park info. You can also purchase vehicle and backcountry permits here. Nearby **Pinewood Museum** (afternoons in July and August, 154 Wasagaming Drive, 204.848.2810) offers more Riding Mountain history, including exhibits about Grey Owl, the British-born naturalist who lived in the park with two pet beavers in 1931 – and pretended he was indigenous. There's also information about a prisoner-of-war camp that operated inside the park during the Second World War.

Non-park-related flicks are screened daily at movie house **Park Theatre** (mid-May to Thanksgiving, 117 Wasagaming Drive, 204.848.2423, parktheatre.ca, $10 adults/$7 kids/seniors), the largest log-cabin cinema in North America. The same rustic

MUST SEE:
Wasagaming
& Onanole
A rustic national-park town on the south side of Riding Mountain and an approach town just outside its limits – with lodges, campgrounds, a log-cabin movie house and even a Clear Lake cruise ship. Clear Lake is pictured here.

structure houses **T. R. McKoy's Italian Restaurant** (daily mid-May to Thanksgiving, 117 Wasagaming Drive, 204.848.2217) a seafood-pasta parlour and steakhouse that positions itself at the upper end of Wasagaming's half-dozen restaurants. Also during high season, you can also tear into cinnamon buns at **White House Bakery & Restaurant** (daily, 104 Buffalo Drive, 204.848.7700) or bison burgers at **Wig Wam** (132 Wasagaming Drive, 204.848.7752).

You can have dinner on the water by boarding **The Martese** (Victoria Day to Thanksgiving, 204.848.1770, theclearlakemarina.com), a cruise ship that encircles Clear Lake from the Wasagaming marina. The 19-metre, 98-passenger yacht plied the waters of Lake Okanagan, BC, before Wasagaming entrepreneur Sheldon Willey trucked it to Manitoba in pieces and reassembled it on Clear Lake. In July and August, the ship leaves four times daily. Cruises at 1 and 3 p.m. are $17 for adults, $11 for youths and $7.50 for kids. The 6 p.m. dinner cruises are $60 for adults and $30 for kids, while the 9 p.m. sunset cruises are $17 per person.

A network of trails allows you see most of Clear Lake on foot or by bike. The 12-km **Southshore Trail** extends from Wasagaming northwest to Keeseekowenin Ojibway First Nation's reserve on the northwest side of the lake. The 3.5-km **Lakeshore Trail** follows the shoreline through the town, while the 9.5-km **Northshore Trail** encircles the east side of Clear Lake. Other trails in town include

Charles Shilliday

Black bears are common in Riding Mountain.

the 5.5-km **Wasagaming Bike Trail**, the two-kilometre **Ominisk Marsh Trail**, and the 3.5-km **South Lake loop**, the latter two located just west of the town proper, and open only to hikers.

The most popular place to stay in the resort town is **Wasagaming Campground** (mid-May to mid-October), which has 508 campsites ($27.40 to $38.70) as well as yurts ($56.50) and cabin-like A-frame tents ($70-$90). Reservations can be made as early as April at 204.848.7275 or reservation.parks-canada.gc.ca.

Hotel options include **New Chalet** (May-October, 116 Wasagaming Drive, 204.848.2892, newchalet.com, rooms $120-$150), boutique hotel **The Lake House** (May-October, 128 Wasagaming Drive, stay-lakehouse.ca, rooms $149-$239) and the year-round **Elkhorn Resort Spa & Conference Centre** (3 Mooswa Drive East, 204.848.2802, elkhornresort.mb.ca, rooms $100-$249, chalets $275 to $940). While the Elkhorn's rooms are somewhat dorm-like and the private cabins are over-priced, the resort redeems itself with an open-air jacuzzi, Solstice Spa, and in the summer, riding stables at adjacent Triangle Ranch. Elkhorn also has the only year-round restaurant option inside the park gate – **Mountain Grill**, where you can tuck into Manitoba lamb, bison short ribs, pan-fried pickerel and wild-boar gnocchi.

Elkhorn also works with Onanole-based **Earth Rhythms** (204.867.7152, earthrhythms.ca), an ecotourism outfit run by former Riding Mountain ranger Celes Davar, which offers wildlife-watching tours and bike trips as well as culinary and cultural tours. Tour prices vary. Earth Rhythms operates all year, with activities dependent on the season.

On your own, there are several trails to check out in the Clear Lake area, within a 10-minute drive from Wasagaming. The short **Arrowhead** (3.4 kms) and **Brûlé** (1.9 kms) trails, the moderate **Kinosao** (7.3 kms), and the long day hike to **Grey Owl's Cabin** (17.4 kms, return) depart from trailheads on either sides of Highway 19, which leaves Highway 10 east of Wasagaming. Both the Kinosao and Grey Owl trails are also open to mountain bikes.

One kilometre farther east of the Grey Owl trailhead, a short access road leads south from Highway 19 to small **Lake Katherine**, where you'll find the 2.4-km **Loon's Island Trail** and also **Shawenequanape Kipi-Che-Win**, a.k.a. Southquill Camp, a replica of a traditional Ojibway village. It offers overnight stays inside tee-pees, and Ojibway cultural programs.

Another five-kilometre east on Highway 19, a side road leads to an unserviced campground at **Whirlpool Lake** ($15.70) and the eight-km **Cowan Lake Trail**, which passes by a single backcountry campsite before hooking up with the Grey Owl trail.

Unlike its Alberta cousins Banff and Jasper, Wasagaming almost turns into a ghost town every winter, with only the Elkhorn resort remaining open. Most winter visitors come to Riding Mountain for the cross-country skiing, although fewer trails are now maintained due to budget cutbacks at Parks Canada. Volunteers now help groom and maintain ski and snowshoe trails.

In the Wasagaming area, the eight-kilometre **Wasagaming Campground**, 3.4-km **South Lake** and 8.2-km **Compound East** ski trails are regularly groomed, as are the 17.5-km **Grey Owl**, 6.7-km **Whirlpool Lake** and 3.2-km **Lake Katherine** trails off Highway 19. The 3.4-km **Arrowhead** and 4.2-km **Brûlé** trails, also off Highway 19, are reserved for snowshoeing.

The Escarpment

Riding Mountain actually looks like a mountain when you're at the eastern fringe of the park, home to some of the steepest inclines on the Manitoba Escarpment. These slopes rise about 400 metres off the low-lying farmland to the east, an elevation gain equivalent to a quarter of the depth of the Grand Canyon.

Highway 19 winds down the escarpment before exiting the park at the **East Gate National Historic Site**, a fort-like wooden structure built in 1933, when the gravel road provided the only vehicle access to Clear Lake. No other road in Manitoba has such steep switchbacks, which makes it a fun, short drive.

Bartley Kives

Bald Hill, on the east face of Riding Mountain.

Five trails allow hikers and cyclists to climb or descend the escarpment in the east side of the park. The most-popular route is the 6.4-km **Gorge Creek Trail,** a dedicated day-hiking route that follows Highway 19; its eastern trailhead sits near the East Gate site.

The longer 11.1-km **Packhorse,** 8.4-km **Bald Hill** and 7.8-km **J. E. T Hill** trails – also open to mountain bikes and equestrians – connect with the hilltop **North Escarpment trail** and a backcountry campsite at **East Deep Lake.** Despite the elevation gain, there are only a handful of lookouts along these trails – this area is a little more rewarding for bikers than it is for hikers. To reach the eastern trailhead for these routes from Highway 5, drive north past Highway 19 and turn left at the gravel road opposite PR 462. When you reach the park boundary, turn left and keep your eyes peeled for the parking lot on the right.

The newest trail on the escarpment, **Reeve's Ravine** (11.5 kms), was built with mountain bikes in mind and actually affords nice views. It connects with the Bald Hill and J.E.T. trails; the trailhead is located north of the East Gate, adjacent the 2.2-km **Burls & Bittersweet** walking trail.

Higher up the escarpment, on the south side of Highway 19, the 37-km **South Escarpment Trail** is no longer maintained, so expect to bush-crash if you use it. It provides access to the seven-km **Muskrat Lake spur trail, Muskrat Lake** backcountry campsite and the seven-km **Robinson Lake loop.**

There are two more trails in the northeast corner of the park. The 6.4-km **Oak Ridge** Trail is a day-hiking route, while the two-km **Scott Creek Trail** leads to a hike-in campsite overlooking the northeast corner of the escarpment. To reach these trails, drive north on Highway 5 to the town of McCreary, then west on PR 261 through the McKinnon Creek park entrance. Keep going until you see the trailhead on the right.

In the winter, the North Escarpment trail is maintained but not groomed for skiing (17.6 kms, return, from Highway 19), while Oak Ridge (10.4 kms) is groomed.

At any time of year, if you're driving up to the escarpment side of the park from Neepawa via Highway 5 and don't have a Riding Mountain park pass, purchase your permit at the Tempo station in McCreary to avoid an hour-long detour to Wasagaming.

The Highway 10 Corridor

The only road straight through Riding Mountain, Highway 10 is the most direct way to get from Brandon to Dauphin – and one of the biggest threats to wildlife in the park. The speed limit along the 50-kilometre stretch between Clear Lake and the park's north entrance is 80 km/h, but it's a good idea to drive even slower at night. Moose head onto the highway in March and April to lick road salt, deer and bears frequently cross during the summer and fall, and coyotes may jog along the shoulder to avoid deep winter snow. For obvious reasons, this is a great place to observe animals, provided you drive slowly and are aware of other motorists, who may not be so careful. If you see a large critter, do *not* get out of your car – bears, moose, and elk are a lot faster than you think.

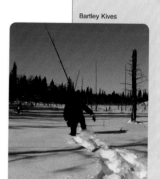

Bartley Kives

Snowshoeing in deep, mid-February powder near the Bead Lakes in Riding Mountain National Park.

There are six trails along this stretch of road. Ten kms north of Clear Lake, the 25-km **Ochre River Trail** heads northwest through the park, descending along the Ochre River most of the way. Along the way, there are two backcountry campsites, one horse camp, and **Cairns Cabin** ($73.50, 204.848.7275) which cross-country skiers in groups of three to 12 may reserve during the winter as an overnight shelter for a 26.4-km (return) trip from Highway 10. The trail is only maintained occasionally during the winter.

Continuing north, the four-km **Bead Lakes loop** makes for an easy summer hike or winter snowshoe excursion, while the one-km **Boreal Trail** is accessible to people in wheelchairs. **Moon Lake** has an unserviced campground ($15.70), a swim dock, and a 9.2-km hiking/snowshoeing loop. There are more short day hikes/ski routes at **Kippan's Mill** (1.2 kms hiking/7.2 kms skiing) and **Beach Ridges** (3.5 kms hiking and skiing), the latter just south of the park entrance.

Bartley Kives

The nearby **Crawford Creek trail** can be used for a 10-km (return) summer day hike or winter cross-country-ski jaunt. Three more ski trails start from this area: **Edwards Creek** (5.6 kms), **Broadleaf** (4.2 kms) and **Hilton** (16 kms, return).

Put in the trail time, and you'll see critters: A bull moose bathes in a bog along the Moon Lake hiking trail.

Bartley Kives

A Thanksgiving morning frost along the Tilson loop (above); an August goldenrod bloom along the Birdtail loop (below).

The Wilder West

Riding Mountain's large and almost-roadless west side is the wildest portion of the park, with few sightseers going farther west than the captive **bison range at Lake Audy,** in the middle of the park. About three dozen of the beasts graze inside the three-square-km enclosure. You can observe the bison from inside your vehicle or from a covered interpretive display. Just don't go walking around – bison can sprint up to 50 km/h, and tend to be very aggressive. Located west of Clear Lake, the range is accessible from a summer road that branches off Highway 10 just north of the lake, or via PR 354 just south of the park. Lake Audy has an unserviced campground ($15.70) – outside the bison enclosure, of course.

Most of the other attractions on the west side of the park are hiking and cycling trails. The granddaddy of them all is the 67-km **Central Trail,** which follows an old logging road from Audy Lake to a western trailhead at Bob Hill Lake. Allow three to five days for hiking, or two or three for mountain biking.

Bartley Kives

Every other trail in the west side of the park connects to the Central Trail. The 10-km (one-way) **Strathclair Trail,** which heads north from Lake Audy, is popular with wildlife watchers during the fall elk-mating season, when bulls issue surprisingly loud bugling noises. The 15-km **Grasshopper Valley Trail** loops around Lake Audy and makes for a relatively easy overnight hike, while just to the west, the 14-km **Long Lake Trail** can be tacked on to Strathclair and part of Grasshopper to create a north-south Riding Mountain through-hike.

Farther west, there are three more spur trails and two long loops. The 39-km **Tilson Lake loop**, which partly follows the Birdtail Creek Valley, makes for a decent two-night/three-day back-packing route. Camp at the Tilson Lake and Birdtail backcountry sites. The Tilson trailhead is just inside the park at the Deep Lake warden station, accessible from PR 264, north of Rossburn.

The **Birdtail loop** is a better choice for a single-night back-packing trip. Listed as 11 kms, it's actually 26 kms, return. Start at Bob Hill Lake, at the end of the Deep Lake Road, and bed down at Kay's campsite, near the northern edge of the park.

If you'd like to visit the west side of the park but aren't into backcountry camping, stay at the unserviced Deep Lake camp-ground ($15.70). There's also a 10-km cross-country ski trail at **Deep Lake** and two more groomed trails further west in the park, north of PR 264, at **Flat Lake** and **Bydak Lake**.

Riding Mountain Gateway Towns

While rustic Wasagaming is a pretty tourist town, there are some things you can't do inside a national park. Only three kms south, the Riding Mountain gateway town of **Onanole** (Highway 10 at PR 262) is the place to buy booze, watch fireworks on Victoria Day and Canada Day, play minigolf and maybe snag a campsite at the height of the summer season.

Motorists in Riding Mountain National Park slow down to watch a black bear cub cross Highway 10. Traffic 'jams' are common in the summer.

When Wasagaming Campground is full, try **Onanole RV Park and Campground** (Highway 10, 204.848.2398, campingmanitoba.com, serviced sites $44.77) or **Sportsman's Park** (Highway 10, 204.848.2520, sportsmanspark. ca, sites $36-$39). The latter has an 18-hole mini-golf course.

Onanole is also home to the highly regarded **Foxtail** (daily year-round, Highway 10 at Victor Avenue, 204.848.2195), whose wood-fired pizzas and paninis are made with ingredi-

Bartley Kives

ents sourced from artisanal Manitoba producers. There are vegan and gluten-free options. **Poor Michael's Emporium** (May-October, Highway 10 & Albin Avenue, 204.848.0336), which started out as a bookstore, now sells decent espresso and light vegetarian snacks.

Fifteen kms northwest of Onanole on PR 354, **Trailhead Ranch** (204.848.7649, trailhead-ranch.com, bed-and-breakfast $35), offers horseback trail rides and multi-day trips in Riding Mountain

National Park. Options range from $38 for a two-hour ride to $235 per day for guided backcountry trips with meals and tent accommodations.

Fifteen kms south of Onanole, **Erickson** (Highway 10) is the best place to load up on groceries on your final approach to the park. A statue of a Viking ship pays tribute to the community's Scandinavian heritage.

West of Erickson, **Sandy Lake** (Highway 45 at PR 250) operates the **Ukrainian Cultural Heritage Museum** (July and August, free admission). On the second weekend in August, volunteers bake bread at an outdoor clay oven.

Continuing west, **Oakburn** (Highway 45 and PR 577) marks the turnoff to Baldy Lake, where you can access the middle of Riding Mountain's Central Trail. If you have time for a diversion, drive north on PR 577, turn right at PR 566 just past the town of Olha and head six kms east until you come to two rustic A-frames covered in straw. These are recreations of the *budda*s used as shelters by Ukrainian pioneers at the beginning of the 20th century.

Still farther west, **Rossburn** (Highway 45 and PR 264) is your exit point if you're heading to Riding Mountain's Deep Lake entrance. West of Rossburn, Highway 45 dips into the scenic Birdtail Creek Valley at **Waywayseecappo First Nation** (pop.

Bartley Kives

Ferns, ferns, everywhere: Lush mid-summer foliage in Riding Mountain National Park.

1,219) before continuing west to **Angusville** (Highway 45 and PR 476), the gateway to Riding Mountain's westernmost Moose Lake entrance. Angusville's **Heritage Hall**, which sports a trio of Byzantine-style domes, is worth a quick driveby.

On the east side of the park, tiny **Kelwood** (east of Highway 5 on Road 110 North) warrants a spot on the map for hosting the **Harvest Sun Music Festival** (theharvestsun.com), a mid-August folk-and-roots music festival. Weekend passes for the three-day event are $75 for adults and $35 for youths, day passes run from $31 to $42 and camping is $16 for tents and $42 for RVs. If you're driving past the town toward Riding Mountain's east entrance during the summer, stop in at **White Rabbit Café** (Tues-Sat seasonally, 8 Mountain Ave., 204.967.2548) for a sandwich or a slice of pie.

Assiniboine River Valley

In southern Manitoba, the meandering Assiniboine River isn't much to look at. But west of Riding Mountain, the river flows through a majestic valley that's roughly two kilometres wide and 100 metres deep. Like many of the province's features, this valley was carved by a torrent of glacial meltwater around 10,500 years ago. Today, the ancient spillway's slopes make for excellent mountain biking, passable downhill skiing and fishing on Lake of the Prairies, a body of water created in 1968, when the Assiniboine was dammed near the mouth of the Shell River.

The main route along the most dramatic stretch of this valley is Highway 83, which runs loosely parallel to the river for 50 kms between the agricultural centres of Russell and Roblin.

Charles Shilliday

Russell

The gateway to the Assiniboine River Valley, Russell (pop. 1,669) is a convenient pit stop at the confluence of highways 16, 45, and 83. As the westernmost Manitoba community of any size on the Yellowhead Highway, the town has a **Travel Manitoba**

Rolling terrain in the Assiniboine River Valley.

information centre (May-September, Highway 16 at 83), and more than its share of places to crash, most notably the large Russell Inn (Highway 83, 204.773.3186 russellinn.com, rooms $94-$184) and **Boulton Manor Suites** (322 Memorial Ave. South, 204.773.3267, rooms $80-$120). The latter is a bed-and-breakfast in an 1894 mansion once owned by Charles Boulton, who fought for the Canadian government against Louis Riel in both the 1869 Red River Resistance and the 1885 North-West Rebellion in Saskatchewan.

Asessippi Provincial Park

Lake of the Prairies is Manitoba's modest equivalent of Utah's infamous Lake Powell. Created by dams, both are narrow, artificial bodies of water that attract boaters and anglers but lack the look, feel and ecology of genuine natural areas.

Most of the development along Lake of the Prairies is concentrated in **Asessippi Provincial Park** (PR 482), a 23-square-km recreation area encompassing the bottom of the lake, Shellmouth Dam, and the lower part of the steep Shell River Valley, another glacial spillway.

From early December to the first weekend in April, there are 21 downhill-ski and snowboard runs on the Shell at **Asessippi Ski Area and Winter Park** (end of Assessippi Avenue, 204.564.2000, asessippi.com). Asessippi has two lifts, a snow-tubing area, a half-pipe and terrain parks for snowboards and a lodge with fast-food franchises and a pub. Lift tickets are $50 a day for adults, $42.50 for youths and $38.25 for kids. Snow tubing is $29.25 for adults, $21.75 for youths and $19.58 for kids. The ski area occupies the southeast corner of the provincial park. From Highway 83, head west on PR 482 for two kms and turn right into the Shell River Valley. There's no lodging at the site, so most skiers stay in Russell or nearby Inglis.

MUST SEE:
Assiniboine & Shell River valleys
Glacial meltwaters carved out spillways through the prairies. They're now home to Lake of the Prairies and the Asessippi Provincial Park.

Keep following PR 482 west to reach the main entrance to the park at the east end of the Shellmouth Dam. The park has a marina, boat launch, beach and a campground (sites $23.10-$27.30, yurts $56.50).

Asessippi also has three short hiking trails. The 1.6-km **Cherry** and 2.3-km **Aspen** trails are flat, but the three-km (return) **Ancient Valley Trail** involves a short climb up and down the Assiniboine River Valley. You'll probably have the trail to yourself – most people come to the park to fish for pickerel (walleye).

Asessippi to Roblin

East of Asessippi, a particularly scenic stretch of the Trans Canada Trail follows a bend in the Bear Creek to the hamlet of **Inglis** (PR 366 at PR 592), home to the **Inglis Grain Elevators National Historic Site**, a collection of five immense wooden structures from the early 20th century. They're worth a passing glance on the way to **St. Elijah Romanian Orthodox Church** (just west of PR 592, five kms north of Inglis), a 1903 structure founded by the only Romanian pioneer community in rural Manitoba.

Eight kilometres north of Inglis on Highway 83, there are 25 kms of challenging cross-country ski loops at **Rivendell X-Country & Uphill Skiing** (Dropmore Road, 204.564.2315, skitrails.ca, $8 donation), a privately maintained trail system one km west of the highway. Call ahead for trail conditions.

Another four kms north on Highway 83, turn east to visit the **Frank Skinner Arboretum** (daylight hours spring through fall, Road 166 North, 866.552.5496 skinnerarboretum.com, admission by donation) where a nursery, gardens, and a short trail celebrate the life's work of the celebrated Dropmore, Man., plant breeder who developed and introduced 150 different hybrids that could withstand the nasty Prairie winter.

You can also ride around most of Lake of the Prairies by taking a **100-km bicycle circle tour** using PR 482, Highway 83, the Trans Canada Trail, and a short section of Highway 5. Start at Russell in the south or in the north art **Roblin** (pop. 1,774), at the junction of Highways 83 and 5.

In Roblin, grab an organic waffle or a sandwich at **The Starving Artist** (Mon-Sat, 126 First Ave. Northwest, 204.937.2914), which also does Tex-Mex on Thursday nights. The other safe bet is **Metal Red's Pizza** (132 Main St., 204.937.4992).

Dauphin and Vicinity

The largest community in the Parkland, tree-lined **Dauphin** (pop. 8,251) is only three years younger than Winnipeg – a fur trade-era fort was established on the Vermilion River, on the plains north of Riding Mountain, in 1741.

Home to Assiniboine and Cree for centuries, Dauphin was visited first by French explorers, then British fur traders, and

Wendy Wilson/Prairie Pathfinders

Dauphin's Ukrainian Catholic Church of the Resurrection.

eventually Ukrainian settlers. It's now the unofficial capital of all things Ukrainian in Manitoba, even if it doesn't boast a single restaurant specializing in perogies, cabbage rolls, or other Carpathian culinary treats.

The city sits at the confluence of highways 5, 10, and 20, 15 kilometres from the northern entrance to Riding Mountain National Park. The best-known attraction is the Byzantine-domed **Ukrainian Catholic Church of the Resurrection** (1106 First St. Southwest, 204.638.5511, guided tours in July and August), a 1939 structure with an impressive interior. The gallery within **Watson Arts Centre** (weekday afternoons, 1104 First Ave. Northwest, 204.638.6231, watsonartscentre.com) hosts exhibits by Parkland artists. **Dauphin Rail Museum** (Thurs-Tues in July and August, 101 First Ave. Northwest) contains one of Canada's last surviving railway-station roundhouses.

Happily, **Fort Dauphin Museum** (weekdays May, June and September; Tues-Sun July and August; 140 Jackson St, 204.638.6630, fortdauphinmuseum.wordpress.com) goes well beyond the usual pioneer/fur trade exhibits typically found in Manitoba museums. Along with the wooden palisades of a recreated fort, Fort Dauphin documents the millennia-old indigenous presence in west-central Manitoba. Its collection includes 10,000 artifacts catalogued by the Parkland Archeological Laboratory. Admission is $4 for adults and $3 for youths.

If you want to stretch your legs in Dauphin, try the 1.4-km walking trail in Vermilion Park, in the middle of the city. If you'd rather put on calories, both of the locally owned **Corrina's** restaurants (daily, 1430 Main St., 204.638.7040 and 28 Memorial Blvd., 204.701.1100) are known for their burgers and, occasionally, Ukrainian platters.

For a bigger dose of Ukrainian culture, drive south from Dauphin on Highway 10 to the north slope of Riding Mountain, where the **Selo Ukraina Site** (open by appointment, 204.638.1554)

has a replica Ukrainian pioneer village and an 11,000-seat outdoor amphitheatre that serves as the focal point for two large summer festivals.

Leading into the Canada Day long weekend, **Dauphin's Countryfest** (countryfest.mb.ca) attracts more than 12,000 cowboys and urban wannabes to the biggest outdoor music festival in Manitoba (yes, it's bigger than the Winnipeg Folk Festival). Headliners at the four-day, three-stage event have included Carrie Underwood, Dierks Bentley, LeAnn Rimes, and Big & Rich. The vast majority of the Countryfest audience camps out at the site all weekend – the sea of RVs alone is something to behold. The massive party also seems to attract every resident of western Manitoba and eastern Saskatchewan between the ages of 16 and 25, so be prepared for a campground scene just as insane as the one at the Folk Fest, albeit with cans of Blue replacing buds of green as the intoxicant of choice. Weekend passes are $239, while day passes range from $79 to $89. Campsite passes are an additional $89.

Over the August long weekend, the far-less-rowdy **Canada's National Ukrainian Festival** (cnuf.ca) attracts Slavic musicians and dancers from across Canada. Weekend passes are $95, day passes range from $35 to $55 and camping costs $50.

MUST SEE: Dauphin's Countryfest
During the final days of June, Manitoba's largest outdoor music festival attracts 12,000 party-goers – some of them country music fans – from across southern Manitoba and eastern Saskatchewan.

Around Dauphin

If you didn't get your fill of Ukrainian heritage in Dauphin, a well-preserved set of hand-built pioneer dwellings stand on the **Wasyl Negrych Farmstead** (daily July and August, 204.548.2326) about a half-hour drive to the northwest. Ten log structures and an outdoor oven, all built between 1897 and 1910, were designed to emulate Ukrainian dwellings in the Carpathian Mountains. To reach the site from Dauphin, drive west on Highway 5 to Gilbert Plains, head north on PR 274 for 17 kms, and turn east on Negrych Road.

Gilbert Plains itself is best known for its giant golf ball. Continue west on Highway 5 and you'll reach the town of **Grandview**, a gateway to Duck Mountain Provincial Park (see below). Highway 5 then criss-crosses the scenic Valley River Valley on the way to Roblin and eventually Saskatchewan.

Southeast of Dauphin, on a northeast slope of Riding Mountain Provincial Park, the **Ochre River** is one of the most challenging whitewater routes in the province – but it's only possible to shoot during a very short window after the April snowmelt. The recommended paddling sections extend 25 kms from the border of Riding Mountain to a takeout on PR 582, south of the town of Ochre River. You'll need to consult a topographical map to find the put-in.

The Ochre River tumbles into walleye-rich **Dauphin Lake**, the smallest of Manitoba's "Great Lakes" at 519 square kms and a big draw for anglers. The most-popular access point is **Rainbow Beach Provincial Park**, 20 kms east of Dauphin on Highway 20. There's a boat launch and campground (May-September, $18.90-$23.10).

Forty kilometres east of Dauphin, **Ste. Rose du Lac** (pop. 1,023) is the most northern francophone town in Manitoba. Make a quick stop to see the stone **Ste. Rose Grotto** at Parc Dollard, just north of Highway 5 on the left side of PR 276. In the winter, the same spot marks the start of a short cross-country ski loop around a bend in the Turtle River.

About 60 kms north of Ste. Rose on PR 276, you'll find the only provincial park named after a mythical sea serpent. **Manipogo Provincial Park**, tucked into the northwestern cranny of Lake Manitoba, takes its name from a snake-like aquatic creature that supposedly frequented Lake Manitoba in the middle of the last century. Reports about Manipogo peaked around the same time people in BC claimed to see a Loch Ness–like sea monster of their own in Lake Ogopogo. Unlike deep, dark Loch Ness or Lake Ogopogo, Lake Manitoba is extremely shallow and thus unlikely to harbour many secrets. As a result, even the kookiest cryptozoologists hold little stock in tales about a Manitoban sea creature. If you visit Manipogo today, you'll find a campground (May-September, $18.90-$23.10), a beach, a boat launch, and a short hiking trail – but probably no plesiosaurs.

Duck Mountain Provincial Park

The highest plateau in Manitoba, **Duck Mountain Provincial Park** is a lot like Riding Mountain's redneck little brother. While Riding Mountain enjoys the protection of strict Parks Canada regulations, Duck Mountain – a tract of densely forested uplands – is scarred by ATV tracks and continues to be logged at a rate that makes con-servationists cry in their hemp-flavoured organic beer.

Almost two-thirds of this post-glacial landscape is open to logging, which is a shame, considering the natural beauty of what locals call "The Ducks." Dozens of little lakes are really puddles left behind by retreating glaciers, while the hills that cover the 1,424-square-kilometre plateau are comprised of sand and gravel carried over here by ice 12,000 years ago.

The tallest of the hills is **Baldy Mountain**, the highest point in Manitoba, which rises up from the southeast corner of the park. Peak-baggers seeking to visit the highest point in every Canadian province will be disappointed by the ease of access to the 831-metre summit: All you have to do is get out of your car and walk a couple of paces. An observation tower provides an even higher vantage point to see the aptly named Valley River Valley to the south. You can reach the Baldy Mountain parking lot from PR 366, the only north-south route through the park.

PR 367, the sole east-west artery, meets PR 366 near the **Blue Lakes**, popular scuba sites for divers training at altitude. Between East and West Blue Lake, there's **Blue Lake campground** (May-October, $18.90-$23.10), a townsite, and a pair of day-hiking trails. The 5.5-km **Blue Lakes Trail** is a decent little workout, while the one-km **Shining Stone Trail** is a just a leg-stretcher.

MUST SEE:
Baldy
Mountain
Manitoba's highest point isn't hard to reach, but you'll want to check it just peakbag the province on your way through Duck Mountain Provincial Park.

To the east of the Blue Lakes, the **Wapiti Trail** is a 4.5-km loop near the junction of PR 366 and 367. Farther east on PR 367, **Singuish Lake** has a beach and campground (May-September, $15.80). To the west of Blue Lakes, a 23-km, ATV-scarred hike-and-bike trail system at **Mossberry Lakes** connects with a built-up area at **Child's Lake**, home to more short hiking/ski loops and **Child's Lake campground** (May-September, sites $18.90-$24.15, yurts $56.50). In the southwest corner of the park, off PR 367, the 4.5-km **Shell River Valley loop trail** hugs the west side of Shell, which flows into the Assiniboine River at Asessippi.

Heading north from Blue Lakes on PR 366, flatwater paddlers can get their feet wet on the **Chain Lakes** and **Beaver Lake** paddling loops; the short distances involved make these flatwater routes attractive to novice canoeists and families with small kids. There are also decent day hikes at the **Spray Lake Trail** (5.5 kms return) and a good view from the 1.2-km **Copernicus Hill Trail**.

Continuing north on PR 366, **Wellman Lake** is the largest built-up area in the park, with a beach, campground (May-September, $18.90-$24.15) and accommodations at **Wellman Lake Lodge** (year round, 204.525.4543, wellmanlakelodge.com, cabins $165-$260). Stretch your legs on the 3.8-km **Glad Lake cross-country ski trail**, which, in summer, doubles as hiking access to Copernicus Hill.

Swan River Region

Almost five hours by car from Winnipeg, the Swan River Valley occupies a flat break in the Manitoba Escarpment between Duck Mountain, to the south, and the steep Porcupine Hills to the northwest. This plain doesn't see many tourists, as southern-Manitoban motorists driving north to Thompson, The Pas, or Flin Flon usually bypass this area by taking faster, relatively featureless highways 6 and 60.

The valley is the northernmost agricultural area in Manitoba, parallel in latitude to the northern Interlake and the Canadian Shield wilderness north of Atikaki Provincial Park. As such, it marks the transition between the tourist-oriented parkland and the lonelier, scruffier towns of Manitoba's north.

Swan River and Around

Sleepy, given its size, **Swan River** (pop. 3,907) is an agricultural hub that can be used as a base of operations for exploring the surrounding area. The town has the requisite pioneer displays at **Swan Valley Historical Museum** (May-September, one km north of Swan River on Highway 10, admission $2), a few chain and independent motels and restaurants including hometown-favourite **Pizza Place** (Mon-Sat, 600 Main St. East, 204.734.9374) and the nine-table, French-influenced **Madoco** (evenings Thurs-Sat, 124 Fifth Ave. North, 204.734.4718).

Southwest of Swan River, **Thunder Hill** rises above the valley alongside the Saskatchewan border. Archeological evidence

Wendy Wilson/Prairie Pathfinders

A view of the Swan River Valley from Thunder Hill.

suggests people first visited this hill 9,000 years ago; more recently, the Cree named it after the Thunderbird. A decent view of the Swan River Valley can be had all year from the **Thunder Hill Ski Area** (December-March, 204.539.2626, skithunderhill.ca, lift tickets $22 adults, $19 youths). From Swan River, head south on Highway 83 to PR 487 and head west until you reach the hill; follow the signs up. The summit is 32 kms from downtown Swan River.

Porcupine Hills Provincial Forest

North of Swan River on Highway 10, the **Porcupine Hills** rise up on the western horizon and continue well into Saskatchewan. The hills are home to the second-highest peak in Manitoba, **Hart Mountain**, at 821 metres above sea level.

Logging is the main activity in these highlands, but Manitoba Conservation & Water Stewardship runs three seasonal campgrounds in the hills. **Whitefish Lake Provincial Park** (May-September, $16.80) is located in the southwest corner of the park, at the end of PR 279, which branches off Highway 10 about 16 kms north of Swan River. Farther north, campgrounds **at Bell Lake Provincial Park** (May-September, $16.80) and **North Steeprock Lake** (May-September, $16.80) are located on PR 365, which snakes up into the hills just north of the town of Birch River.

There's also one long hike up the Manitoba Escarpment that may be tackled on foot or on a mountain bike. The 10-km (one-way) **Bellsite Trail** follows an old logging road into the hills from a trailhead off Highway 10, about one km north of the town of Bellsite.

Kettle Stones Provincial Park

One of the weirder places in Manitoba, **Kettle Stones Provincial Park** is a four-square-km island of grassland and mixed forest surrounded by the dense Jack pine, spruce, and aspen stands of Swan Pelican Provincial Forest. The main attractions are kettle stones — large sandstone boulders glued together by dissolved calcium carbonate from ancient seashells. These rare geological formations, sacred to the Cree, emerged about 8,500 years ago, when wave action on post-glacial Lake Agassiz broke up the surrounding muck.

Kettle stones ranging in diameter from 50 centimetres to five metres stand out like eerie monuments within this small park, located about 70 kms northeast of Swan River. Getting here, however, is a nightmare: Even locals get lost on the way, so it's a good idea to travel with a guide, if you can find one.

If you're hell-bent on making the trip on your own, the following directions may or may not actually get you there: From Swan River, take Highway 10 east to PR 268, then follow the road north 20.8 kms to an unmarked gravel road (if you reach Lenswood, you've gone too far). Turn right and follow a terrible dirt track east for about 25 kms. Do not attempt this in a regular passenger car or van. An off-road 4×4 truck should do the trick, but take a compass, GPS and topographical map, just in case. It's easy to get lost, as there are many other dirt tracks in the area.

Once again, this place is not easy to reach, so driver beware.

Lake Winnipegosis Salt Flats

North of the Porcupine Hills, Highway 10 follows the shore of Dawson Bay and Overflowing Bay, the westernmost corners of Lake Winnipegosis. Just north of the 53rd parallel, on the east side of the road, the **Lake Winnipegosis Salt Flats Ecological Preserve** protects an unusual area of pink, orange, and brown saline flats that are home to salt-tolerant plants, and, in late summer, thick mats of colourful microbial growth. Visitors to the site are asked to tread extremely lightly.

A similar site on the southwestern corner of Sagemace Bay, northwest of the town of Winnipegosis, was heavily mined for its salt more than a century ago.

Katarina Kupca

Parkland Daytrips

The author along the Riding Mountain's Tilson Loop, with the October foliage of the Birdtail Creek Valley in the distance.

A Taste of Riding Mountain

Begin and end: Wasagaming.

When to go: Victoria Day-Labour Day.

1. Start your day in Riding Mountain National Park with cinnamon buns in Wasagaming at **White House Bakery & Restaurant** (daily, 104 Buffalo Drive, 204.848.7700). Then head six kms east on Highway 10 to start of Highway 19.

2. Descend the Manitoba Escarpment on Highway 19, taking the gravel road 29 kms to the park's historic **East Gate**. Walk up and down a section of either **Gorge Creek trail** or **Reeve's Ravine** to stretch your legs for the morning; do an entire trail if you have time.

3. Back at the park's east gate, take Highway 19 five kms east to Highway 5. Drive seven kms south to Road 110 North and head east into Kelwood for a sandwich or a slice of pie at **White Rabbit Café** (Tues-Sat seasonally, 8 Mountain Ave., 204.967.2548).

4. Back on Highway 5, drive south 21 kms to PR 357, also known as **Mountain Road**. Ascend the escarpment on PR 357, driving 35 kms to Highway 10. Drive seven kms north and head west on Highway 45 for seven kms. Drive north on PR 270 for 14 kms until it merges with PR 354 and continue 18 kms north and west to Audy Lake Road. ✳

5. Drive nine kms north into the park to the **Audy Lake bison enclosure** to view Manitoba's symbolic creature.

6. Retrace your route to PR 354 and take it all the way east to Onanole, where there might be a seat and pizza waiting for you at **Foxtail** (daily, Highway 10 at Victor Avenue, 204.848.2195).

Parkland Peaks and Valleys

Begin and end: Dauphin.

When to go: May-September.

1. Start off with breakfast in Dauphin at **Corrina's On Main** (daily, 1430 Main St., 204.638.7040). Then prepare to head west of town.

2. From Dauphin, head west on Highway 5 45 kilometres to Grandview. Then head north on PR 366 for 34 kms, into **Duck Mountain Provincial Park** and up to **Baldy Mountain**, the highest point in Manitoba. Marvel at the Himalayas-like heights and try not to struggle with vertigo.

3. Back on PR 366, continue north 19 kms until it merges with PR 367. Follow PR 367 west 30 kms to the **Shell River Valley Trail** and go for a walk.

4. Continue west on PR 367 seven more kms until the junction with PR 594. Follow it 19 kms south until the junction with Highway 83. Head south 18 kms to **Roblin** and grab a sandwich at **The Starving Artist** (Mon-Sat, 126 First Ave. Northwest, 204.937.2914).

5. From Roblin, take Highway 5 west 13.5 kms, crossing the Assiniboine River Valley. Head south on PR 482 for 46 kms, at first straddling the Saskatchewan border before crossing the **Shellmouth Dam** at **Lake of The Prairies** and rolling through **Asessippi Provincial Park** before reconnecting with Highway 83.

6. Take Highway 83 north for 1.6 kms to PR 366. Drive east 3.5 kms to **Inglis** and check out one of the largest collections of big **grain elevators** still standing on the Prairies.

7. Continue east on PR 366, zigzagging 63 kms back to Highway 5 at Grandview —you're your return to Dauphin.

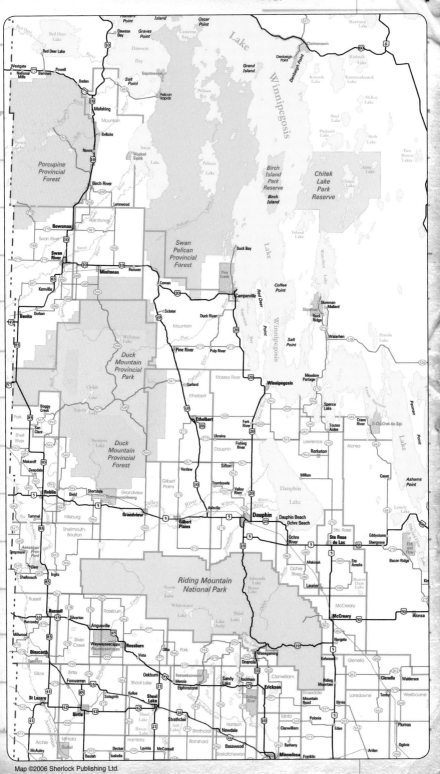

THE NORTH

11

Despite its image as a Prairie province, more than half of Manitoba is a rugged landscape incapable of growing so much as a stalk of wheat. The rocky Canadian Shield covers most of northern Manitoba, with the exception of a strip of tundra along Hudson Bay and the swampy limestone lowlands around Cedar Lake and the northwest side of Lake Winnipeg.

Cree and Dene have hunted and fished in this vast area for hundreds, if not thousands, of years. The first European explorers travelled up canoe routes from Hudson Bay in the 17th century. Fur traders followed in the following decades, and trapping took off, but most northern First Nations clung to hunter-gatherer lifestyles until the 20th century. The last truly nomadic people in the region, the Sayisi Dene, were forcibly removed from their traditional caribou-hunting lands in 1956.

Though some indigenous people continue to hunt, fish, and trap, northern Manitoba's economy is now based on mining, logging, hydroelectric power and tourism. There are few road-accessible communities, but the towns with industry are relatively large – Thompson, The Pas and Flin Flon are Manitoba's fifth-, 10th-, and 11th-largest cities.

There are four major highways in the region: Highway 6 runs up from the Interlake to Thompson; Highway 10 connects the Parkland to The Pas and Flin Flon; and Highways 39 and 60 connect the two north-south routes. Narrower roads lead to the mining towns of Snow Lake, Sherridon, and Lynn Lake, hydroelectric centre Gillam and Norway House Cree Nation, the latter at the north end of Lake Winnipeg. All other northern communities are only served by rail, floatplane, or ice road, including 16 economically depressed and extremely isolated First Nations.

Up until the 1980s, tourists visiting the North came primarily to hunt or fish. But lower-impact activities such as wilderness travel and wildlife-watching are on the rise, especially in Churchill, the Hudson Bay port town built next to the largest concentration of polar bears in the world.

Opposite: Polar bears are the main tourist draw up in Churchill, but the unusual outpost also boasts beluga whales, migratory birds, wildflowers, and spectacular northern lights.

Obviously, anyone visiting The North is coming for more than a daytrip. It takes 7.5 hours to drive from Winnipeg to Flin Flon or Thompson, while getting to Churchill by any means other than air travel will consume more than a day. But if you have the time, there are many fascinating sights up here, including unusual limestone formations at Clearwater and Iskwasum lakes and along northern Lake Winnipeg, two significant waterfalls along the Grass River, inquisitive beluga whales in the Churchill River estuary; and, in almost every town, the unusual, scruffy culture unique to Manitoba's north.

Manitoba Lowlands

Back in the 1990s, Parks Canada was instructed to establish a national park for all 39 ecological areas in the nation. They had 22 covered, and needed 17 more to go. One of those areas without a representative park was the Manitoba Lowlands, a huge crescent of very flat land that extends up from the US border, across the Central Plains and Interlake, and northwest into Saskatchewan.

Seeing as it didn't make sense to build a park on top of prime agricultural land, biologists, conservationists, and bureaucrats nominated two sparsely populated patches of land along lonely Highway 6 to become Manitoba's third national park. Plans were made, maps were drawn – and then absolutely nothing happened, as communities near the proposed park decided they didn't want a protected area in their backyards.

The proposed Manitoba Lowlands National Park, which would have been given a Cree name, was supposed to cover two sections of Lake Winnipeg's western shoreline above and below the town of Grand Rapids. The park would have protected hundreds of kilometres of pristine shoreline, one of the world's longest freshwater sand spits, stunning limestone cliffs, a unique colour-shifting lake, bat hibernacula, and nesting grounds for bald eagles, white pelicans, and blue herons. The park also would also have been the only place in North America where you could find all five of the continent's big ungulates – moose, elk, deer, caribou, and even a herd of reintroduced wood bison.

The park failed to materialize when four First Nations expressed justifiable concerns about losing access to traditional hunting and fishing areas – as well as potential restrictions on future development. Happily, the natural features that were to be protected by a park aren't going anywhere. On a trip north to Thompson or Churchill, there are a handful of attractions accessible by vehicle from Highway 6. Just make sure you have plenty of gas in your tank, as this is the loneliest road in Manitoba – Grand Rapids has the only gas station for 350 kms along a stretch of road from St. Martin Junction, in the northern Interlake, to Ponton, at the confluence of Highways 6 and 39.

Chitek Lake Provincial Park

While every Manitoban recognizes the bison as a provincial symbol, there's some confusion about the two subspecies of North America's largest land animal. The bison most know is the plains bison, which once numbered tens of millions and roamed across southern Manitoba until the 1850s. The larger and less woolly wood bison, restricted to northwestern Canada, only numbered in the hundreds of thousands before it was believed have gone extinct a century ago.

The subspecies was found alive in 1957, when a few wood bison were spotted in the Mackenzie River delta in the Northwest Territories. They formed the seed population for a recovery program that brought a few of the ungulates to Manitoba in 1984, when they were placed in a pen at Skownan First Nation in the northwestern Interlake. Descendants of these creatures were released in 1991 and 1996 near the shores of Chitek Lake, between Lake Winnipeg and Lake Winnipegosis, even though the wood bison likely never roamed free in Manitoba before. They did well enough to warrant the creation of a park reserve that was to be incorporated into a Manitoba Lowlands national park.

Since the park didn't materialize, the province created **Chitek Lake Provincial Park** in 2014 in a co-management deal with Skownan First Nation. The park now protects habitat for a wood bison herd estimated at 300 animals. There are no roads into the park, whose poorly drained terrain can only be readily visited during the winter. But there were plans to develop some form of ecotourism. While no guided trips were initiated when this book went to print, check with the Skownan band office (204.628.3373, skofn.com) to learn of tour possibilities.

Lowlands Sights Along Highway 6

Driving north from the Interlake, the first Lowlands sight you *can* actually visit is **Long Point,** a large peninsula jutting into Lake Winnipeg's wild and wavy northern basin. About two kilometres north of North Twin Creek, at a 90-degree bend in Highway 6, the gravel Long Point Road provides access to a fishing-boat launch and a rugged beach where there's an excellent chance of seeing bald eagles and herons during the summer.

About 40 kms north on Highway 6, gas up at **Grand Rapids,** a hydroelectric town on the spot where the Saskatchewan River empties into Lake Winnipeg. The rapids were tamed by the huge **Grand Rapids Generating Station Dam**, which you can visit via an access road on the north side of the river. During the summer, there are usually pelicans at the spillway, which makes for a decent picnic spot.

About 32 kms north of Grand Rapids, another gravel road leads east to **Sturgeon Gill Point**, a small fishing marina next

The limestone cliffs at Sturgeon Gill Point, a feature of the proposed Manitoba Lowlands National Park.

to a rocky beach. You can walk south from the beach to a set of limestone cliffs that rival the impressive formations at Steep Rock on Lake Manitoba. The best time to visit is midwinter, when you can walk on to the lake to view the cliffs. In the summer, you'll need a canoe (and calm water) to get the same view. You can also approach the cliffs on foot by walking around the edge of a marsh that sits between the parking lot and beach. Take waterproof boots and gaiters if you want to remain dry.

Another 30 kms north, on the west side of Highway 6, pull over to view **Little Limestone Lake**, one of the world's most unusual karst lakes. *Karst* refers to limestone areas with underwater cavities, but Little Limestone has something even more fascinating than caves: the lake changes colour when the temperature rises or drops, as lime precipitates out of the lake or gets dissolved back into it. Little Limestone Lake can appear clear, turquoise, or bluish-white, depending on the temperature. The lake and its shore were protected in 2011 as **Little Limestone Lake Provincial Park**, in co-operation with Mosakahiken Cree Nation. There are no services here and no plans to develop any. For a closer view of the lake, a short road on Mosakahiken land connects Highway 6 to the east shore of the lake.

The Pas

Six hours northwest of Winnipeg, **The Pas** (pronounced "the paw") is actually two communities rolled into one. There are 5,513 residents of the paper-mill town on the south side of the Saskatchewan River, while 2,319 more dwell north of the river in **Opaskwayak Cree Nation** (OCN), one the most entrepreneurial reserves in Manitoba.

As recently as 30 years ago, the two communities didn't trust each other, as racism divided the indigenous and non-indigenous populations. Today, the situation has improved to the point where two of the most important institutions are shared: Pas residents cheer on the Manitoba Junior Hockey League's **OCN Blizzard** (ocnblizzard.com), who play at the 1,100-seat Gordon Lathlin Memorial Centre, while Opaskwayak residents play an integral role of **The Pas Trappers Festival** (trappersfestival.com), a February shindig featuring dogsled races, ice-fishing competitions, and other rustic traditions.

The main tourist attraction is on the OCN side of the river. **Aseneskak Casino** (Highway 10, 204.627.2250, aseneskak.ca), the first indigenous casino in Manitoba, offers the usual games plus a gift shop selling Cree crafts. OCN also runs the **Kikiwak Inn** (Highway 10, 204.623.1800) and hosts **Opaskwayak Indian Days** in August.

On the south side of the river, the **Sam Waller Museum** (daily, 306 Fischer Ave., 204.623.3802, samwallermuseum.ca) houses natural and regional history exhibits inside a 1916 brick building, which once served as the local courthouse. Admission is $4 for adults and $2 for seniors and students.

You'll find genuine local colour when you chow down at diners in The Pas. **Miss The Pas** (daily, 158 Edwards Ave., 204.623.3130) is the kind of spot where there are so many pictures and knickknacks on the walls, you don't need to bring anything to read. Rival **ShylannaH's New Hawaiian** (daily, 202 Fischer Ave., 204.623.3555) offers wild rice, harvested in the area, as a side-dish alternative to potatoes – and does chili & bannock during the Trappers Festival. If a pub atmosphere if more your thing, **Good Thymes** (Mon-Sat, 1607 Gordon Ave., 204.623.2412) does pizzas, burgers and pasta.

Clearwater Lake Provincial Park

While The Pas isn't the prettiest city in Manitoba, there's plenty of natural beauty nearby. Immediately north of town, 590-square-km **Clearwater Lake Provincial Park** (Highway 10 at PR 287) is dominated by a cold, almost circular, and – as the name suggests – unusually clear body of water, teeming with trout. Fishing is a big deal here.

Take PR 287 into the park to reach **Sunset Beach, Campers Cove campground** (Victoria Day-Labour Day, sites $18.90-$23.10, yurts $56.50) **or Pioneer Bay campground** (Victoria Day-Labour Day, 23.10). There's an excellent short walking trail between the two campgrounds – **Clearwater Caves**, an 800-metre loop around crevices formed by masses of dolomite limestone that broke away from shoreline cliffs. As well, the **Jackfish Creek Fishway**, east of Campers Cove, is worth a stop in the early spring to watch northern pike swim upstream to spawn.

Flin Flon

MUST SEE:
*Flin Flon,
The Pas, and
Thompson*
Hardscrabble
northern log-
ging and mining
towns with a
still-thriving
frontier spirit.

Heading north from The Pas on Highway 10, the flat, swampy Manitoba Lowlands landscape gives way to rugged and rocky Canadian Shield shortly before **Flin Flon**, a quirky mining town on the Saskatchewan border.

Like The Pas, Flin Flon is really two communities living side by side. About 5,400 people live in houses scattered among the granite hills on the Manitoba side of the border, while another 1,500 live in Creighton, Saskatchewan, to the immediate southwest. The Hudson Bay Mining and Smelting Company, just west of downtown, dominates the twin communities. The massive open-face pit is not visible from Highway 10, but you can see the main stack several kilometres away. At 251 metres, it's the tallest free-standing structure in western Canada. To put that in perspective, the Eiffel Tower in Paris stands 320 metres.

Between 1930 and 1992, HBM&S removed 63 million tonnes of mostly zinc and copper ore from the open-face pit and two main shafts, including one extending more than a km below the surface. A new shaft called 777 Mine started up in 1999, but much of the ore refined at the plant today is shipped in from other northern Manitoba mines. The company's shuttered Trout Lake Mine, east of Flin Flon, was briefly used to grow a government-approved crop of medical marijuana. For a while, some Main Street shops sold T-shirts trumpeting Flin Flon's dubious status as Canada's marijuana capital.

As if a big mine wasn't enough, Flin Flon's topography adds to the hardscrabble feel of the town, as Canadian Shield greenstone is everywhere. Houses and streets are built on the sides of outcroppings, while long wooden boxes are used to insulate above-ground sewer lines – it's simply not economical to drill holes in solid granite just to carry human waste around.

Given the steep inclines, it's more fun to walk around Flin Flon than any other Manitoba city. The best route is a **five-km trek around Ross Lake**, a body of water in the middle of the community. Park at **Mike's Ice N Burger Hut** (April-September, One Island Drive at 3rd Avenue, 204.687.8600) and walk counterclockwise around the lake – you'll cross a flat wooden boardwalk, hike up steep cliffs with wooden stairs, and then descend along 3rd Avenue to gloriously greasy fast food. Feel like something more local? Pick up a pickerel burger with cranberry mayo at the **Kelsey Dining Room** at the Victoria Inn (daily, 160 Highway 10-A North, 204.687.7555).

Other places to check out in Flin Flon include the **waterfowl sanctuary** at **Hapnot Lake** (Bellevue Avenue at Ross Street); modest **Joe Brain Children's Petting Zoo** (June-August, Green Street between Balsam Avenue and Spruce Avenue); and the **Flin Flon Tourist Park** (Highway 10A at the east end of town), where you can pick up regional tourism info, or visit the **Station Museum** (June through August) and nab a sample of copper ore as a free souvenir.

Bartley Kives

Flin Flon takes its name from Flintabbatey Flonatin, a character in a pulp fiction novel found by a prospector. The statue at the entrance to the town was designed by cartoonist Al Capp of *L'il Abner* fame.

Wendy Wilson/Prairie Pathfinders

A five-kilometre-long walking trail encircles Ross Lake in the heart of Flin Flon.

Outside the museum, an oversized **statue of Flintabattey Flonatin,** designed by *L'il Abner* cartoonist Al Capp, explains how the town's unusual moniker is taken from a character in a pulp novel found by an early prospector.

Around Flin Flon

Just south of Flin Flon, across the Saskatchewan border, the **Flin Flon Ski Club** (flinflonskiclub.com, $10 daily trail-use fee) maintains 28 kms of trails that extend down to the northwest arm of Schist Lake. The hilly Shield topography makes for excellent cross-country skiing and decent mountain biking, especially on sections of bare greenstone. To reach the main parking lot from Third Avenue, head south on Boam Street and follow Cemetery Road, and then Saskatchewan Road.

Southeast of the city, Highway 10 crosses cool, clear **Athapapuskow Lake** at **Bakers Narrows Provincial Park**, a popular campground (Victoria Day-Labour Day, sites $18.90-$23.10, yurts $56.50) with two beaches and an observation tower offering views of Canadian Shield scenery. If you're looking for peace and quiet, there are six unserviced campsites along the lake at the north side of the park, away from all the RVs and rowdies. Immediately across the highway, you can belly up to the buffet or a walleye dinner at fishing outfitter **Bakers Narrows Lodge** (204.681.3250, bakersnarrowslodge.com, cottages $120-$160).

Southwest of Creighton, meanwhile, Saskatchewan Highway 167 heads to **Amisk Lake**, a large Canadian Shield lake used as a summer resort by Flin Flon residents. **Denare Beach**, 18 kms southwest of Creighton, is a good spot to buy locally processed wild rice, rent a houseboat for lazy trips on Amisk Lake or simply hang at the beach.

From Denare Beach, Highway 167 continues south along the east shore of Amisk Lake, exiting the Canadian Shield on its way past a series of **limestone caves** to the put-in for a **paddle down the Sturgeon-Weir River**. From here, it's a two-day, whitewater paddle to Sturgeon Landing, Sask., which straddles the Manitoba border 25 kms west of Highway 10. You'll need to arrange a car shuttle; the trip is described in Laurel Archer's *Northern Saskatchewan Canoe Trips*.

Grass River Corridor

The relatively tame Grass River was once a valuable and easy-to-paddle link between traplines in northwestern Manitoba and trading posts along Hudson Bay. The 450-kilometre-long river, which flows from the Cranberry Lakes southeast of Flin Flon to the Nelson River near Split Lake, is the Goldilocks of waterways; it

Bartley Kives

doesn't meander like a typical Manitoba Lowlands river but also doesn't tumble over violent rapids like Canadian Shield. For paddlers in middle gear, it may be just right.

There are far fewer people on the Grass River today than there were during the 18th and 19th centuries, which is surprising, considering two major roads – highways 39 and 6 – effectively parallel the route all the way from Cranberry Portage to Thompson.

A Class I rapid along the Grass River, which cuts across north-central Manitoba.

Driving along the river, you'll pass historical and natural attractions that include a karst spring inside Grass River Provincial Park, a stunning pictograph site at Tramping Lake, and Manitoba's biggest waterfalls, Pisew and Kwasitchewan Falls.

Canoeists and kayakers can also tackle portions of the route, enjoying surprisingly clear water and well-marked portages. Hap Wilson's *Wilderness Rivers of Manitoba* has a good description of the first 370 kilometres, from Cranberry Portage to Paint Lake Provincial Park. That entire route would take about three weeks to paddle, but smaller chunks can be broken up into trips as short as two days.

Grass River Provincial Park

The largest road-accessible park in northern Manitoba, **Grass River Provincial Park** protects 2,300 square kilometres of forests, wetlands, and lakes in the transition zone between the Manitoba Lowlands and the Canadian Shield. The main attractions are fishing, camping, paddling and wildlife watching. Woodland caribou range all the way through the park and usually choose to calve on tiny, predator-free islands in the middle of the summer. The park also boasts sizable moose, deer, beaver, otter, black bear, heron, pelican, and cormorant populations, as well as smaller numbers of wolves, lynx, martens, fishers, and elusive wolverines.

Motorists can access the park in four places. At the west end of the park on Highway 10, the town of **Cranberry Portage** (Highway 10 between The Pas and Flin Flon) offers water access to **First Cranberry Lake**, and is the only sizable place to load up on supplies such as fishing gear and groceries. Cranberry Portage is also the access point to **McCracken's Elbow Lake Lodge** (204.271.1713, elbowlakelodgemanitoba.weebly.com), located downstream on Elbow Lake.

Bartley Kives

Heading east from Highway 10 on Highway 39, **Simonhouse Lake** offers an alternate entry point to the backcountry as well as boat launch and beach at **Gyles Campground** (Victoria Day-Labour Day, $16.80).

A campsite above the rapids near Kwasitchewan Falls.

Next up is **Iskwasum Lake**, which has another boat launch, a **campground** (May-September, $16.80) and the detour-worthy **Karst Spring Trail**, a 3.2-km hiking loop that passes by one of the weirder sights in the province: a stream that surges out of solid limestone before it drains into the Grass River.

The last sizable body of water in the park is large and turbulent **Reed Lake**, which can stymie paddlers heading downstream. There's another boat launch at **Reed Lake campground** (Victoria Day-Labour Day, $16.80). Fishing excursions can also be arranged through **Grass River Lodge** (late May-September, Highway 10, 204.358.7171, grassriverlodge.com), while there are also four cabins to rent on Four Mile Island through **Petersons' Reed Lake Lodge** (mid-May-September, 204-688-8346, reedlake.com).

Tramping Lake and Wekusko Falls

One of the most dramatic set of pictographs in Manitoba appears on a rock face in the northern channel of **Tramping Lake**, which sits downstream from Grass Lake Provincial Park on the Grass River system. The ochre paintings, which may be more than a thousand years old, depict birds, mammals, snakes, and humanoid figures. They stretch for metres up the rock face, which is unusual for pictographs, which normally appear only at canoe level.

The only way to see the pictographs is from the water. If you're not paddling down the Grass River, you can rent a canoe or motorboat at **Wekusko Falls Lodge** (PR 392 between Highway 39 and Snow Lake, 204.358.2341, wekuskofallslodge.com), on the east side of Tramping Lake. Alternatively, there's a boat launch on the south end of Tramping Lake, at the end of a muddy track that leads

MUST SEE: Tramping Lake pictographs One of the largest assortments of indigenous rock art in Manitoba, accessible via motorboat or canoe from Wekusko Falls.

north from Highway 39; you may need a high-clearance vehicle to reach this put in.

Wekusko Falls itself is worth a visit, as the Grass River drops 12 metres between Tramping and Wekusko lakes. Wekusko Falls Lodge occupies the upstream side of PR 392, while **Wekusko Falls Provincial Park** sits on the opposite side of the highway, occupying both sides of the river downstream. The park has a small beach and a campground (Victoria Day-Labour Day, $17.85-$22.05) with 10 relatively secluded walk-in tenting sites scattered along the falls, a fair distance from the standard drive-in campground sites.

Pisew Falls and Paint Lake

East of Wekusko Lake, Highway 39 merges at Ponton with Highway 6, which connects southern Manitoba with Thompson, the largest city in Manitoba's north. No drive up Highway 6 is complete without at least a pit stop at **Pisew Falls**, a 13-metre Grass River waterfall on the east side of the highway, about 40 kms northeast of Wabowden. Boardwalks leading right up to the falls offer close-up views of the torrent, as well as the ferns and mosses that thrive off the spray. It's an even more dramatic sight during the winter – even –30 C temperatures can't freeze the flow.

At the opposite end of the parking lot, the 22-kilometre (return) **Upper Track Hiking Trail** leads to **Kwasitchewan Falls,** Manitoba's highest at 14 metres. There are four backcountry campsites along the Grass River at the north end of the trail, the nicest sitting above the falls at a gorgeous set of rapids. The walk makes for an excellent dayhike or a fantastic overnight, albeit with one

The Grass River tumbles 14 metres at Kwasitchewan Falls, Manitoba's highest waterfall, accessible via canoe or the twenty-two kilometre Upper Track Hiking Trail.

Bartley Kives

potential hazard – there are no bear boxes at the campsites, so be prepared to hang your food from a high tree limb.

No camping is allowed at the Pisew Falls trailhead. The nearest car camping is 40 kms south at **Setting Lake Wayside Park** (Victoria Day-Thanksgiving, across Highway 6 from Wabowden, 204.689.2362) or 50 kilometres north at **Paint Lake Provincial Park** (Highway 6 at PR 375), the usual take-out for longer Grass River canoe trips and a destination unto itself.

Paint Lake Provincial Park also has a large marina, two beaches, three short cross-country ski loops, an outdoor skating rink, a winter toboggan run, and two campgrounds: **Paint Lake campground** (Victoria Day-Labour Day, $18.90-$24.15) and the **smaller Lakeview campground** (Victoria Day-Labour Day, $16.80). There are also two island canoe-camping sites and year-round accommodations at **Paint Lake Resort** (204.677.9303).

Norway House and the Hayes River

At the height of the fur trade, most of the goods and people moving between Manitoba and Europe passed up and down a trade corridor that connected the Red River settlement with Hudson Bay through Lake Winnipeg, a short stretch of the high-volume Nelson River and the length of the much tamer Hayes River. Two centuries ago, this freshwater highway was the busiest place in Manitoba – and **Norway House** (pop. 4,758) sat midway along the journey.

This Nelson River community sat at the crossroads of the Hudson's Bay Company trade network in the 1800s. Most of the traffic passing through came and went in York boats, flat-bottomed vessels capable of handling both the shallow rapids on the Hayes River and the waves of Lake Winnipeg.

Today, Norway House is connected to the rest of Manitoba by PR 373, which branches off Highway 6 about 30 kms northeast of Ponton and the junction with Highway 39. The modern community encompasses both Norway House Cree Nation and the adjacent non-treaty settlement.

Three structures from the Hudson's Bay Company's transhipment post survive at the main Norway House townsite near the end of PR 373. **Archway Warehouse**, completed in 1841, is the oldest log structure in Manitoba that remains at its original site. The granite **jail** dates back to 1856 and is the oldest lockup in the province. The ruins of a limestone 1838 **powder magazine** sit in a wooded area nearby.

In early August, Norway House celebrates both its fur-trade history and indigenous roots during **Treaty & York Boat Days** (nhcn. ca/yorkboatdays), which includes boat races and strongmen/women competitions.

The community also serves as the launch point for a 600-km **canoe trip to Hudson Bay**, which follows the lower portion of the old York-boat trade route. The trip encompasses a short downstream section of the Nelson River, an upstream paddle along the

MUST SEE:
Pisew & Kwasitchewan Falls
Manitoba's two tallest waterfalls, connected by a 22-kilometre hiking loop through the northern boreal forest.

MUST SEE:
The Hayes River
Follow the historic fur-trade route between Lake Winnipeg and Hudson Bay on a Canadian heritage river that retains its natural flow.

Echimamish River and then a paddle down the Hayes River, which includes crossings of windy Oxford and Knee Lakes. The three-week-plus trip terminates at York Factory, where the remains of HBC storehouses still stand between the mouths of the Hayes and Nelson rivers.

Unlike the Nelson River, whose flow is controlled by hydro-electric dams, the Hayes continues to flow as naturally as it did during the height of the fur trade. Although its volume is much smaller – the Hayes discharges eight per cent of what the Nelson sends into Hudson Bay – the paddle is sufficiently arduous, long and remote to demand whitewater paddling skills and prior wilderness-camping experience. Toward the end of the trip, Hudson Bay tides and polar bears present dangers. Some paddlers break it up into shorter sections, either to save time or avoid wind on the two large lakes.

Fifteen-day guided Hayes trips, including charter flights, can be arranged through **Northern Soul Wilderness Adventures** (866.425.9430, northernsoul.ca), starting at $4,800 a person.

Thompson

At the end of long, lonely Highway 6, **Thompson** (pop. 12,829) emerges from the wilds of the boreal forest. Manitoba's fifth-largest city is also one of the newest communities in the province: there was nothing here before 1956, when a massive body of nickel ore was discovered near the Burntwood River. Over the next five years, mining giant Inco created a city from scratch, building a mine, smelter, refinery, and all the amenities needed to serve the humans working all the machinery. As a result, Thompson looks a lot like a 1960s suburb plopped into the middle of the wilderness, with an inner commercial core ringed by neatly planned residential streets and then ... well, nothing. Except trees, and a massive nickel mine.

From the air, the open-face portion of the mine looks like an ugly brown scar on a dark-green landscape. From the ground, it's a little less freaky because you won't see it driving in.

Aside from mining, Thompson serves as a transportation hub for the rest of northern Manitoba. Scheduled flights and charters from **Thompson Municipal Airport** (eight kms north of downtown, off PR 391) serve isolated First Nations and remote fishing lodges across the North. The **Via Rail Station** (Station Road, one kilometre east of downtown, arrivals & departures 204.677.2241, viarail.ca) offers the cheapest means of getting to Churchill – the 16-hour ride from Thompson costs as little as $67.20 each way if you book well in advance.

Whatever you do, *do not leave your vehicle at the train station!* Anything of value inside likely will be removed during your visit to Churchill. For a small fee, the staff at **McCreedy Campground** (17 Jasper Dr., off PR 391 just north of the Burntwood River, 204.778.8810) will look after your car and provide shuttle service to the train station.

If you're spending time in the city, the best diversion is **Thompson Zoo** (daily, 275 Thompson Drive North), home to northern and boreal species such as Canada lynx, both Arctic and timber wolves and snowy owls. Admission is free, but donations are appreciated. A one-kilometre interpretive trail also begins at the zoo.

If real wolves aren't enough, a much-larger *Canis lupus* is painted on to a side of **Highland Towers** (274 Princeton Drive), an apartment building on the east of town. The 10-storey timber-wolf mural is a reproduction of a painting by wildlife artist Robert Bateman. There are also 35 brightly painted concrete wolves scattered about Thompson.

Heritage North Museum (daily, July and August; afternoons Mon-Sat, September-June, 162 Princeton Drive, 204.677.2216, heritagenorthmuseum.ca) offers a mix of natural and cultural history inside two hand-built log cabins.

To see Thompson on foot or by bike, the 15-km **Millennium Trail** passes by the museum, the zoo and **King Miner**, the city's requisite oversized statue. About 20 minutes north of Thompson on PR 280, non-profit **Mystery Mountain Winter Park** (winter weekends, 204.778.8624, mysterymountain.ca) has four lifts, 18 downhill runs, and 10 kms of cross-country ski trails. Daily tickets are $35 for adults, $25 for students/seniors and $15 for kids.

Refuel with pizza at **Santa Maria** (daily, 11 Station Rd., 204.778.7331), Greek food at **The Hub** (daily, 111 Churchill Drive, 204.778.5630) or burgers and fries at **Popeye's** (summer only, 300 Mystery Lake Rd., 204.677.5575).

Thompson's annual fair, **Nickel Days** (nickeldays.ca), is usually held the fourth weekend in June. The week before Christmas is reserved for the **Thompson Fur Table** (manitobatrappers.com), a two-day event where about 300 trappers from across northern Manitoba show off their wares in the same room for prospective buyers. This unique event, held since the 1970s as a means of maximizing trappers' earnings, offers a rare glimpse into northern trapping culture – and the opportunity to buy a pine marten, beaver or weasel pelt, if you're not squeamish about dead animal skins.

Beyond Thompson

As remote as it may seem, Thompson is not the end of the line for Manitoba highway driving. From the hub of the north, PR 391 winds hundreds of extremely lonely kilometres northwest to the Saskatchewan border.

Gas up before you go. From Thompson, it's 213 kilometres to **Leaf Rapids**, a faded mining town that had more than 2,000 residents in the 1970s but now has a mere 453. It's another 106 kilometres to **Lynn Lake**, another faded town whose population dwindled from 3,500 to 482.

So why drive up? Seven kilometres north of Lynn Lake, PRs 394 and 398 bring you to tiny **Burge Lake Provincial Park**, a pike-fishing spot with a free, eight-site campground (Victoria Day-Labour Day). Another 14 kilometres up PR 394, Zed Lake Provincial Park has a little-used sandy beach and another free campground (Victoria Day-Labour Day). There's also trout in Zed Lake.

If you're one of those people who must drive as far as you can just for the hell of it, PR 394 continues another 79 kilometres to **Kinoosao, Sask.**, an outpost on the eastern shore of **Reindeer Lake**, the 20th-largest freshwater body in the world. If you've come this far, **Grand Slam Lodge** (204.356.8648, grandslamlodge.ca) charges $75 per person, per night for cabin rentals.

Now if you're one of those people who must drive as far as you can in the worst imaginable conditions possible, just for the hell of it, at the height of the winter you can exit PR 394 north of Vandekerchove Lake and drive another 332 kms to **Sayisi Dene First Nation** at Tadoule Lake. This is as far as you can drive in Manitoba – it's only 133 kms from the Nunavut border. You may see caribou herds along the way, but do not attempt this trip unless you've made arrangements to stay at Tadoule Lake.

Northeast of Thompson, PR 280 travels 305 kms to the hydro-electric town of **Gillam** (pop. 1,317) The trip takes four hours under optimal conditions along a very lonely road but can cut 6.5 hours – and half the price – off a Via Rail ride from Thompson to Churchill.

Bartley Kives

Sunset over Prince of Wales Fort, which sits opposite the town of Churchill. Kayaking the mouth of the the Churchill River is possible with a guide; tides are considerable at Hudson Bay.

Churchill

MUST SEE:
Churchill
Polar bears in the fall, rare birds in the spring, and beluga whales in the summer at one of the world's top ecotourism destinations.

Aside from Winnipeg, Manitoba's premiere international destination is tiny, remote **Churchill** (pop. 813), an isolated Hudson Bay port that's become one of the top ecotourism spots in Canada. This end-of-the-railway outpost's embarrassment of natural attractions includes beluga whales, birds, and wildflowers in the summer, polar bears in the fall, and northern lights and caribou in mid-winter. Factor in a colourful history that encompasses fur-trade-era naval intrigue, a Depression-era megaproject, Cold War military paranoia, and even a short-lived stint as a rocket-launching pad, and you have a weird and wonderful town worthy of a visit any time of year.

Churchill's Unusual History

Ecologically speaking, the tundra around Churchill is the newest piece of the province. The Hudson Bay Lowlands only emerged from glacial ice about 8,000 years ago, a full 4,000 years after Turtle Mountain and other parts of southwestern Manitoba. Compressed by a couple of kilometres of ice, the Churchill region has been rebounding upwards at a rate of 1.3 metres every century since the ice disappeared. When the first indigenous people moved into the area – no later than 2,900 years ago, according to archeological evidence found at Twin Lakes, southeast of Churchill – the Hudson Bay coastline was located several kilometres south of the current shore. Geographers have found at least 185 former beach ridges between the original coast and the modern waterline.

For about a millennium, Dene hunters followed herds of barren-grounds caribou around the taiga west of Hudson Bay, occasionally coming into conflict with Cree from the south and Inuit from the north. The first European to see the region was British explorer Thomas Button in 1612, followed by Danish sailor Jens Munck in 1619 and inland adventurer Henry Kelsey, who ventured up the Churchill River in 1690.

In 1732, British fur traders began building Prince of Wales Fort on the west side of the river to protect Hudson's Bay Company assets from the French. The massive stone fort, which had 12-metre-thick walls and 40 cannons, was finally finished 40 years later. Comically, the French navy didn't show up for another 10 years, finally surprising the hapless Brits in 1782. The mighty fort fell without a shot being fired, but the French soon returned the strategically useless property in a peace treaty.

For the next century, British merchants continued to trade with Dene trappers at Churchill, but the end of the fur trade saw the fort slide into obscurity. Luckily for Churchill, the Manitoba, Saskatchewan, and Alberta governments devised an ambitious plan to build a railway across the muskeg to a new Churchill seaport. Grain from western Canadian farms would then be shipped from Churchill to the UK across the shortest transatlantic shipping route yet.

The rickety Hudson Bay Railway was completed in 1929, when a new port, grain elevator, and town were built on the east side of the Churchill River. But since the shipping lanes were only ice-free three months a year, the port would never become very profitable.

Still, the town got lucky again, as Cold War tensions led the Canadian and American military to build air and naval bases at Churchill to keep an eye out for invading Soviets. A binational aerospace effort even led to the creation of a rocket-launching range in 1956. By 1965, the town's population had swollen to almost 7,000. Unfortunately, advances in radar technology made the airbase obsolete, and the military bases closed down and were soon dismantled. The town's population had shrunk to 1,600 by 1970, and has slowly been declining ever since.

Adding to the town's misery was the most shameful event in Manitoba's modern history: the forced relocation of the Sayisi

Dene. In 1956, the Canadian government airlifted the nomadic people from its traditional caribou-hunting grounds near Duck Lake in north-central Manitoba and settled them on the outskirts of Churchill. Ostensibly, they were moved to protect the caribou. It was a horrible mistake with disastrous consequences.

Accustomed to living off the land, the 1,100-member band suddenly found itself with no food, shelter, or means of support. Alcoholism, violence, and sexual abuse became norms in the exiled community, which endured a miserable 17-year stay in Churchill. A third of their numbers died from suicide, murder, disease, and misadventure.

The Sayisi Dene were finally returned to their traditional lands in 1973, when the survivors set up a new settlement at Tadoule Lake. With the benefit of hindsight, the entire sad episode is considered an act of cultural genocide. It's recounted in *Night Spirits*, a moving non-fiction account by Dene author Ila Bussidor.

On a less-sombre note, Churchill's fortunes have improved since the end of the '70s with the advent of polar-bear-watching tours. Today, ecotourism brings in tens of thousands of visitors a year, outshining even the port as the driving force of the local economy.

Getting to Churchill

Unless you own an icebreaker, the only way to Churchill is by air or rail, with neither option being cheap or easy. There are no roads across the muskeg to Hudson Bay, though Manitoba and Nunavut are talking up building a permanent road from Gillam up to Churchill, and eventually along the west coast of Hudson Bay to the high Arctic.

In the meantime, return flights from Winnipeg to Churchill on **Calm Air** (calmair.com) start around $845. During the summer and peak polar bear-watching season, there are up to three flights per day. The 1,000-kilometre plane ride takes about two hours. In contrast, a **Via Rail** (viarail.ca) trip from Winnipeg takes 45 hours *each way* along a circuitous route that actually curves west into Saskatchewan before heading northwest. The cheapest return ticket is $426. To save money – and time – the best way to reach Churchill from Winnipeg is to drive up to Thompson, park your vehicle at McCreedy Campground (see *Thompson*) and then take the 16-hour, $134 (return) Via Rail trip north across the muskeg.

Regardless of whether you travel by plane or train, make sure the tours and accommodations you desire aren't booked up during your visit. If that sounds too complicated – and money is not an issue – you can book a combination flight/motel/ecotourism package through tours companies (see below) and save yourself the logistical headache.

Gregg Shilliday

Churchill Ecotours

So what makes Churchill such a desirable place to watch wildlife? Mostly, it's a fluke of geography.

East of the town, along the coast of Hudson Bay, hundreds of polar bears spend the summer lazing about the tundra in protected Wapusk National Park, home to the largest concentration of denning sites in the world. The bears can't hunt for seals, their main food source, without ice on the bay. So every fall, they head to the one place where the bay freezes up earliest – the Churchill area, where fresh water from the Churchill River dilutes the seawater.

On any given day in late October and early November, dozens of polar bears are usually visible on the tundra to the immediate east of the town. For decades, the human residents used to bemoan the presence of these ferocious and extremely intelligent carnivores that occasionally wander into the community in search of an easy meal. Too often, aggressive bears were killed for being too curious. But in 1979, following another period of economic stagnation, some locals finally got the bright idea to offer tours of the surrounding tundra and show off the massive creatures to the world. They use oversized vehicles with massive, bog-eating wheels and windows well above the (usual) reach of polar bears.

Today, two tour companies – Frontiers North and Great White Bear – have the right to operate tundra vehicles between Churchill and the northwest border of Wapusk. You'll pay in the hundreds for a day of polar-bear watching – and thousands for a package tour. To many people, the chance to watch the world's most dangerous land predator is a once-in-a-lifetime experience. Along with bears, you're likely to see Arctic foxes, Arctic hares, and ptarmigans out on the tundra. Just don't come expecting solitude, as you'll be sharing your ride with several dozen other tourists. As well, the

Most tourists come to Churchill for bears and belugas but don't miss out on visiting the impressively reconstructed Prince of Wales fort.

237

bears appear to be quite used to the vehicles – some of the critters even try to drink the wastewater that leaks from portable tundra lodges, which are buggies linked together and equipped with beds and kitchens.

Of course, it's possible to see polar bears in the wild without paying big bucks for a tundra vehicle tour, but unlikely if you don't plan to rent a car. Travelling on foot is suicidal during polar bear season, though most bears that venture too close to Churchill are captured by provincial conservation officers and locked up in a "bear jail" east of town until the ice freezes or the opportunity arises to move them by helicopter.

While bears are the main draw in Churchill, the summer congregation of beluga whales at the mouth of the Churchill River can be more rewarding. In July and early August, about 3,000 of the four-metre-long whales feed on small fish called capelin in the partly saline estuary, with grey-coloured whale calves swimming circles around their bright-white mothers in an amazing displays of aquatic grace.

Most tourists see the whales on a tour boat or on zodiacs, packaged with tours of Prince of Wales Fort on the west side of the river. You're guaranteed to see whales this way, but anyone who's slightly fit should also try kayaking or snorkeling with beluga whales. There are few experiences more profound than being surrounding by a pod of these highly intelligent mammals as they chirp like birds, vent their blowholes, and, if you're really lucky, playfully nudge your kayak. The downside is that some day-paddles may not result in whale encounters.

Other summertime sights around Churchill include spectacular blooms of wildflowers from June through August, and fantastic birding from mid-April into July. Churchill is one of the top bird-watching spots in North America, with loons, tundra swans, eiders, mergansers, and gyrfalcons among the most sought-after species. Some of the top birding spots include upriver, in the Churchill River estuary; Bird Cove, east of town; and Akudlik Marsh to the southeast (see *Around Churchill*, below). Unfortunately, there's no safe way to wander on foot for any distance, as encounters with stealthy and silent polar bears are possible at any time of year. All guides are equipped with bear bangers or firearms.

Tours of the Churchill area by dogsled, snowmobile, helicopter, and Bombardier – a tank-like covered snowmobile – may also be arranged.

If you can, book your polar-bear excursion toward the beginning of the season, as an early freeze-up might mean no bears at all if you show up at the tail end. Here's a list of Churchill ecotour operators, guides and package-tour companies, as of 2015:

Arctic Wolf Adventures (204.675.8298): Guided nature tours and wildlife photography of the Churchill area. Call for rates.

Aurora Domes (204.675.2532): Northern lights viewing from inside heated, optically correct domes. Call for rates.

Blue Sky Expeditions (204.675.2001, blueskysmush.com): Full and half-day dog-sledding excursions and indigenous education. Tours $90 to $400.

Churchill Nature Tours (204.636.2958, churchillnaturetours.com): Bird-watching, wildflowers, polar-bears and beluga whales. Tours $4,400 to $5,600.

Churchill Northern Studies Centre (204.675.2307, churchillscience.ca): Scientist-led study tours on birding, arctic wildlife, winter survival, northern lights, astronomy, beluga whales and polar bears. Tours $1,200 to $4,300.

Churchill River Mushing (204-675-8176): Sled-dog tour packages, plus northern lights, winter camping, igloo building, trapline and arctic wildlife viewing by sled dog teams.

Churchill Subarctic Tours (204.675.2474) Snowshoe and snow-mobile tours around Churchill from December until the late April freeze-up. Call for rates.

Churchill Wild (204.878-5090, churchillwild.com): All-inclusive tours to see polar bears, northern lights, beluga whales, birds and caribou at four remote wilderness lodges within a short flight from Churchill: Nanuk Polar Bear Lodge, North Knife Lake Wilderness Lodge, Dymond Lake EcoLodge and Seal River Heritage Lodge. All-inclusive packages, $8,800 to $17,500 per person.

Frontiers North Adventures (204.949.2050, frontiersnorth.com): One of two licensed tundra-vehicle operators. Summer single-day tundra buggy tours, $179 adults, $139 kids. Fall single-day polar-bear tours, $459 adults, $359 kids. The latter books up quickly. All-inclusive polar bear and beluga-watching packages, $1,500 to $11,500.

The Great Canadian Travel Company Ltd. (204.949.0199, greatcanadiantravel.com): All-inclusive polar-bear-watching packages, $1,400 to $9,700.

Great White Bear Tours, Inc. (204.675.2781, greatwhitebeartours.com): One of two licensed tundra-vehicle operators. Day-long polar bear tours, $472.50. These book up months in advance. All-inclusive packages, $5,700 to $8,900.

Heartland International Travel & Tours (204-989-9630, heartlandtravel.ca): Single-day, there-and-back Churchill polar-bear-watching tours from Winnipeg, $1,400. These book up months in advance.

Hudson Bay Helicopters (204.675.2576, hudsonbayheli.com): Helicopter sightseeing tours of Churchill area. Call for rates.

Lazy Bear Lodge (204.663.9377, lazybearlodge.com): Three-hour snorkelling and kayaking with beluga whales, $135. All-inclusive summer beluga/polar bear tours, $400 to $5,900. All-inclusive winter polar-bear tours, $5,600. Zodiac charters.

Nature 1st Tours (204.675.2147, nature1sttours.ca): Highly recom-mended hiking, birding and natural-history tours, led by a local naturalist, fully armed for your protection. Half-day tours $95, full days $165, and multi-day all-inclusive tours, $2,150.

North Star Tours (204.675.2356): Historical and indigenous-culture tours. Call for rates.

Sea North Tours Ltd. (204.675.2195, seanorthtours.com): Beluga-whale watching from zodiacs and Prince of Wales Fort tours, $115 adults, $57.50 children. Three hours of snorkelling with belugas, $220. Two hours of kayaking with belugas, $160 adults, $60 children. Private zodiac charters, $350 an hour.

Tamarack Vehicle Rentals (204.675.2192, tamarackrentals.ca): Truck and van rentals for self-directed sightseeing, $75 to $140 a day.

Wapusk Adventures (204.675.2887, wapuskadventures.com): Dog-sled tours and indigenous education. Call for rates.

Wat'chee Lodge (204.675.2114, watchee.com): Tour polar-bear denning sites from a lodge 60 kilometres south of Churchill. Call for rates.

The Churchill Townsite

When you live in a place where the neighbours are capable of killing and eating you, you tend to develop a weird personality. That's part of the allure of Churchill, the only town in Canada where gun-toting escorts take kids trick-or-treating on Halloween, and police ignore ATV drivers who cruise down the main drag with shotguns strapped to their back.

From a very young age, Churchillians are taught to fear and respect polar bears, one of the few creatures actually known to prey on people, if given the chance. During polar bear season, the townsfolk are incredibly wary – they take cabs to travel even short distances at night and don't even poke their noses outside their homes until they're sure no bears are lurking in the area.

Their vigilance has been rewarded with a remarkable statistic: No human has been killed by a polar bear in Churchill since 1983, when a hapless drunk tempted fate by wandering into a burned-out building to relieve himself. Bears will snack on humans even though we don't have enough fat to *really* interest them (they much prefer a tasty meal of rich seal blubber). Nonetheless, attacks on pedestrians in town have occurred; the most recent incident occurred in 2013.

In daylight, the Churchill townsite is safe to negotiate, especially during the long summer days. Attractions in the compact town include interpretive displays at the **Parks Canada Visitor Reception Centre** (in the Via Rail Station); incredible Inuit art at the **Eskimo Museum** (Mon-Sat, 242 Laverendrye Ave., 204.675.2030); indigenous art of all stripes for sale at **Northern Images** (spring through fall, 174 Kelsey Blvd., 204.675.2681); and handmade crafts at **Arctic Trading Company** (Mon-Sat, 141 Kelsey Blvd., 204.675.8804). It's also fun to jump around the rocks on the

Hudson Bay coast behind the sprawling **Town Centre Complex** (Laverendrye Avenue) but even here, polar bears can be a danger.

Churchill hotels tend to be expensive during the fall polar-bear season and much cheaper the rest of the year. Only the wooden **Lazy Bear Lodge** (313 Kelsey Blvd., 204.675.2969, lazybearlodge.com) has some esthetics going for it. Other options include **Tundra Inn & Hostel** (34 Franklin St., 204.675.8831, tundrainn.com), **Seaport Hotel** (215 Kelsey Blvd., 204.675.8807, seaporthotel.ca), **Bear Country Inn** (126 Kelsey Blvd., 204.675.8299), **Churchill Motel** (Kelsey & Franklin, 204.675.8853), **Iceberg Inn** (184 Kelsey Blvd., 204.675.2228, iceberginn.ca) and four B&Bs. Call for rates, which fluctuate with the seasons.

You can grab a meal in Churchill at the **Lazy Bear Café** (hours vary, Lazy Bear Lodge), which doesn't serve alcohol, or the **Reef Dining Room** (daily, Seaport Hotel), which does. They both serve Arctic char, and sometimes caribou, at tourist-trap prices. More-economical meals can be found at the cafeteria-like **Gypsy's Bakery & Restaurant** (Mon-Sat, 253 Kelsey Blvd., 204.675.2322) where you can get sandwiches, fresh baked goods and a few Portuguese dishes. You can also buy groceries here, which is a godsend considering the cost of food in Churchill.

If you fancy a drink, Churchill bars can be a little gritty, but locals know the value of the tourism industry and tend to leave visitors in peace. The **Seaport Hotel** has the largest bar, but the atmosphere is funkier at the **Royal Canadian Legion** (23 Hudson Square, 204.675.2272). If you can get a Churchillian talking, you'll be entertained for hours – there isn't a person in town who doesn't have some kind of tale to spin about a close encounter with a bear.

Bartley Kives

Around Churchill

To explore the area around the Churchill townsite, you'll have to rent a car or hire a cab for the day. It simply is not safe to walk around in polar bear country. But if you are spending several days in town, it's fun to go driving around on your own, packing a pair of binoculars to watch birds and scan for polar bears. You should also take an air horn and hope like hell a little blast of noise will deter any polar bear that sneaks up on you.

The rocks along Hudson Bay, immediately north of Churchill's town centre complex. Due to a process known as isostatic rebound, the shore is rising at a rate of several centimetres a century.

West of town, the monstrous grain elevator at the **Port of Churchill** dominates the landscape, rising up from the tundra like an otherworldly monolith. Tours can take you to upper floors, where there are amazing views of the coast. Farther west, **Cape Merry** offers a view of the mouth of the Churchill River and of **Prince of Wales Fort** across the strait. You'll need to hire a boat or take a tour if you want to get across and see the impressive but slowly disintegrating stone structure.

Bartley Kives

The wreck of *Miss Piggy*, east of the the Churchill townsite.

Driving east of Churchill along the Hudson Bay coast, sights include the remains of cargo plane *Miss Piggy* (west of Amundson Road at Robert Crescent) which crashed in 1979 on an approach to Churchill Airport, and further east, the rusted-out hulk of the *MV Ithaca*, a British steamship that ran aground west of Bird Cove during a storm in 1960.

At low tide, you can walk right up to the wreck and inspect the interior – but only if you have an armed escort, and even then, the locals may chide you for your risk-taking behaviour. Nearby **Bird Cove** is a good birding spot, while the next point to the east makes for an excellent shoreline walk, but again, only with an armed escort.

Continuing east, the former **Churchill Rocket Research Range** is now a national historic site, though there isn't much to see besides an old metal silo. The site is now home to the **Churchill Northern Studies Centre** (churchillscience.ca), a base for biologists, archeologists, and other researchers. You can stay here and take tours – See *Churchill ecotours* for information about educational trips.

Southeast of the Northern Studies Centre, the road continues on to a small cottage area at **Twin Lakes,** where archeologists discovered 2,900-year-old remains of pre-Dorset culture fishing camps. Again, you need to take special care walking around here.

Driving due south from Churchill, you'll pass by **Akudlik Marsh**, where serious birders try to spot the rare Ross's Gull, and continue to the former site of **Dene Village**. When the Sayisi Dene were moved to Churchill, they were first deposited on the banks of the Churchill River, and later put up in houses next to a graveyard – ignoring a cultural taboo against visiting gravesites, and were finally put up in

The wreck of the *MV Ithaca,* grounded in the shallows of Hudson Bay east of Churchill. Thanks to polar bears, it's unsafe to visit without an armed escort.

Bartley Kives

this suburb, where all the plate-glass windows were soon smashed and the people descended into madness. All that's left today are the concrete foundations of the old homes and a grim plaque that remembers the dead and pointedly uses the term *genocide*.

If you continue south, you'll eventually reach **Goose Creek**, a fishing spot and birding area 10 kms up the Churchill River. Farther south of Churchill, accessible only by train and a short ride on a Bombardier, **Wat'chee Lodge** (watchee.com) offers the most-secluded wildlife-watching opportunities in the Churchill area that don't require a plane ride from town.

The Seal River

Tumbling across northern Manitoba to Hudson Bay, hundreds of kilometres from any permanent road, the **Seal River** is the one of the wildest and most pristine major rivers in Canada. It's also one of the three most highly regarded whitewater-paddling routes in Manitoba, along with the Bloodvein River and the Hayes River.

It's a 315-km paddle from Sayisi Dene First Nation on Tadoule Lake to the mouth of the Seal River at Hudson Bay. Most paddlers take two weeks to descend the river, allowing for lousy weather. There are 42 sets of rapids along the way and the vast majority are considered difficult; canoes must be outfitted with spray decks to shed water from standing waves. There are also very few portages along the way.

Paddlers who do attempt the Seal will be rewarded with immense beauty. The river's features include Shield forests in its upper reaches, peaty Hudson Bay lowlands on the lower portion and the chance to explore massive eskers, the sandy remains of glacial meltwater, on foot. It also offers a chance to see caribou, harbour seals, and if you're lucky, beluga whales at Hudson Bay. If you're unlucky, you may see polar bears. You must travel with a firearm, just in case. For protection from polar bears, there's a gated enclosure at a campsite above the final sets of rapids before Hudson Bay.

To reach the Seal River, fly **Perimeter Aviation** (800.665.8986, perimeter.ca) from Thompson to Tadoule Lake. Paddle down the Seal to the river mouth at Hudson Bay, where it's recommended you arrange a boat to carry you to Churchill. Paddling on the bay is dangerous due to the combination of tides, very shallow water, the potential for heavy waves and the threat posed by polar bears. From Churchill, you can take Via Rail back to Thompson.

Fifteen-day guided Seal trips, including charter flights, can be arranged through **Northern Soul Wilderness Adventures** (866.425.9430, northernsoul.ca), starting at $4,800 a person.

***MUST SEE:
The Seal River***
Nerve-rattling rapids, massive sandy eskers and the chance to see harbor seals, beluga whales and maybe polar bears await paddlers who take on one of Canada's most pristine and awe-inspiring whitewater rivers.

Jason Sorby

NORTHWESTERN ONTARIO

12

For all intents and purposes, Northwestern Ontario can be considered part of Manitoba. Kenora, the biggest community in the region, is only 205 kilometres from Winnipeg and an excruciating 1,900 from Toronto, the Ontario provincial capital.

Thousands of Winnipeggers own cottages in and around spectacular Lake Of The Woods, a Canadian Shield lake dotted with 14,500 islands, while many more Manitobans treat the area as a weekend getaway destination.

Northwest Ontarians, meanwhile, see Winnipeg as a place to shop, visit a medical specialist or go out for a night on the town. The bonds between the two areas are so strong, some people in the Kenora-Rainy River region periodically threaten to secede from Ontario and start sending their taxes to Winnipeg instead of Toronto.

This ambiguity is hardly a recent phenomenon. When Europeans first visited the region, Lake Of The Woods was a no-man's land where the Cree, Sioux and later Anishinaabe struggled for dominance. One of the bloodier episodes in early Canadian history took place on Lake Of The Woods in 1736, when a French-Canadian canoe party was ambushed by Sioux near what's now the Canada-US border.

During the fur trade, Northwestern Ontario witnessed a rapid influx of traders and settlers, as Lake Of The Woods and it upstream source, the Rainy River, comprised part of the main trade route between what was then the Northwest Territories and Upper Canada.

After Canada became a sovereign nation, the region again became the subject of dispute, as Manitoba and Ontario both claimed the pioneer settlement of Rat Portage — later the "ra" in "Kenora" — as their own. Between 1870 and 1881, each province built rival courts and jails and enlisted rival police officers to enforce rival sets of laws. At one point, a band of Ontario agitators burned down the Manitoba jailhouse.

The jurisdictional jockeying finally ended in 1889, when Ottawa awarded the Lake Of The Woods region to Ontario. To this day, some Kenorans still refer to their western neighbours

Opposite: A rockfall at Point Lake, in the southeastern extreme of the Experimental Lakes Area. Much of northwestern Ontario is best experienced on the water.

as "Tobans" in less-than-flattering tones, but Manitobans, by and large, are oblivious to the insult.

Up until the last few decades, logging and mining formed the backbone of the region's economy, but tourism now serves that role. In the summer, Kenora's population swells from a town of 15,400 to a boreal-forest metropolis of 40,000 or more.

If you love fishing, sailing, canoeing, kayaking, or racing around in a motorboat, you can spend a lifetime exploring the wider area, which boasts some of world's best flatwater paddling and some of the Canadian Shield's most attractive scenery. Backcountry travel is increasingly popular on Crown land across northwestern Ontario, to the point where fishers and wilderness travellers are actually beginning to put stress on once-isolated lakes.

Jason Sorby

Dusk in the ELA.

Tourism is such a strong component of the economy, you're just as likely to meet Winnipeggers and Americans on the water as you are Ontarians.

Just one word of warning: the locals may still be holding some sort of quiet grudge. Burgers ordered at northwestern Ontario greasy spoons sometimes come slathered with an amazingly thick layer of relish.

What else could explain that, besides a grudge?

Kenora

MUST SEE:
Kenora
A sort of Venice in the centre of the Canada, this resort city has five beaches and a half-dozen harbours that serve as the main gateway to Lake of the Woods.

One of the most unusual resort towns in North America, **Kenora** is a marine community misplaced in the middle of the continent. The municipality encompasses both a mainland component and thousands of island cottages spread out among Lake Of The Woods' densely populated northern basin.

As a result, the city's Safeway has motorboat parking, the municipal police patrol the waters by speedboat and Domino's Pizza delivers in 30 nautical minutes or less. This place is like a Canadian Shield version of Venice, with channels, bays, beaches and marinas making the city an attractive port of call during the summer.

Geographically, Kenora's mainland component is located at the north end of Lake Of The Woods, where the Winnipeg River begins to flow northwest toward Manitoba. It's spread out along a 30-kilometre crescent of Highway 17, about two hours east of Winnipeg on the Trans-Canada Highway.

Driving around mainland Kenora, you'll find the city is really four neighbouring communities. What the locals call **Kenora** is the main built-up area in the centre of town, home to the largest of several marinas. **Jaffray Melick** encompasses the suburbs on high Canadian Shield rock to the north. **Norman** is an island neighbourhood located to the west of downtown Kenora, while **Keewatin** occupies the extreme west end of the municipality.

Main Street in
downtown Kenora.

Historically, First Nations referred to the entire area as "Portage of the Muskrats," which was later shortened to Rat Portage by the French and English. In 1905, the name was changed to Kenora — an amalgamation of Keewatin, Norman and Rat Portage — to appease a flour mill that didn't think consumers would purchase baking supplies with the word "rat" stamped on the bags.

Although some tourists merely pass through on their way on to Lake Of The Woods, the city itself is worth a visit. Early 20th century architecture has been preserved along Main Street, the main drag in downtown Kenora. If you're interested in learning more about the city's colourful history, **the Lake Of The Woods Museum** (daily July & August, Tues-Sat June & September, 300 Main St. South, 807.467.2105, lakeofthewoodsmuseum.ca) only charges $4 for adults and $3 for seniors and students.

Main Street is also where you'll find **Plaza Restaurant & Tavern** (Tues-Sat, 125 Main St. South, 807.468.8173), a beloved Greek institution where the calamari rivals any in Winnipeg. Next-door neighbours **Cornerstone** (daily, 154 Main St. South, 807.468.7787) and **Bijou Steakhouse** (Wed-Sat, 152 Main St. South, 807.468.2463) sling burgers and walleye, while you can grab caffeine at **HoJoe Coffee & Books** (Mon-Sat, 103 Main St. South, 807.468.6111).

Main Street is also where you'll find three-storey clothing and outdoor retailer **The Hardwear Company** (Tues-Sat, 106 Main St. South, 807.468.1226), where you can pick up camping gear you left behind in Winnipeg.

Parallel to Main Street, Kenora's **Harbourfront** is the largest marina in town and the place to catch a ride on the **MS Kenora** (807.468.9124, mskenora.com), which cruises around Lake Of The

Woods three times daily from Mother's Day to Labour Day. You can purchase tickets ($27.43 adults, $26.55 seniors and $14.16 kids) at Thistle Pavilion in the middle of the Harbourfront. You can also grab a water shuttle south of the harbourfront at Wharf Marina (south end of Water Street) to **Coney Beach** on Coney Island, located in the bay across from downtown; boats at other Kenora marinas may also offer rides.

During the August long weekend, the Harbourfront turns into party central for **Harbourfest** (harbourfest.ca), the annual town fair, which usually coincides with the start of the Lake Of The Woods International Sailing Association Regatta, better known as the **LOWISA** (lowisa.org), a week-long circumnavigation of Lake Of The Woods by a fleet of 70 boats.

Bartley Kives

East of Main Street, **Ye Old Chip Truck** (daily during summer, Chipman Street and Second Street South) slings fries in the parking lot at Kenora Market Square while brewpub **Lake Of The Woods Brewing Co.** (daily, 350 Second St. South, 807.468.4337), will serve you a walleye BLT or send home with a growler of an excellent pilsner or ale.

Still farther east, you can take in a good view of Safety Bay and Coney Island from the restaurant up on the ninth floor of the **Lakeside Inn** (470 First Avenue South, 807.468-5521). The circular lakefront hotel is the quirkiest place to stay in Kenora; chain hotels and independent motels are scattered along Highway 17 east of downtown. During the summer, it's best to reserve ahead, as space is scarce around Canada Day and during a two-week stretch in late July and early August that includes Harbourfest, LOWISA and the Kenora Bass International fishing tournament.

A cow moose observes human interlopers on Rupert Lake, southeast of Kenora.

Between the Lakeside Inn and the Safeway with the motorboat parking, **Laurenson's Creek** extends east from the lakefront, through the centre of the city and into **Laurenson's Lake** on the east side of town. You can explore the creek by canoe, kayak or stand-up paddleboard; rentals are right along the creek at **Green Adventures** (806 River Drive, 807.407.8683, greenadventures.ca, $10 per hour) or downtown at The Hardwear Company.

Continuing southeast, **Anicinabe RV Park & Campground** (Miikana Way at Golf Course Road, 807.467.2700, anicinabepark. ca) has a beach, 83 campsites ($27-$39) and another Green Adventures canoe/kayak/paddleboard rental kiosk.

West of downtown Kenora, past the Harbourfront, **McLeod Park** has an artificial geyser that spouts every 15 minutes during the summer, plus an oversized statue of a muskellunge, an aggressive relative of the northern pike.

Continuing west, Lakeview Drive – also known as Highway 17 – crosses a bridge on to Tunnel Island and then across a second bridge on to the island neighbourhood of **Norman**, home to the new **Lake Of The Woods Discovery Centre** (daily, 931 Lakeview Drive, 807.467.4655, kenora.ca), a tourist-information kiosk with a couple of free museum exhibits, including a collection of vintage lake boats and a display about the 1907 Stanley Cup champions the Kenora Thistles. Nearby **Norman Park** has another public beach.

Farther west, in the **Keewatin** neighbourhood, take a quick gander at the **Keewatin Potholes** (end of Sixth Street, south of Highway 17), a series of unusual pits carved out of the Canadian Shield granite by swirling postglacial sediments. Stop in for burgers, pasta or curries at **901 Westside** (Mon-Sat, 901 Ottawa St., 807.547-2901), chill out at **Keewatin Beach** (Keewatin Beach Road on the lakefront) or continue further west to MacKenzie Portage Road and drive six kms south to reach to the **Vernon Nature Trails**, a five-km hiking and cross-country ski loop.

A more extensive set of trails can be found northeast of Kenora at **Mount Evergreen Ski Club** (Mount Evergreen Road, south of Airport Road, 807.548.5100, skikenora.com), which maintains eight downhill runs (lift tickets $30 adults, $20 children) and grooms 50 clicks of cross-country trails ($8 day passes) during the winter. Some of Mount Evergreen's trails are open for summer hiking and mountain biking.

Also in northeast Kenora, there's another public beach along **Rabbit Lake** at **Garrow Park** (Birchwood Road, off Rabbit Lake Road). The lake is also home to **Log Cabin Tavern** (daily, 201 Rabbit Lake Rd., 807.548.8778), an old-school barbecue joint with a mini-golf course.

Lake Of The Woods

If you're spending any time in the Lake Of The Woods region, you should do everything in your power to actually get out on the lake, where there are 14,500 islands, 104,000 kms of shoreline, dozens of sand and slate-rock beaches and several sections of sheer granite cliffs to explore among six large basins and hundreds of smaller bays in Ontario, Minnesota and Manitoba waters.

Gregg Shilliday

The fishing is excellent, the birding is fulfilling and there is plenty of history to discover, from centuries-old indigenous rock art to fur trade-era forts, 19th-century steamship wrecks and 20th-century goldmines.

This maze of a lake can be explored by canoe, kayak, paddleboard, powerboat, houseboat, sailboat, yacht or even tug, all of which may be rented or chartered out of Kenora. Boats may also be rented out of a dozen other gateway communities, most notably

Clearwater Bay, Sioux Narrows, Nestor Falls and Morson, Ont. as well as Warroad, Minn.; all are described in brief later in this chapter.

Large stretches of open water on Lake Of The Woods can present a headache for canoeists, though island-hopping remains possible in the heaviest of waves. The absence of portages make this lake ideal for kayaks and paddleboards. The main challenges for self-propelled exploration of the lake are navigation (it's easy to get lost on a lake where all the islands look the same at a distance) and run-ins with powerboats in the heavily used harbours and straits. Paddlers should take along a compass, GPS unit and topographical maps – know how to use them all.

Powerboats, houseboats and sailboats face the same navigational challenge, plus the risk of running aground on rock outcroppings or destroying motors or keels on underwater reefs can strand houseboats, damage powerboat motors and destroy sailboat keels. Nautical charts are highly recommended for anyone piloting watercraft with any sort of draft. Pleasure-craft operating cards and licenses are compulsory.

Despite these warnings, there are few more exciting freshwater lakes to explore in North America. If you're interested in the history of many of the islands you'll visit, pick up a copy of *The Explorer's Guide to Lake Of The Woods*, on sale at the Lake Of The Woods Museum as well as Winnipeg bookstores.

The following Kenora-based companies provide rental services and/or guided tours of the lake:

Board Anyone (329 Second St. South, 807.468.3211, boardanyone.com): Paddleboard and wakeboard rentals.

Green Adventures (806 River Drive, 807.407.8683, greenadventures.ca): Motorboat, canoe, kayak and paddleboard rentals, plus guided fishing, paddling and climbing trips.

Hook 'n Bullet (807.548.2037, hooknbullet.ca): Houseboat, powerboat, pontoon boat and kayak rentals, plus guided fishing trips.

Houseboat Adventures (800.253.6672 houseboatadventures.com): Houseboat and motorboat rentals.

Lake Escapes (807.465.5812, lakeescapes.ca): Guided canoe and kayak daytrips and longer trips.

Lakeside Watersports (807.547.2026, lakesidewatersports.ca): Powerboat, pontoon boat and Seadoo rentals, plus guided fishing trips.

Northern Harbour (807.548.5719): Sailboat rentals.

Perch Bay Resort (866.495.4545, perchbay.com): Powerboat rentals.

Tall Pines Marina on Cameron Bay (855.543.2167, tallpinesmarina.com): Powerboat, pontoon boat and Waverunner rentals.

The Hardwear Company (106 Main St. South, 807.468.1226, hardwearco.lightspeedwebstore.com): Canoe and kayak rentals.

Highway 17 Corridor

East of the Manitoba-Ontario border, the Trans-Canada Highway switches designation from Highway 1 to Highway 17 – and forms the only road link between eastern and western Canada. This vital, two-lane artery is infamous for occasional closures due to washouts or motor-vehicle collisions. Driving it at night also may mean avoiding wildlife; white-tailed deer and moose are common along the road during the summer.

Bartley Kives

Highway 17 is also a highly scenic, winding drive through Canadian Shield country, especially between Kenora and Vermilion Bay, Ont. The following are some of the destinations along the route, which is slated to be widened to four lanes in 2015 and 2016.

Clearwater Bay

The first significant Lake Of The Woods entry point heading east into Ontario is **Clearwater Bay**, home to a pair of marinas and a liquor store prized by Winnipeggers as the closest place they can purchase Canadian craft beers unavailable in Manitoba. West of the town, the log-cabin restaurant/gift shop **Pinewood Lodge** (daily, Highway 17, 807.788.2581) has all the tourist trinkets your kids want but never, ever need.

Dawn at difficult-to-reach Waterfall Lake.

Gordon Lake Loop

There are dozens upon dozens of flatwater paddling options in northwestern Ontario. The **Gordon Lake loop**, a flatwater circuit on Crown land north of the Trans-Canada Highway, has the advantage of easy road access and no requirement to double back. This three-to-four-day loop runs from the Gordon Lakes up to Canyon Lake and back. Access it from Gordon Lake Road (40 kms east of the junction of Highway 17 and Highway 71); there's a put-in and unsupervised parking lot at Little Gordon Lake west of the Gordon Lake Road and a takeout east of the road at Gordon Lake. There are no fees.

Experimental Lakes Area

In the late 1960s, a team of Canadian freshwater scientists grappling with questions about the environment had a crazy but brilliant idea: Use a series of pristine and relatively isolated lakes

Bartley Kives

Sometimes, flatwater really is flat: A calm day in Winnange Lake Provincial Park.

east of Kenora as a living laboratory where they could conduct "whole-lake manipulations" – that is, experiments on entire living ecosystems, rather than just inside a lab, where only a handful of variables come into play.

The result was **Experimental Lakes Area,** a network of lakes where federal scientists and university researchers have conducted decades of research that's had a profound effect on water management and industrial development around the world. The ELA's two most famous discoveries involved demonstrations of the way acid rain can destroy entire food chains and how phosphorus loads from agricultural waste and urban sewage-treatment, among other sources, promotes the growth of blue-green algae that deprive lakes of oxygen and ultimately destroy their ecosystems. Given the ELA's record of immense success, it was only natural Ottawa sought to shut the field station down in an effort to save $2 million a year ... without realizing the environmental-remediation costs of restoring all the lakes to their natural states would cost at least $50 million. A deal was brokered to keep the field station alive in 2014.

You cannot visit the station without an invitation, but much of the area is also a premiere flatwater paddling destination, as the network of portages maintained by ELA staff adds to the efforts of thousands of canoeists who paddle here every year.

The primary access to the north side of the Experimental Lakes Area is **Pine Road** (2.3 kms east of Gordon Lake Road on Highway 17), the length of which is open only to ELA staff. Paddlers can drive as far south as the put-in on the west side of **Upper Stewart Lake**; an unsupervised parking lot is located up a hill to the south and around the corner; a stop sign will warn anyone who isn't on ELA business not to travel any further.

Popular paddling routes include the overnight **Stewart Lake Loop**, which usually involves camping on Manomin Lake or Winnange Lake, itself protected by **Winnange Lake Provincial Park**. With three or four days, venture to **Teggau Lake**, the deepest in the ELA, with a stunning campsite at a mid-lake point and centuries-old indigenous pictographs at its upper neck. With five or six days to spare, a longer loop can encompass large **Dryberry Lake**, south of the formal ELA region. Topographic maps are a must for navigation; pick them up at Canada Map Sales in Winnipeg or outdoor retailers.

And don't worry about what scientists have actually done to the ELA's lakes: most of the bodies of water they've manipulated are small and out of the way. The volumes of added substances, which have included mercury, estrogen and flame retardants over the years, are also so small they must be measured by scientific instruments.

Alternate access to the north side of the ELA is available from the West Arm of Eagle Lake at **Stanley's Lodge** (End West Arm Road, 15 kms east of Pine Road, 807.227.2199, stanleys.com), where they'll watch your vehicle for a fee; call to arrange ahead of time.

Jason Sorby

Vermilion Bay and Vicinity

Farther along the Trans-Canada Highway, the former railway town of **Vermilion Bay** sits on the north edge of Eagle Lake, one of the larger bodies of water that isn't Lake Of The Woods. Use Vermilion Bay as an alternate ELA access point, the launch of a flatwater paddling excursion along the **Eagle-Dogtooth Provincial Waterway** (see *Highway 71 corridor*) or a 10-day paddle south through a popular and remote route that encompasses **Hawkcliff Lake**, **Atikwa Lake** and amazing **Waterfall Lake** on the way to Kakagi Lake (see *Highway 71 corridor*).

If you don't plan to leave the Trans-Canada Highway, stop in at **Busters Barbecue** (Highway 17 at Highway 647, 807.227.5256) for pulled-pork poutine.

Highway 647 also provides access to **Blue Lake Provincial Park**, which has a beach, campground, four short walking trails and access to a 97-km flatwater backcountry paddling route.

Northwestern Ontario and southeastern Manitoba mark the northern range of the fragrant water lily, which grows in shallow, still water. The flowers usually open up in early June.

Highway 71 Corridor

A few clicks east of Kenora on Highway 17, the junction with Highway 71 offers you a chance to snake south along the east side of Lake Of The Woods. This 140-km ribbon of asphalt, another very pretty drive, offers several access points to the both big lake and the smaller ones in canoe country to the east, as well as several provincial parks, fishing lodges and resort towns catering primarily to US fishers.

Bryan Scott

Rushing River
Provincial Park is
attractive to car
campers – and
as the gateway to
the wilderness of
Eagle-Dogtooth
Provincial Park.

Eagle-Dogtooth Provincial Waterway

One of the most popular destinations along Highway 71, **Rushing River Provincial Park** is a pretty provincial campground curving around the western edge of Dogtooth Lake. There's set of falls right along the highway, 5.6 kms south of Highway 17.

You may also use the park as an access point to paddle the **Eagle-Dogtooth Provincial Waterway,** a provincial park of sorts that connects the lakes on Crown country between Highway 71 and Vermilion Bay on Eagle Lake, including part of the Experimental Lakes Area and Winnange Lake Provincial Park (see *Highway 17 corridor*).

Another 13.5 kms south on Highway 71, Highwind Lake Road can take you right into the heart of the ELA; drive 13 kms east for direct access to Hillock Lake or Highwind Lake as an access point to paddle the five-or-six day **Dryberry Lake loop**. There's also camping and beach at **Highwind Lake Camp** (highwindlakecamp. ca, sites $40-$50), which will also watch your vehicle for a fee while you're out for days.

One word about camping directly on Highwind Lake road: Due to careless car campers, habituated bears have been a problem in this area.

Sioux Narrows

About 50 kms south of the Highway 17, the 71 crosses entrances to two eastern bays of Lake Of The Woods, Long Bay and Regina Bay. The area is known as Sioux Narrows thanks to a centuries-old battle between northern Cree and Anishinaabe and a Siouan war party from the south.

On a large island between the two crossings, **Sioux Narrows Provincial Park** has a beach, boat launches and a campground.

Five kms down the road, across "the world's longest wooden single-span bridge," the town of **Sioux Narrows** offers touristy gift shops, fishing-supply shops and most importantly, lake access. There are houseboat rentals at **Floating Lodges** (807.226.5476, floatinglodges.com), **Lake Of The Woods Houseboats** (807.226.5462, lowhouseboats.com) and **Tomahawk Resort** (807.226.5622, tomahawkresort.com). All three also offer fishing-guide services.

Bryan Scott

Sioux Narrows can also serve as the access point for a 10-day kayak trip around the Aulneau Peninsula, the large island in the middle of Lake Of The Woods. Outfit yourself in Winnipeg or Kenora, however.

If you need a break, grab a beer, burger or fried walleye on the patio at **Big John's Mineshaft Tavern** (Highway 71, 807.226.5224) or try to get the corner table with the best view of the lake.

Kakagi Lake

About 30 kms south of Sioux Narrows, Highway 71 runs alongside the western edge of **Kakagi Lake**, a large and unusually clear spring-fed lake with the cold waters favoured by lake trout. This is prime fishing territory but also a great access spot for paddlers.

Kayakers can enjoy large, portage-free Kakagi, while canoe-ists can use to begin or end a 10-day flatwater paddle from Vermilion Bay (see *Highway 17 corridor*). Kakagi is also a good access point for a seven-day **Pipestone Lake loop** paddle that terminates at Nestor Falls (see below) and access to **Stephen Lake**, home to a small but spectacularly well-preserved pictograph site, as well as shockingly clear **Isinglass Lake**. Grab some topographic maps and get planning.

There's free access to Kakagi Lake from an unsupervised government dock; lodges along the water, such as **Boreal Bay Lodge** (807.484.2940, bblodge.ca), may look after your vehicle for a fee.

Nestor Falls

Roughly 45 kms south of Sioux Narrows, Nestor Falls provides access to southeast Lake of The Woods as well as Pinus Lake, a backcountry entry point to Kishketuna Lake, Pipestone Lake and other pristine lakes in Crown country. You can rent houseboats at **Canada Houseboat Vacations** (807.484.2448, canadahouse-boatrentals.com). Off the water, **Monique's Lawg Cabin** (Highway 71,

807.484.2402) is the requisite burger spot within, you guessed it, a log cabin.

Five kms south of Nestor Falls, **Caliper Lake Provincial Park** has a beach, campground and a three-km walking trail.

North of Kenora

Unpopulated to begin with, northwestern Ontario gets even lonelier north of the Trans-Canada Highway. Only some of the following destinations are accessible by road.

Minaki

Among dozens of cottage communities north of Lake Of The Woods, the most famous is **Minaki**, a fishing resort 45 kms northwest of Kenora on Ontario Highway 596.

From 1927 to 2003, the Winnipeg River community was dominated by **Minaki Lodge**, a spectacular wooden structure built in the same grand style as railway jewels like the Banff Springs Hotel, Jasper Park Lodge and Chateau Lake Louise. Unlike those luxury institutions, this boreal-forest lodge never had access to the large numbers of wealthy tourists required to keep it solvent. Over a tumultuous, 76-year existence, Minaki opened, closed and reopened numerous times as a string of owners — including the swank Four Seasons hotel chain and Whitedog First Nation — tried and failed to keep the place going.

The landmark closed for good in 2003, when a fire destroyed the main lodge and the owner had no insurance. A subsequent police investigation did not result in charges, and the cause behind the ignominious end to this grand structure remains a mystery.

Dawn at Teggau Lake.

Jason Sorby

Today, most of the Minaki Grounds are off limits, as roads through the grounds are blocked by barricades. You can still see the ruins of the main lodge and a series of metal sculptures that survived the fire.

The other Minaki attraction involves accommodations that actually exist. One kilometre south of town, **Minaki Yurt Adventures** (807.466.1191, minaki.ca) maintains a 25-km cross-country ski and bike trail system for day users ($5 per person, $10 per family).

Overnight visitors stay in one of six yurts, circular structures modelled after portable dwellings used by Mongolian yak-herders. They range from rustic structures with stoves and bunk beds to a main lodge with full amenities. Rentals range from $25 per person, per night to $400-plus per night for the main lodge. There's also a sauna and wood-fired pizza oven at the main site. MYA also has ski, snowshoe, kayak and climbing-gear rentals. Guiding services start at $180 per day.

Another 12 kms northwest of Minaki on Highway 525, experienced climbers can tackle the **Gooseneck Rocks**, which consists of three cliff faces. The Alpine Club of Canada's Manitoba section maintains a guide to this site and other climbing spots north of Kenora at alpine-club.mb.ca.

Ear Falls and Red Lake

North of Vermilion Bay, Ontario Highway 105 leads north 100 kms to the town of **Ear Falls**, which sets at the northwestern edge of Lac Seul. The outpost is best known for the **Trout Forest Music Festival** (troutfest.com), a three-day roots-music gathering typically held during the second week of August at Waterfront Park. Passes are $70 for adults, $60 for students/seniors and $22 for kids; camping is another $22.

Continuing north from Ear Falls on Highway 105, there's a beach and campground 25 kms up the road at **Pakwash Provincial Park.**

Another 52 kms up, the highway terminates at **Red Lake**, an access point for canoeists intending to paddle the entire length of the Bloodvein River, which terminates at Lake Winnipeg (see *The Shield*), as well as Woodland Caribou Provincial Park.

Woodland Caribou Provincial Park

The eastern neighbour to Manitoba's Atikaki Provincial Wilderness Park, Ontario's **Woodland Caribou Provincial Park** offers is very similar. There are no roads into this wilderness park, which is crisscrossed by hundreds of kms of paddling routes, several significant pictograph sites and one of the largest caribou herds south of Hudson Bay.

The easiest way to access the park from Manitoba is by paddling in from Nopiming Provincial Park. Bloodvein River visitors often start their trips by landing floatplanes on Artery Lake.

MUST SEE: Woodland Caribou Provincial Park
The eastern neighbour of Manitoba's Atikaki Provincial Wilderness Park is a roadless protected area home the upper reaches of the Bloodvein River and hundreds of kilometres of flatwater-paddling routes.

There's also road access to the eastern edge of the park from Red Lake, where **Red Lake Outfitters** (807.727.9797, redlakeoutfitters.com) offers guided excursions.

Unlike Atikaki, Woodland Caribou is not free. Daily fees at $10.17 for adults, $8.14 for seniors and $4.80 for kids aged six to 17.

Rainy River Corridor

South of Lake Of The Woods, the rocky Canadian Shield suddenly flattens out into an area of lowlands that looks more like southern Manitoba. Forests open up into farmland in this grassy transition zone above the Rainy River, a former steamship route that still serves as the border between Ontario and Minnesota and between Lake Of The Woods and Rainy Lake.

Jason Sorby

The main route through this area is Ontario Highway 11, which follows the river 99 kms to the mill town of Fort Frances on Rainy Lake to the Minnesota border.

Beautiful, inedible fungi. When in doubt, don't.

Fort Frances

The massive mill operated by paper giant Abitibi Consolidated looms over **Fort Frances** (pop. 7,952), the second-largest city in the Manitoba-adjacent corner of northwestern Ontario. The city sits on the southwestern edge of Rainy Lake and sports two waterfront parks, a number of restaurants slinging walleye and more than its fair share of touristy knickknack shops; Fort Frances is a border town, sitting on the opposite side of Rainy River from International Falls, Minn.

If you find yourself here, head downtown to **The Lighthouse** (328 Scott. St., 807.274.1084) for walleye and fries. There's a better view at **The Harbourage** (1230 Second St. East, 807.274.6611), as well as some Ukrainian dishes.

Manitou Mounds

MUST SEE:
Kay-Nah-Chi-Wah-Nung Historical Centre
The largest intact set of ancient burial mounds in Canada, an indigenous spiritual centre and an archeological site dating back 5,000 years on the north side of the Rainy River.

Downstream from Fort Frances sits the only bona fide tourist attraction along the Rainy River. **Kay-Nah-Chi-Wah-Nung Historical Centre** (807.483.1163, manitoumounds.com), also known as the Manitou Mounds, preserves Canada's largest collection of indigenous burial mounds, built along a three-km stretch of the Rainy River between 300 BC and 1100 CE.

The grounds can be visited all year, but come during June through September to visit the interpretive centre, which explains the significance of this spiritual and archeological site, where human habitation dates back 5,000 years. Kay-Nah-Chi-Wah-Nung, which means "place of the long rapids," is maintained by Rainy River First Nations.

Access to the site is from Shaw Road, which runs south of Highway 11 15.5 kms west of the junction with Highway 71 – or 3.4 kms east of the town of Stratton. From Highway 11, drive 3 kms south on Shaw Road, make a right on River Road and drive another 1.5 kms east.

Morson

The main access point for Lake Of The Woods' southern basin is **Morson**, located 45 kms north of Highway 11 at the end of Highway 621. Morson-based **Ontario Wilderness Houseboat Rentals** (807.488.5594, wildernesshouseboats.com) will rent you floating living quarters.

Morson is the water access point to visit the undeveloped islands of **Lake Of The Woods Provincial Park** and **Sable Islands Provincial Nature Reserve**, the latter home to nesting grounds for the endangered Piping Plover.

Unlike other portions of Lake of The Woods, the southwestern basin is shallow, wavy and featureless; boating here is more like tooling around Lake Winnipeg or other shallow Manitoba great lakes.

Rainy River/Baudette

The westernmost Canadian town on Highway 11, **Rainy River** actually marks the beginning of the road that eventually becomes Yonge Street in Toronto. This is of particular interest to people from Ontario's capital.

The fastest way to reach Manitoba from this involves crossing the toll-free international bridge over Rainy River to **Baudette**, Minn. and cutting through northeastern Minnesota along Highway 11.

Consider a detour at Minnesota's Highway 50 to drive 13 kms north to **Zippel Bay State Park** at the south end of Lake Of The Woods. The park has a beach, campground, a nine-km summer hiking trail and 18 kms of winter cross-country ski trails.

The last Minnesota town of significance before the Canadian border is **Warroad**, the access point for Muskeg Bay, the shallowest and most dangerous section of Lake Of The Woods. Head north on Highway 313 to reach Sprague, Man. and the Northwest Angle, an orphan section of Minnesota whose only road access is from Manitoba. It's listed in the *Canadian Shield* chapter.

Camping Ethics

It's safe to assume visitors to Manitoba will spend some time out-doors. But while almost every human has a profound respect for nature, few agree on the best way to enjoy it – one person's soli-tude can be another's redneck bonfire.

In the interest of protecting natural areas and making wilder-ness trips more enjoyable, the Leave No Trace Centre for Outdoor Ethics, in Boulder, Col., has formulated an excellent series of camping guidelines. The following camping guidelines have been reprinted with permission from Leave No Trace.

1. Plan Ahead and Prepare
- Know the regulations and special concerns for the area you'll visit.
- Prepare for extreme weather, hazards, and emergencies.
- Schedule your trip to avoid times of high use.
- Visit in small groups. Split larger parties into groups of four to six.
- Repackage food to minimize waste.
- Use a map and compass to eliminate the use of marking paint, rock cairns, or flagging.

2. Travel and Camp on Durable Surfaces
- Durable surfaces include established trails and campsites, rock, gravel, dry grasses, or snow.
- Protect riparian areas by camping at least 65 metres from lakes and streams.
- Good campsites are found, not made. Altering a site is not necessary.
- In popular areas: concentrate use on existing trails and campsites; walk single-file in the middle of the trail, even when it's wet or muddy; keep campsites small; and focus activity in areas where vegetation is absent.
- In pristine areas: disperse use to prevent the creation of campsites and trails; avoid places where effects on the eco-system are just beginning.

3. Dispose of Waste Properly
- Pack it in, pack it out; inspect your campsite and rest areas for trash or spilled foods. Pack out all trash, leftover food, and litter.
- Deposit solid human waste in catholes dug 10 to 15 centime-tres deep, at least 65 metres from water, camp, and trails. Cover and disguise the cathole when finished.
- Pack out toilet paper and hygiene products.

- To wash yourself or your dishes, carry water 65 metres away from streams or lakes and use small amounts of biodegradable soap. Scatter strained dishwater.

4. Leave What You Find

- Preserve the past: examine, but do not touch, cultural or historic structures and artifacts.
- Leave rocks, plants, and other natural objects as you find them.
- Avoid introducing or transporting non-native species.
- Do not build structures or furniture, and don't dig trenches.

5. Minimize Effects of Campfires

Jason Sorby

- Campfires can cause lasting consequences to the backcountry. Use a lightweight stove for cooking, and enjoy a candle lantern for light.
- Where fires are permitted, use established fire rings, fire pans, or mound fires.
- Keep fires small. Only use sticks from the ground that can be broken by hand.
- Burn all wood and coals to ash, put out campfires completely, then scatter cool ashes.

6. Respect Wildlife

- Observe wildlife from a distance. Do not follow or approach them.
- Never feed animals. Feeding wildlife damages their health, alters natural behaviours, and exposes them to predators and other dangers.
- Protect wildlife and your food by storing rations and trash securely.
- Control pets at all times, or leave them at home.
- Avoid wildlife during sensitive times: mating, nesting, raising young, or winter.

As annoying as the job may be, hang or otherwise secure your food in bear country. Bonus: You'll also keep it away from rodents.

7. Be Considerate of Other Visitors

- Respect other visitors and protect the quality of their experience.
- Be courteous. Yield to other users on the trail.
- Step to the downhill side of the trail when encountering pack stock.
- Take breaks and camp away from trails and other visitors.
- Let nature's sounds prevail. Avoid loud voices and noises.

Acknowledgements and Thanks

The basic structure of this guidebook is a shameless rip-off of the excellent *Lonely Planet* formula. Thank you for making the first version a Canadian bestseller and thanks for purchasing this new edition.

Many facts, figures and dates cited in this book were derived from materials published online by Statistics Canada, Travel Manitoba, Manitoba Conservation & Water Stewardship, the Manitoba Historical Society, and Environment Canada, as well as dozens of municipal websites and other online sources. A more complete bibliography can be found in *Selected Sources*.

Overall, this guidebook would not exist without the initiative, hard work and patience of Gregg Shilliday, Catharina de Bakker, Mel Marginet and Ingeborg Boyens at Great Plains Publications, as well as the creativity and diligence of Suzanne Braun's design team at Relish New Brand Experience.

A Lake Winnipeg-sized ocean of gratitude must also be extended to my editors at the *Winnipeg Free Press* for providing me with the flexibility to pursue a wide range of interests and to take time out from reporting to pursue book projects. I'm indebted to Paul Samyn, Scott Gibbons, Shane Minkin and Alan Small for allowing me to go AWOL in February 2015 to complete the revision of this guidebook.

Many thanks to Katarina Kupca, Sean Kavanagh, Jen Skerritt, Mary Agnes Welch, James Turner, Rob Williams and Bryan Scott for ferreting out flaws and inconsistencies in the new edition. Thanks as well to Bryan Scott, Ken Frazer, Brenda Schritt, Charles Shilliday, Travel Manitoba, the Prairie Pathfinders and others for graciously contributing photos.

Other people deserving of kudos are Alexis McEwen and Dene Sinclair at Travel Manitoba and Gillian Chester at Tourism Winnipeg for suggesting additions to the latest edition. Also helping out with info or advice were Colin Corneau, Wally Daudrich, Mike Green, Lisa Kehler, Wab Kinew, Kevin Smith, Tim Smith, Kristin Westdal, and dozens of helpful people on Twitter who responded to requests for restaurant recommendations. Adam Wazny warrants special mention for recommending "Boston Pizza" as the best place to eat, everywhere.

Additional thanks to my family – Eema, Cheryl, Ronni, and Shai – for tolerating my inattentiveness throughout the winter of 2014–15. Thank you as well for the support of Stefan and Eta Kupca, Andre Iwanchuk, Karen Burgess, Michael Koch-Schulte, Jason Sorby, Leone Banks, Chris Boyce, Holly Caruk, Dave Danyluk, Chris Debicki, Rea Kavanagh, Ewan Umholtz, Marnie Old, Amanda Harris, Sean Irving, John K. Samson, Bob and Lindsay Somers, Virinder Gill, Scott Farlinger, Sara Stasiuk, Lynne Skromeda and Jason Old.

Thanks, *todah*, *merci*, *miigwetch*, *danke*, *dakuyem*, and *dhanyavaad*. I think that just about covers it.

Selected Sources

Ames, Doris, Peggy Bainard Acheson, Lorne Heshka, et al. *Orchids of Manitoba*. Winnipeg: Native Orchid Conservation Inc., 2005.

Archer, Laurel. *Northern Saskatchewan Canoe Routes*. Erin, Ont.: Boston Mills Press, 2003.

Buchanan, John. *Canoeing Manitoba Rivers — Vol. 1 South*. Calgary: Rocky Mountain Books, 1997.

Canada's Historic Places. Federal-provincial online registry at historicplaces.ca.

City of Winnipeg. Statistics, historical documents and other records at winnipeg.ca

Environment Canada. Climate data at weatheroffice.gc.ca.

Ernst, Trent. *Manitoba Backroad Mapbook: Outdoor Recreation Guide*. Coquitlam, BC: Backroad Mapbooks, 2010.

Everything Churchill. Listings at everythingchurchill.com.

Kives, Bartley and Bryan Scott. *Stuck In The Middle: Dissenting Views of Winnipeg*. Winnipeg: Great Plains Publications, 2013.

Lake of the Woods Museum. *The Explorer's Guide to Lake of the Woods*. Kenora, Ont.: The Lake of the Woods Museum, 2000.

Manitoba Historical Society. Articles and documents at mhs.mb.ca.

Manitoba Lodges and Outfitters Association. Listings at mloa.com.

Parks Canada. Documents at pc.gc.ca.

Prairie Pathfinders. *Hiking The Heartland*. Winnipeg: Prairie Pathfinders, 2007.

Province of Manitoba. Parks brochures, economic data and other documents at gov.mb.ca.

Statistics Canada. Census and survey data at statcan.gc.ca.

Stewart, Kenneth W., and Douglas A. Watkinson. *The Freshwater Fishes of Manitoba*. Winnipeg: University of Manitoba Press, 2004.

Stunden Bower, Shannon. *Wet Prairie: People, Land and Water in Agricultural Manitoba*. Vancouver: University of British Columbia Press, 2011.

Taylor, Peter, ed. *The Birds of Manitoba*. Winnipeg: Manitoba Naturalists Society, 2003.

Travel Manitoba. Listings and other documents at travelmanitoba.com.

Welsted, John, John Everitt, and Christoph Stadel, eds. *The Geography of Manitoba — Its Land and its People*. Winnipeg: University of Manitoba Press, 1996.

Wilson, Hap, and Stephanie Aykroyd. *Wilderness Rivers of Manitoba*. Erin, Ont.: Boston Mills Press, 2004.

Winnipeg Free Press. Electronic and physical archives, 1872-2015.

Index